How to Raise a Happy Child

(and be happy too)

Heather Criswell, Kid Whisperer
Taryn Voget, Cofounder of the Everyday Genius Institute

Publisher's Disclaimer

The material in this book is for informational purposes only. The authors and publisher expressly disclaim responsibility for any adverse effects that may result from the use or application of the information contained in this book.

Published by the Everyday Genius Institute, in partnership with WiseInside®, San Francisco, California.

Contact the authors at *hello@raiseahappychild.com*.

ISBN-13: 978-0-9844545-7-0
ISBN 10: 0-9844545-7-8

Printed in the United States of America

First Edition

Editing and interior layout and design by Joanne Shwed, Backspace Ink
(www.backspaceink.com)

Visit these websites for more information:
www.raiseahappychild.com
www.everydaygeniusinstitute.com
www.wiseinside.com

Heather Criswell

To my mom and dad, thank you for seeing me as a miracle in your lives, always. Although you are no longer here in physical form, I get to witness the presence of your spirit every day. I am love because I was so loved.

To my husband Brian, words will never describe the true love, connection, and trust I share with you. I am so thankful to share this journey with you ... over and over again!

To my son Jacob Alan, thank you for choosing me as your mom. I am honored to share this life with you. Words will never express the love and appreciation I have for you. Your light shines so bright on this planet. You are a miracle!

To my brother-in-law Keith, I couldn't pick a better brother! Our conversations light up my life and fill my heart with love.

To my "blood sister" Stacy, I am so blessed to have you as a constant source of love and light in my life. You are so loved and valued.

To all the beautiful teachers who have worked by my side, especially Miss Myra, Miss Colleen, Miss Krista, and Miss Brady. Thank you for your continued support, love, and willingness to "practice" together. I am so thankful for our time together!

To my Cinderella Fairy Godmother, Wendy Dearborne, thank you for your continued inspiration, guidance, support, and love. Thank you for listening to Mary Robie when I can't hear her for myself. You remind me to "Live like there is no midnight." I will always love and appreciate you.

For all the children I have had the opportunity to learn from and grow with, I am eternally grateful for your trust and love. You have all inspired me beyond words.

Taryn Voget

For my mom and dad, thank you for always helping me make my dreams a reality. This book is here because of your love and support. I love you both eternally.

To my five siblings Denika, Tristen, Paden, Kendall, and Cameron Voget, you are my most valued treasures and my best friends. You bring so much joy to my life and help me keep it real. Lovies always.

To my beloved nieces Adalie and Emmersen, and nephews Oliver, Dashiell, and Baylor, you bring such incredible happiness to my life. Thank you for teaching me so much more than I could ever teach you.

To Tim Hallbom, my cofounder, teacher, and friend, thank you for everything you have taught me about human behavior and the power of modeling. This book is possible because of you.

To all of my friends, family, colleagues, clients, customers, readers, and fans, thank you for your encouragement, ideas, feedback, contributions, and support. My gratitude for you is beyond words.

kid whisperer (*n.*) a person who uses deep rapport and communication skills with children to work in harmony, agreement, and cooperation, while honoring and respecting their feelings and their children's feelings equally.

kid whispering (*v.*) child-raising technique rooted in the principle of developing deep rapport with children, and honoring the feelings of the children and the adults equally. Kid whispering is a radical departure from "traditional" techniques of punishment, rewards, threats, fear, and time-outs, which use force or manipulation to gain obedience. Alternatively, kid whispering (and kid whisperers) decide on the energy they bring to every situation, listen to feelings, focus on what is wanted, honor choices, and believe in greatness ... *always.*

Contents

Explanation of Videos

This book comes with eight "how-to" videos that you can easily access with your phone, tablet, or computer. These videos show many of the parenting techniques in action and convey body language, voice tonality, and dialogue in a way that words in a book simply can't express. Our hope is that these videos provide a rich experience with real-world examples that you can use in your own life.

At the end of the chapter, you will see a box with a link to the video corresponding with that chapter. To access the videos, simply click on the Quick Response (QR) code (using a free QR code reader on your phone) or follow the URL link to our website to see the video with the teachings in action.

If you aren't familiar with QR codes, they look like this:

Using a QR code reader application on your phone, you can click this image and it will take you directly to the video, which is optimized for smart phone playback. You can also type in any browser the URL link, which looks like this:

www.raiseahappychild.com/intro-video

In addition to videos at the end of the chapters, we've included a summary of the videos at the back of the book (see "List of Videos"), so you can access and reference them all in one place.

Now, let's get started ...

Preface

"There is an instinct in a woman to love most
her own child—and an instinct to make any
child that needs her love, her own."

—*Robert Brault, writer and blogger*

It was more than a dream. It was more than a passion. It had to happen. I lined up my dolls as a small child and practiced. I dedicated all my education, energy, and effort to it.

I knew what I was born to do: *Teach children.*

My dream became a reality. When I was just 21 years old, I opened See World Learning Center, a unique preschool. I named it "See World" because I wanted the children to *see* a different world—a world where they are safe, their opinion matters, they are loved, they are valued, and they are equal. I wanted them to *see* a world of possibilities and wonder. I wanted them to *see* their own greatness.

We teach what we need to learn the most. I soon realized that I was actually learning more from the children than I was teaching them. I now know that the children had much more wisdom than I had originally thought.

I always believed that children were amazing, beautiful gifts. For years, I was "schooled" in the belief that we have to "teach" children—especially young ones—how to "be" (e.g., teach them to be nice, share, be a good friend, and have good manners).

I quickly learned that children already have these qualities. My job as a teacher is to remind, encourage, and support the children of who they really are: amazing little souls on this planet who came here to explore, expand, and love.

See World Learning Center was different. Our focus was far from lesson plans, learning the ABCs and 123s, saying sorry, or being nice to each other. Posters in typical preschools say, "A is for apple." Our posters said, "Stand up for what you believe in, even if you are standing alone."

My favorite poster—"I believe I am"—had a home in every classroom, and the name soon became our pledge. We didn't pledge our allegiance to the United States. It was not for lack of love for our country; it was because I felt that it was more important for my children to pledge allegiance to themselves … *first.* They can't be anything for their country if they are not that for themselves. I wanted every child to leave my preschool remembering, feeling, embracing, and knowing the mantra, "I believe I am."

We didn't follow a strict plan for the day; instead, we rolled with it on a day-to-day basis. We had the normal times in school (e.g., story time, naptime, snack time, outside time, and free time); however, if the "planned schedule" was not working, we changed it.

It was more than a school. It was a place for children to *be:* Be happy, be mad, be crazy, be sad, be excited, be tired, be silly, be bored, be yourself, and be alive.

Our school was decorated with spirit. We had a rainbow of handprints on the outside of the building. (Yes, it was my idea to do this in the middle of the summer in Las Vegas at approximately 107 degrees F.) I thought it would be awesome to have all the kids put their hands in paint and make a rainbow on the outside of our school. We went through an entire bulk box of popsicles that day, but we did it! We also decorated a hallway with the handprints of each child who came to the school. They picked the color and the handprint went

I Believe I Am...

a unique and precious human being

my own best friend and my

 own worst enemy

a loveable and loving person

capable of realizing my potential

self respecting

responsible for my own behavior

learning from my mistakes

creating a joyful life

an important part

of the universe!

 I LOVE ME.

www.WiseInside.com   Robert Valett

on the wall. Each handprint was unique; some used one color and others used every color.

Our school was decorated inside and out with spirit and love. At the time, I thought it would be cute and fun. I now know that it was actually a brilliant idea. The children knew that they were valued and important enough to put their handprint in permanent paint on the wall—on the inside, for everyone in the school to witness, and on the outside, for the world to know that this was their school, a place where they were valued, appreciated, and, more importantly, a place where they mattered.

We were invested ... invested in each other.

We were learning ... learning from each other.

We each had a purpose in this experience together. The children were here to remind me of all the lessons that adults "forget" as we get wiser with age. I was here to show the children how to communicate and cooperate in this society without losing their sense of self (e.g., self-worth, self-esteem, self-value, self-awareness, and self-confidence).

> We each had a purpose in this experience together.

I have learned from the best teachers in the world: our children—over 30,000 of them! For the past 25 years, I have practiced how to communicate and connect with children from every culture and every age.

"When you learn, teach. When you get, give."

—*Maya Angelou, American author and poet*

I have learned. I am excited to teach. I have been given so much by so many. I am excited to give you the love, value, and truth that these 30,000 children have given me.

How to raise a happy child ... and be happy too!

Introduction

"Certain things in life simply have to be experienced—
and never explained. Love is such a thing."
—Paulo Coelho, best-selling fiction author

I had to decide: Do I want to live or die?

My parents have done their fair share of making—what seemed to be at the time—mistakes with me. My father would choose to watch television instead of interact with me. My mother would have meltdowns and breakdowns frequently. They chose to get a divorce against my wishes. They neglected their own needs and health, and they died too early (at least for me).

Death is an interesting process. The only death I experienced as a child was the death of PaPa Bill (my mother's father) when I was 11 years old. He had massive strokes and was bedridden for over a year before he passed away. I remember it as a terribly difficult time for my mother, and so much indescribable pain lingered in our home for much longer than I wanted.

In the last 12 years, we have lost 13 family members. My husband Brian and I had our first miscarriage, which started the chain of "death" events. Within a couple of years, we were blessed to get pregnant again—this time carrying twins—and, within a few months, they decided to leave my body. A couple of years later, my beloved Grandma Hazel (my mother's mom) left. Within 11 months of her passing, my mom Mary passed at 52 years old. Shortly after, Grandpa Ralph (my father's dad) was diagnosed with Alzheimer's disease and passed within a few months. Brian's vivacious Grandma Marge died shortly after. Brian's Aunt Hannah left the planet three months after her mom Marge. Then, we were pregnant again—twins again—gone again. The next year, Grandma Pat (my father's mom) left her body for good. Within 11 months, my father Alan, at 61, decided to leave this planet.

> I never anticipated losing my entire family—and future family—so quickly.

I never anticipated losing my entire family—and future family—so quickly. I barely had time to breathe between each passing. I would get up and start going, only to be knocked down again and again. I lost every family member I had in those 12 years. It feels so strange to live here, on this planet, feeling like I am all by myself.

My husband Brian always says, "What am I? *Chopped liver?*"

Of course not. It's just odd to have everyone who mattered in my life—the people who knew me and loved me anyway—leave so quickly.

It was very difficult to live with so much pain and loss. I felt like a failure as a mother, incapable of providing a safe, nurturing womb for my children. I felt like an ungrateful grandchild; I didn't call my Grandma Pat and thank her for the fruitcake she sent me before she died. I felt like a failure as a daughter. Maybe I could have done more, such as helping my parents get in shape. I felt lost. I felt alone. I couldn't imagine living this life, here on Earth, without the love of my family. I was dying physically, emotionally, and spiritually.

I had to decide: live or die ... literally. I was about 265 pounds, eating my way through each crisis. I had diabetes. I was losing feeling in my feet. I had eye problems from the complications of diabetes. I had high blood pressure. I had kidney problems. I was 36 years old and dying.

The signs are there.

I had to look beyond the physical. I had to look deeper for the love that I thought I was missing. I had to love myself enough to look for it and believe it.

One day, while I was driving, and when Grandma Hazel was sick, I asked for a sign from the universe—God—to know if I should visit her in Texas. (I lived in Las Vegas at the time.) I pulled into a Burger King drive-through and there was a car in front of me with a Texas license plate. This was the sign I was asking for, and it showed up within minutes of my request.

My mom was very spiritual but not so religious. She said that she would always be with me, and she was right. She knew the license-plate story about Grandma Hazel and, close to her passing, she told me to look for, be aware of, and pay attention to the signs.

She said, "I will always be with you, Heather. All you have to do is pay attention and feel the love."

Shortly after her passing, I was flooded with Texas license plates. They were everywhere and I was in Nevada! I started getting mail, addressed to my mom, at my home. I got mail from a Catholic Charities organization but not just any Catholic Charities. It was from Sacred Heart Catholic Charities. (PaPa Bill was an architect who built Catholic churches throughout Texas. One of the churches and schools he built was Sacred Heart, where I attended school as a young girl.) I still get mail addressed to my mother—three moves and 12 years later! I feel her with me. I feel her presence. I feel her love.

I shared the mail and license-plate experiences with my dad. He thought I was crazy. He said it was just a coincidence and had no meaning whatsoever. He often laughed, made fun of, and mocked it. However, when he was in hospice, after his "day of enlightenment" (you will hear all about that in *Chapter 1: How Do You Define "Success" As a Parent?*), he looked at me.

"Heather, I don't think I will be able to do the mail thing like your mom, but I think I can do the license-plate thing. So, when you see a Nevada license plate, know that I am there with you."

I laughed, smiled, and cried. Not a day goes by that I don't see at least one Nevada license plate; usually, there are three to four a day. I feel him with me. I feel his presence. I feel his love. Love is constant. It continues on, without the body.

> Love is constant. It continues on, without the body.

Love surrounds me.

The more I pay attention, the more I am aware of the love that surrounds me, embraces me, and fills me each and every moment.

The love I have felt and experienced from the children in my life has carried me through every challenge. They remind me of the love that is hidden to me but so obvious to them.

They remind me to love myself. They remind me of the true meaning of life. Like the license plates, the more I look for the love in each child—in their eyes, in their words, in their heart, in their actions, and in their spirit—the more I know why I am here.

I am here to experience and feel love.

I am here to love and be loved.

I am here because I have purpose and value to add to this planet.

I am here.

I matter.

> "This is no ordinary love."
> —*Sade, Grammy Award-winning artist*

Life Lesson #1: There is one constant in my life: a knowing that has never been questioned. I was and I am loved. It's not unconditional love. It's genuine love. Compassionate love. True love. Abundant love. Powerful love. Meaningful love. Authentic love.

"Believe nothing, no matter where you read it or who has said, not even if I have said it, unless it agrees with your own reason and your own common sense."

—*Buddha, spiritual teacher*

Over the years, I didn't consciously think about how I communicated or connected with children, and I didn't have a desire to explore it. I felt that it was a special gift with which I came to this world. It seemed very natural and, moreover, intuitive. I felt like an artist with an empty canvas, a chef with raw ingredients, or a gardener with a bunch of seeds and acres of land to fill.

I am at home with children. I feel at peace in their presence. I feel like the world is the way it is supposed to be when I see it through the eyes of a child. Children remind and encourage me to see the wonder in small things, feel pure joy, and look at each experience in life with fresh eyes, an open mind, and a loving heart.

I met Taryn Voget, cofounder of the Everyday Genius Institute, several years ago. Her sisters have small children, and she would often call me up and ask for parenting advice on behalf of her sisters.

> I am at home with children. I feel at peace in their presence.

"What do you do when your child bites you?"

"What do you do when your child refuses to pee in any toilet except for the one near her room?"

"What's your opinion on giving sugar to kids?"

... and on and on. I loved sharing all of this advice.

One day, Taryn asked if she could formally interview me and deconstruct how I get such great and consistent results with children. That is how this book began.

A new approach to parenting is revealed.

The truth is that I honestly never considered the idea of doing an Everyday Genius Institute project on parenting. I couldn't fathom the possibility of finding a "model parent" whose strategies would work for any parent on the planet with any child. It seemed impossible. Then the universe chuckled at my limited thinking and, one day, I "found" Heather.

We started off as friends. As Heather mentioned, I kept calling her for advice as my sisters would share the latest developments with their small children, my beloved nieces and nephews.

Two things always amazed me. The first was Heather's advice, which was completely counterintuitive to what I would have done. Secondly, it *always* worked—and she had never even met my nieces and nephews! I was simply fascinated at how she thought. Everything she did was rooted deeply in the universal human emotion of love. Being a person who notices brilliant strategies when I see them, I picked up right away on the genius of her communication style and approach.

One day, we had a particularly fascinating conversation where I said, at least a dozen times, "Wow! Let me wrap my head around that. I never really thought about it *that* way before."

At that moment, I knew that we had to share a revolutionary new model—a new way of thinking—with parents and families everywhere.

I knew that we had to share a revolutionary new model – a new way of thinking – with parents and families everywhere."

I never knew there was a method to my madness.

As Taryn and I deeply discussed and explored my unique ability to understand children—regardless of age, language, or cultural differences—she recognized a specific pattern of communication that I was using. I was completely surprised. In fact, I initially argued that I did not have a "gift" but just an intuitive and unexplainable ability to talk with kids. After many hours of conversation and examples, she discovered a pattern of specific strategies that I use without conscious awareness.

Taryn began to deconstruct each example and define individual strategies that I had mastered over the past 25 years to get the desired results in any given situation with any child. She explained how, over time, I would "test" different techniques until I eventually found the pattern that offered consistent results. Put another way, she figured out what I do, step by step, which always works.

Eventually, I saw the patterns she saw and understood the structure of my intuition. The number of years invested, and the shear volume of children with whom I have been lucky to work, provided the opportunity to practice and master the art of communication, connection, and cooperation with children.

We all have the answers inside.

I also believe there is a sprinkle of intuition—a gut feeling—that I take into account when working with each child. We all have the answers inside. When I am quiet, patient, and willing to listen, I can tune into that "inner knowing" and experience the desired result every time.

The first time a child hit me, spit on me, kicked me, cursed at me, ran away from me, threw a shoe at my head, threw my computer monitor across the room, heaved an office chair across my office, bit me, pinched me, ignored me, or colored on the walls, it gave me a chance to practice one more time. The first time leads to the second, and continues forever!

Professionals know best ... right?

At the beginning, I tested every method suggested by the "professionals." I was young and not extremely confident in my abilities. They offered step-by-step directions for success with any child in any given situation—a formula to follow, guaranteeing success for every child.

The promise was, "This is the right way to ... educate/discipline/praise [fill in the blank] your child." In other words, "If you do what I say, and do it right, it will work for every child." The flaw in this theory is that most of the "expert" parenting methods are based on external forces (e.g., bribery, rewards, punishment, shaming, comparing, and time-out) to get the desired results.

Fortunately, I attracted kids to my school who would challenge the system and eventually disprove every method of discipline and communication suggested by the experts.

At the time, I was not thankful for the child who threw his shoe at my head. I didn't understand why he wouldn't conform to the standards. Why couldn't he just behave? Why wasn't he a good boy? Why couldn't he be like all the other kids? Why can't he just go with the flow?

When I look back, many of the suggestions didn't feel good or resonate with me intuitively, but I was taught—*convinced*—that this was the right way to raise these children. I reasoned that they were the professionals; they knew what was best for the children.

The answers are always inside.

The children at See World Learning Center helped me own my greatness. They helped me get in touch with the natural intuition we all posses inside. It is a knowing that, when something doesn't feel right, is not working, or just doesn't feel good, there are other options. It is the courage and strength to seek these other options out, practice them, and often get results that are considered "miracles," "chance," a "gift," or "luck."

My kids offered many opportunities to seek alternatives to the typical child-rearing advice. The alternative methods that we offer in this book will shift your experiences from "behavioral problems" to "successful communication and cooperation."

Although I will map out a path to success, please keep in mind this has been my path. Each of us is on our own journey, gathering support and love along the way. If these ideas feel good, take them, use them, and embrace them. If you like certain parts, and do not like other parts, take the parts you like and modify it for yourself and your experience so it feels good to you. This book is offered as an alternative and something different. We all ultimately know what is best for us in any given moment if we just trust the voice inside. The children always let me know what was best for them, one way or another.

> This book is offered as an alternative and something different.

It took me a long time, a lot of children, and many modifications to trust *myself* over what the authorities or professionals said. I wasn't proud of every interaction I had with every child. I would constantly beat myself up. I would replay situations in my head and get frustrated with how I handled them, how I could have said something better, how I may have hurt the child's feelings, or how I may have hurt their development in some way, shape, or form. At the time, I thought I was a perfectionist; now, I know that I was just learning, growing, and expanding.

I am now more kind, patient, and gentle with my spirit. I know that I am doing my best and can see an opportunity for growth when I make a mistake. When I am easier on myself and my own expectations, it trickles down to the children. It makes it easier on all of us. I am doing my best, and that's all I can do. I believe that we are all learning and growing, albeit some faster and more diligent than others.

I am a work in progress. I am always looking for better ways to communicate and cooperate in love. Each challenge is another opportunity to do it better than the last time. It will never be done. The learning continues. By the time I leave this planet, I hope that there will be a 100th edition of this book. I am alive, aware, and always ready to raise happy children and be happy too!

Kid whisperers see the world differently.

When I research and write about someone's strategy, I literally have to *become* that person and see the world through their eyes. It's more than just writing out the steps of a strategy; it's also understanding the worldview in which the person operates. This has been easy for me as I have written about study strategies of top students, marketing strategies of top marketers, and copywriting strategies of top advertisers. These are all topics I innately understood; the topic of parenting with Heather was different.

In working with Heather, I realized that she sees the world of adults and children completely differently than most of us do. She sees the world between parents and children as a dance—a co-creation—where both parties are equal in their right to create and express themselves in the relationship and in the world.

She sees herself as a parent, walking hand in hand alongside her child and enjoying the ride next to them. She sees children as even more capable than adults, here to teach us and not the other way around. She doesn't believe in punishment, rewards, time-outs, or the use of the word "no" with children. She has far more effective ways of creating the experiences she wants with them.

This book is the result of hundreds of hours of interviewing, discussing, and understanding how Heather approaches children. It took over a year to create—by far the longest it has taken to complete any of the other books on "genius strategies" that I have written.

It took a long time but not because it was hard to understand *what* Heather did. I had to completely shift how I viewed the relationship between adults and children so I could communicate it effectively to you. I had to change my worldview so I could truly see things through Heather's eyes. I had to reprogram just about every belief I had acquired around parenting and build a new model for how to view parents and children. I can honestly say that I love Heather's worldview so much more than the one from which I was initially operating.

For example, I was interviewing Heather one day and trying, for the dozenth time, to understand what she meant by a phrase that she had said over 100 times in the past few days:

"I always hold children in their greatness. I remember who they really are."

I quizzed her by asking, "Heather, how can you hold a child in their greatness when they haven't yet achieved anything that would make them great?"

In my mind, "greatness" was reserved for people like Walt Disney, Mother Teresa, or Steve Jobs—people who had made great contributions and achieved something on this planet.

> "I always hold children in their greatness. I remember who they really are."

Heather looked at me and answered simply, "Do you think greatness comes from achieving; that once you've achieved something, then you are great? I look at children as great and, because they are great, they are able to achieve things."

I was speechless.

It was the smallest reframe, and yet it completely changed my whole worldview in an instant. I had it backwards the whole time! In working with Heather over the past year, I have had this experience over and over again. She would say something small that would shift how I was raised to think.

Since meeting Heather, I have probably uttered these words a thousand times: "You know, I never really thought of it *that* way before!"

How does this book work?

The following chapters break down the strategies step by step, and give explanations and examples to offer you the opportunity to explore and sample techniques that might help you raise a happy child ... and be happy too!

This information is offered so you can try it on, test it, explore it, and modify it to fit your needs and situation—all with a desire to ultimately help make the parenting and child-rearing experiences fun, lighthearted, meaningful, and expansive. These techniques and suggestions have been practiced (and perfected) for years and with many children.

While reading this book, my great hope is that you will have many moments where you get a chance to think differently and try on another way of viewing the world and children. You may find that, like me, your belief system and how you view the world is different from Heather's. I invite you to ask yourself which belief would feel better to hold: hers or yours. In every instance where I asked myself this question, I decided that it felt better to share Heather's belief and view of the world, so I shifted my thinking.

Parenting is a large topic. Our goal is to provide parents everywhere with a model of parenting—an approach—that will work with every child, in every situation, every time. This book is about the *ingredients* that every parent can bring to every parenting situation. It's kind of like Mexican food, where the same five ingredients can be mixed a thousand ways to get totally different recipes.

Heather cooks with five ingredients in every parenting situation and combines them differently based on the scenario or situation:

1. Choose the Energy You Bring to Every Situation

2. Honor Your Feelings First and Then Your Child's

3. Focus on What You *Do* Want

4. Honor Every Choice Your Child Makes

5. Remind Your Child of Their Greatness ... Always

We've organized this book into four parts:

- In *Part 1: Decide Who You Are as a Parent,* we set the stage for parenting and offer an opportunity to really think about what you want your role to be in your child's life.

- In *Part 2: Discover the 5 Ingredients for Parenting Success*, we look at each ingredient to bring to every parenting moment with your child.

- In *Part 3: Put Happiness into Action*, we'll combine all of the ingredients so you can see them in action (and we'll give you a few staple phrases that can be used in many situations).

- In *Part 4: Feel Like a Parenting Pro with These Proven Scripts*, we'll share 22 specific scenarios—with carefully honed scripts—that you can use with your child to get amazing results.

After working with over 30,000 children for 25 years, I've discovered that Heather has mastered the words, the body language, the tone of voice, and the approach. I've tested her techniques with my own nieces and nephews and, when I used the exact techniques, I got the same results as she gets.

This is a different kind of parenting book. Heather and I invite you to share in a new model for parenting—one where old ways of discipline are tossed out the window, and where love and innate greatness trumps all.

Meet us!

We've shared many step-by-step techniques and scripts, and included links to videos to see them in action. You can click on this Quick Response Code (using a code reader on your phone) or follow the URL link to our site to see the videos.

Check out this Introduction video

VIDEO

VIDEO

or visit
www.raiseahappychild.com/intro-video

PART 1

Decide Who You Are as a Parent

I am so much more than a parent.

I am a friend, a lover, a companion, a teacher, a learner, a daughter, a soul sister, an employer, a granddaughter, a speaker, a massage therapist, an inventor, an entrepreneur, a caregiver, a consultant, a coach, a cheerleader, a writer, a great chef (some may argue), a great baker (really ... organic carrot cake ... YUM!), a lover of life, and the list goes on and on.

When I own and acknowledge that I am the sum of many titles, I feel less pressure to be perfect with any. It gives me permission to make a mistake, learn, and proceed with a greater understanding of life.

The greatest parenting experience to date was to be a parent to other people's children. It's one thing to mess up my child, but to make a mistake with another parent's child ... well, that was a lot of pressure! I expected perfection from my staff and myself.

Honestly, we were with these children for 10 to 12 hours a day. Eight to 10 of those hours were waking hours to fill with constant entertainment, learning experiences, meals, compassion, and fun. In my mind, I was doing the most important job on the planet. I am actually glad that I started my school so young. I was just 21 years old, invincible, ready for the challenge, and extremely naïve.

One day, I was in the playground at my preschool, watching the children enjoy life. Emma, one of my four-year-olds, loved gymnastics. She often climbed on the swing set and "hung like a monkey in a tree." On this particular day, the teachers were not focused on Emma. It only takes a moment. I heard Emma's voice across the playground.

"Look at me, Miss Heather!"

As I focused my attention in Emma's direction, I saw her at the top of the six-foot-high swing set, hanging by her legs. Before I could speak or move, I watched Emma come crashing down on a bed of pea gravel, flat on her back. Mind you, "bed" is a generous word. Pea gravel is just a fancy way of saying "a bunch of rocks."

Everything seemed to go in slow motion. I ran to Emma and asked if she was okay, which were the first words that came to my mind, but I just wanted to make sure she was coherent.

"Are you able to move your feet, Emma"?

My immediate thought was that she might have broken her back or neck.

"I'm okay!"

I didn't believe her. I had just watched a little girl fall six feet, on her back, on rocks, and she says that she is okay. I led her away from the playground and literally took off every ounce of clothing, looking for bumps, blood, or even a single bruise. Nothing.

> We love our children. I have never met a parent who has consciously wished illness, struggle, or ill will on their children.

I still was not satisfied. I called her parents and asked them to come to the school to evaluate Emma. I was in total disbelief. Her parents indulged my request and checked her out, head to toe. Same conclusion: nothing.

Emma taught me two very valuable lessons that day:

1. *Giving birth to a child is not necessary to have an unimaginable love for them.* The pain of seeing Emma drop from the sky, unable to catch and save her, was a terrible feeling. In that moment, Emma was my child, loved and valued.

2. *Greater forces exist beyond my own vision and control.* Later that day, another child came to me and said, "Miss Heather, the angels helped Emma down from the swing set. They are always here, flying around to help us. Ones in gold dresses, orange dresses, and purple dresses. All colors. They are here all the time."

We love our children. I have never met a parent who has consciously wished illness, struggle, or ill will on their children. We can all benefit from tools, tips, and strategies in order to be our best in any relationship. Children give us the opportunity to see and love the best and worst in ourselves.

This book is a chance to learn from thousands of children and to remember something simple but profound that most adults have forgotten.

Ready?

I believe I am ... a unique and precious human being.

CHAPTER 1

How Do You Define "Success" As a Parent?

"What would you do if you knew you could not fail?"
—*Unknown*

I am successful regardless of the outcome.

M y success as a human being on this planet is not determined by my parenting failures or successes. I am an important individual who came to play the game of life. I have a unique set of ideas, dreams, and visions that are being expressed minute by minute, day by day, year by year.

Parenting holds a large space in my heart. I see all children as my own. I feel a deep connection to their little spirits. Even at Costco, I look at a little guy, we look eye to eye, and we speak without words. It's a language of love ... a language that we all have. Of course, it is easier to see and feel that love when they are smiling at me rather than throwing a shoe at me; regardless, the love is there.

A few years ago, my father was in hospice. He was dying too early for me at only 61 years old. My father was not religious or spiritual and believed that "when the lights go out, you are worm food."

A few days before his transition, he had what we called his "day of enlightenment." When I visited him in the morning, he said that he had to talk to me about something very important. I sat by his side as he described an amazing experience, using his endearing nickname for me.

"Doodle, it was the most wonderful, beautiful place. I was wrapped in a cocoon of love and taken to a place that was *more* than love. It was a place that was indescribable LOVE. There were so many colors and smells, and a feeling of love, but it was more than love. There are no words in our vocabulary to describe it."

He went on for at least 30 minutes, describing the experience. I was initially in a state of disbelief until I felt his words in my heart—clear, authentic, and true. At the end of the day, he called in the chaplain and told her that he was ready to go. All he wanted to do was kiss his daughter on the forehead, say goodbye, and be with his parents.

Two days went by, and I called my father to say goodnight.

"Hi, Doodle. I won't be able to talk to you on the phone anymore. I am going on a mission, like in space. I love you so much."

The next morning, my father left this planet for his "mission."

We were very close. During the last seven months of his life in hospice, we had daily talks about life: successes, failures, and dreams. When I asked him what made him a successful parent, his answer was extremely enlightening.

"I am not successful. I am lucky ... the luckiest parent to have such a great, loving daughter."

The gift of this answer was that his success as a parent was not determined by external indicators. His description was not based on my level of education, my success as a businesswoman, my appearance, or even my character. He didn't consider me a trophy to be

> ... his success as a parent was not determined by external indicators.

displayed to the world. He felt blessed to have the love in his life that we shared for each other. So do I.

In truth, I would describe some of my father's choices in parenting as "successes" and some as "failures."

- *Success = Finding a preschool to purchase and supporting me in the business, even when the world said it couldn't be done.*

- *Failure = Telling me for 30+ years that I needed to lose weight.*

- *Success = Walking me down the aisle at my wedding, telling me how happy he was for me.*

To be fair, I would describe some of my choices as my father's daughter as "successes" and some as "failures."

- *Success = Building a successful preschool filled with love and good vibes.*

- *Failure = Hating myself for being fat for most of my life.*

- *Success = Marrying an amazing guy and truly enjoying each other over the past 15 years.*

When I think about and describe parenting, I want to highlight a very important—small but subtle—word choice. When I say "my father's choices" and "my choices," I define "choices" as successes or failures, but I cannot define "human beings" as successes or failures.

When I think of my life's memories, I fast forward to that "day of enlightenment" in hospice. All that mattered was love. We were not talking about how much money we had, our houses, our credit score, our cars, or even work. We were talking about family, friends, and the love we shared with each and every one. At the end, all he wanted to do was tell his daughter that he loved her and kiss her goodbye.

So, let's look at the question again with new eyes:

"How do I define my success as a parent?"

I have found an interesting way to reframe that question with a little twist. After testing it on parents and in my own heart, it has a profound way of uncovering the authentic truth that lies deeply in our heart and spirit:

"At the end of your life, how will you know that you were a successful parent?"

Seems easy enough. The most popular answers I received were, "My child is happy, healthy, successful in their career, educated, a good parent, a good friend, financially responsible, has a nice home, married," and the list goes on.

All of these answers seem reasonable, and even desirable, but here's the twist:

"At the end of your life, how will you know that you were a successful parent, leaving your perceived successes and failures of your child out of the answer?"

In other words, "How will you know that you are a successful parent, leaving your child's conditions, behaviors, health, well-being, decisions, and experience as a human on this planet out of the answer?"

> "How will you know that you are a successful parent, leaving your child's conditions, behaviors, health, well-being, decisions, and experience as a human on this planet out of the answer?"

I recently had an experience where I was put to task. I was given the opportunity to embrace the essence of this question and experience it for myself. I spent the day with Gavin, a 19-year-old boy, who was in my preschool from one to seven years old and whom we fostered on and off for about eight years. Gavin played video games all day instead of getting a job and providing for himself (my perception, not his). Even when he was motivated to get a job, he had no luck.

In the moment, I was frustrated. I knew that he was an incredible human being, here on purpose and important to this planet. Because his actions were not showing me who I knew him to be as a person, I had to recall everything I knew him to be. I had to recall moments in my memory that reminded me of his brilliance, character, kindness, and genuine heart of gold. As I recalled all of those events in a short amount of time, I was instantly reminded that, when he played video games, it didn't represent who he is: a unique and precious human being. My job as a parent was to remind him *who he is* when he has lost faith, hope, and belief in himself.

I reminded him of his greatness. I recalled numerous examples of success in his life. I reminded him that he is a gift to this world and (as Grandma Hazel would say) "This too shall pass."

I blamed myself in part for his behavior and choices. I questioned whether I could have done something more as a parent to help him have a good life. If I thought that he was ecstatic playing video games all day, I would be okay with that, but I knew that he wanted more for his life. I held him high, and it was painful to watch him suffer.

There was nothing I could do to turn around the circumstances for Gavin. I couldn't shame him. I couldn't threaten him. I couldn't provide him with a job. The only way I knew how to turn around the pain for myself was to change my mind in that moment. I changed my mind to believe in him—not in his circumstances—by supporting him, being a role model, and telling him a true story.

"You know, Gavin, when I was eating pizza at Pizza Hut every day, working as an order taker, I never believed that I would own a successful preschool, or a wellness center, or be writing a book, but my parents believed in me. They held that space for me—both of them—and look at how great I turned out!"

I held him in greatness and knew that it would all work out. In the end, it *will* all work out.

This chapter started with the statement, "My success as a human being on this planet is not determined by my parenting failures or successes." We are all so much more than any role we play, including the important role of parent.

When I asked friends and colleagues how they would define their success as a parent, the challenge for many of them was to separate *their* success from *their child*. After a few minutes (or a few days), they offered responses that actually made them smile while they were saying them, such as, "I listened to my child," "I did my best as often as possible," "I loved with all my heart," "I valued my time with my child," or "I invested energy in my well-being so I could be my best."

When I fast forward to the end of my life, I think of all the children with whom I have had the honor to communicate, connect, and love.

How will I know if I was successful?

- I know that I did my best to show my love and appreciation for their existence in my life.

- I know that, even when I disagreed with their decisions or felt disappointed with their circumstances, I held them in a space of greatness.

- I was grateful for the time we shared and the experiences we had—the easy ones *and* the challenging ones.

- I was a better person for sharing this life together, and the cocoon of love we shared was indescribable.

> "… to know even one life has breathed easier
> because you have lived. This is to have succeeded."
>
> —*Ralph Waldo Emerson, American essayist, lecturer, and poet*

Put your success inside of your control.

People often how ask me, "How do you pick the 'geniuses' you interview for your Everyday Genius projects?" This is a simple question with a somewhat complicated answer.

I look for everyday people who get extraordinary results by thinking and acting differently than just about everyone else in the field. I look for people who make complicated things look easy and who get consistently superior results with effortless grace.

It didn't take me long to realize that Heather has a unique genius. She is a special person on this planet and definitely thinks differently than just about anyone else in the field of child psychology. I wanted to see her parenting genius shared with the world.

Early in my interviews with Heather, I asked her a simple question: "How do you know that you are successful with kids? What's your evidence?"

Her answer floored me at first, and then I realized her genius right away:

- "With all of the kids I work with and parent, I know that I am successful because, at the end of my life, I will be able to look back and see that I was happy most of the time throughout my child's existence in my life.

- "No matter what the outcome, I loved my child no matter what he did (or didn't do).

- "In every moment, I let my child know that my love is not dependent on her behavior.

- "I have done everything in my power to let my child know that he is in control of his life and is responsible for what he creates in his life.

- "I experienced a lot of joy while my child was growing up and when we spent time together after he left home.

- "I showed my child my love in a meaningful way in every moment I could."

Amazing!

Read this list again and notice how every item is within Heather's control. She has defined her criteria for success as a parent and is in control of achieving her own definition. She bases her success on how she interacts with her kids every day. She intuitively knows what high performers know: If you want to achieve something big, put your success within your control.

Parents often define their success by how their child "turns out" as an adult. They believe they are successful parents if their child gets a certain type of job, marries a certain type of person, leads a certain type of lifestyle, makes certain kinds of choices, and behaves in certain kinds of ways.

Parents also base their own happiness on the behaviors and choices of their children. They define their success based on criteria outside of their control, such as how well their children do in school, what kind of friends they have, how well behaved they are in public, and how much money they make in their career. In doing this, they put an unfair burden on themselves and on their child.

Imagine sitting on a bed with your mother in the last days of her life. She was a good mother and did everything in her power to raise you well. Imagine if she turned to you and said the following words:

"Dear, I am a total failure as a parent. I am a failure because, try as I might, you have not made good choices. I am a failure because you have a job that I don't think is right for you, your health is not what I believe is best for you, your friends aren't worthy of you, and where you are living doesn't make me happy. I am dying, leaving this planet, knowing that I am a failure as a mother because I did everything I could for you, yet the choices you made have not made me happy."

Ouch.

It feels bad to have someone expect us to be a certain way in order to make them happy. It feels bad to know that we have disappointed our parent. It feels bad that we caused someone else to feel like a failure.

Our job is not to make our *parents* happy but rather to make *ourselves* happy—just as your child's job is not to make *you* happy but to make *herself* happy. We cannot control our children's behavior and choices any more than our parents could control ours. We all came to this planet to have our own experience and be our own person.

Let's play out the above scenario a little differently. Imagine your mother, at the end of her life, saying this to you instead:

"Honey, I am so proud of you! I know that, whatever you decide to do, it will be what's best for you. If the outcome doesn't turn out like you hoped, I know that you'll learn from it and create something new. I believe in your greatness and I always have. Thank you for being in my life."

It's much easier and more fun to go through life as Heather does: by defining our own success criteria and putting all of it inside our control.

If you want to achieve something big, put your success within your control.

What last words would you like your child to hear from you?

Stop for a moment and consider how you would define your success as a parent. Play out a scenario where your child turned out beautifully and see how you answer the above question. Then, try on the scenario where your child didn't have the life you would have wished for her, and answer the question that way. Keep working at it until you arrive at a set of success criteria about which you can feel good and against which you could measure yourself. Feel free to borrow from Heather's list or create your own.

Look through your list and reword anything that is outside of your control in a way that is completely inside of your control. For example, if you wrote "I see that my child is happily married and in a job she likes" as something that would make you feel successful as a parent, consider what would happen if your child never marries or marries someone and doesn't need to work.

You might think about changing the earlier example to "I knew I was a successful as a parent because I supported my child to the best of my ability in school and in activities that interested him." This statement is inside your control. What your child does with schooling and activities is totally up to him. Your child is responsible for creating his own life, just as you are responsible for creating yours.

> We all came to this planet to have our own experience and be our own person.

Heather's list is genius. Like Heather, I am for empowerment. I am for every person putting their happiness inside their control. I am for people determining *for themselves* what success looks like and being successful because they have created a definition of success they can achieve by their own actions. I am excited to see how *you* define your success as a parent!

> "Success is the sum of small efforts,
> repeated day in and day out."
>
> —*Robert Collier, best-selling author of The Secret of the Ages*[1]

Review of Chapter 1: How Do You Define "Success" As a Parent?

- It's important to decouple our feelings of "parenting success" from how our child "turns out." We cannot control their choices in life.

- We each have the opportunity to create our own definition of "parenting success." Achieving our definition of success must be entirely within our control of choices and behaviors.

- *Choices* can be successes or failures, but *human beings* are so much more than these labels.

- It is not our child's job to make *us* happy but to make *themselves* happy; it is not our job to make our *child* happy but to make *ourselves* happy.

CHAPTER 2

What Are Your Goals for Yourself and Desires for Your Child?

"Have the courage to follow your heart and intuition.
They somehow already know what you truly want
to become. Everything else is secondary."

—*Steve Jobs, founder and chief executive officer of Apple*

Miracles happen when we get out of the way.

I was a surprise to my parents (the good kind) when my mother found out that she was pregnant. She had cervical cancer at 22 years old and part of her cervix was removed. Many doctors told her that she would never get pregnant and, if by some strange chance she could get pregnant, she would never carry the baby to full term.

My parents eventually accepted the diagnosis and did the next best thing to parenting: They were going to become truckers. Yes, *truck drivers*. They were searching for the perfect semi truck, looking at the future on the road, traveling America, and being wild and free!

A few months into the search for the best truck on the market, guess who was pregnant? The doctors were not optimistic or even hopeful. I was determined to come into this world: two weeks late, 10 pounds and 4 ounces ... *here comes baby Heather!*

I think the best gift my parents ever received was the early diagnosis from the doctors because they didn't have time or energy to think about goals and desires for me. They were just so glad that I was born! All the doctors who worked with my mother considered me a "medical miracle."

Throughout my life, I feel that my parents always had the "miracle" thought in their head, which may have been an unconscious guiding foundation of their love. Mind you, my mother wasn't thinking (consciously, at least) that I was a "miracle" when:

- I stole my friend's wallet from Girl Scouts (actually Brownies ... I never made it to Girl Scouts because of this incident);

- I traced the outline of my mom's handprint where she slapped me on the leg for talking back to her, and then threatened to call Child Protective Services to report her for abuse. (In my mind, I knew I had a case. I traced her handprint on my leg with a pen and, when Child Protective Services came, they would be able to match the handprint. I thought I was pretty smart!); or

- I was 17, and I told my dad that I was moving out to live with my boyfriend because we were in love and going to be together forever (not so much, although I still love him dearly).

Even during these moments, I believe that my parents had a knowing deep inside that I *was* a miracle. I—as a human—was not the behaviors I was displaying. They did not see me as a stubborn, opinionated, defiant child. They looked at the behavior as separate from me as a human being; in other words, I was *acting* stubborn, opinionated, and defiant.

Because my parents didn't put a lot of thought into the job of parenting, I believe they had few "defined" goals and desires for me. With the space they provided, I defined my goals and desires as a young child. From 12 years old, I spent an entire summer—10 hours a day—babysitting for a family. I earned $1,500, which was a fortune to a 14-year-old.

Over the next decade or so, I explored many ways to take care of children. I was a nanny, preschool teacher, youth counselor at the MGM Grand Hotel and Casino (when Las Vegas was still marketing itself as a "family destination" city), and was eventually presented with the opportunity to open my own preschool at 21.

They said that opening a preschool at age 21 couldn't be done; I said it could.

The preschool was my #1 goal and desire. I had a lot to prove. I could:

- Do it without a degree.
- Generate clients.
- Pay my mortgage with less than $300 in my account to start.
- Be the youngest director and owner in the city.
- Provide an amazing space in which children could love and thrive.
- Run a business.
- Communicate effectively with parents.
- Build a client base to fill the school without marketing dollars or experience.
- Make it happen!

I was doing my best to prove it to my parents, my friends, the city inspectors, the city council members, and the world.

As I invested time, money, energy, and effort, I started to see the children's successes as a direct reflection of me. I told this story in my mind: "If it weren't for my school, the children would not be who they are." I measured my worth and value on how the children "performed" and considered their success as my own.

My thoughts and perception altered as my first graduating class entered public school. When I thought of my graduating class, I envisioned the teachers at the public schools saying something like, "Wow! The See World kids are amazing! We couldn't ask for better kids in our classrooms!" (Remember: One can dream in the learning process.)

However, reports came back with a range of comments regarding each child, such as "excessive talker," "easy to distract," and "nice to friends but very outspoken." I wanted my students to be successful—the way in which public school defines "success"—so I could be proud of them and myself.

I remember thinking, "This doesn't make any sense! These are amazing kids. Over the years, they taught me so much about life and authentic love."

In that moment, I realized that it wasn't about me. It wasn't about how I looked as a teacher or owner. The children were not a direct reflection of my success. They were successful beyond my imagination. I spent 10–12 hours a day, every day, with these children. I knew them for who they were, not for their behavior. I reminded myself of all the great times we shared, all the challenges we shared, and all the wisdom we gathered along the way.

I had a shift ... a moment where I embraced what I could control: my expression of genuine love, my support, my attitude, and my feelings. I decided to feel good about the time we had; the joy we shared; and the amazing, self-confident, authentically individual children I had the honor of "playing" with for the seven years I had them (and many more for years to come).

I set *goals* for myself. I have *desires* for my children.

I originally set a goal for my children to be the "star students" in public school. I learned quickly that it was unrealistic to set a goal for another human being. When the public school teachers didn't respond to See World kids in a positive light, I was initially disappointed in the children and their performance/

behavior. It was unfair to set a goal for each child in order to meet my expectations so that I felt better as a teacher, a preschool owner, and an overall person.

Throughout the years, the children gave me plenty of opportunities to "practice" setting goals. They taught me to set my own goals—those specific to my achievements and desires—and to honor the goals they set for themselves by supporting them, regardless of success or failure.

> I had a shift ... a moment where I embraced what I could control: my expression of genuine love, my support, my attitude, and my feelings.

It was freeing to let go of goals for my children. I felt a sense of unnecessary responsibility lifted from my shoulders. When I let them create their own goals, I didn't have as much of an emotional investment. It was no longer determining my self-worth or value. It was easier to support them from an authentic heart space when I was removed from the equation.

Thoughts bubbled up in my mind, such as, "Does this mean that I don't care about their success in life? Will they even want to set a goal? What if I don't like their goals?"

I flashed to the primary goal my father had for me from the age of four—to be thin—and this goal haunted me over the next 30 years. It certainly was not his intention to hurt me; he believed that being overweight was a death sentence and not a desirable wish for any young lady being raised in the South.

The more he focused on the "problem," it grew ... *literally.* He would comment on my choice of food, my clothes, and my overall appearance. Again, he didn't do it to hurt me; in his mind, he was motivating me to change so that I could achieve the goal he had in mind for me.

The problem with his goal—not mine—was that *it was his goal for me.* He could not shame me, encourage me, bribe me, or force me to achieve his goal when the goal was not inspired intrinsically by me. In other words, I could not be something for him that I was not willing to be for myself. Over time, it certainly became a goal for me but for different reasons. At 36 years old, I owned my goal by shedding 85 pounds within one year. *I did it for me.*

Over the years, the children gave me many opportunities to practice the "goals" concept. I quickly learned that, as humans, we all have the desire to learn, grow, and expand. The children often set higher goals for themselves than I thought they were capable of achieving. On many occasions, I was surprised and delighted when they would accomplish a goal that I perceived as impossible. At the same time, I learned how to support them (or stay out of it) when they failed or even quit altogether.

By letting go of goals for my children, I could fully embrace my desires for my them.

In my mind, desires are hopes, dreams, and wishes for my children. Not to be confused with goals, desires are more general and speak to the overall well-being for my child on this planet.

Desires can easily be disguised as goals. I had to be aware and clear when I was thinking of a desire for any given child. It was important for me to have a desire for each child born in love, not fear. When fear would enter the picture, I could shift the desire to a goal for the child in a matter of minutes. Desires need to feel good. When they start to feel bad, it is a big clue that they are beginning to shift to a goal. For another human being, a goal is completely out of my control.

> Not to be confused with goals, desires are more general and speak to the overall well-being for my child on this planet.

Gavin, my video game master, put me to task on this subject. Before we met for lunch, I was clear on my desires for his well-being. My desires were basic and not too far from other people's desires for their own children. My biggest desire for Gavin was to know that he is heard, valued, and loved by me. Another clear desire was that he knows he has purpose on this planet—unique and specific to him.

My goal during lunch was to stay true to my desires for Gavin, regardless of what he was "doing" in the moment. This was personal and specific to me, and what I could control.

As our conversation progressed, I felt my thoughts shifting very fast and morphing into goals for Gavin (e.g., "He needs to get a job," "He needs to research what he wants to do for a living," and "He needs to support himself financially"). They were all very worthy goals but, again, these were *my* goals for him.

Then, I remembered that I couldn't set a goal for Gavin ... period. He had to set goals for himself. I immediately came back to my desires. I wanted Gavin to know that he is heard, valued, and loved by me. I wanted him to know that he has purpose on this planet—unique and specific to him.

My dialogue with Gavin was now directed from:

- "You should ..."
- "You need to ..."
- "What are you thinking?"
- "How are you going to support yourself?"
- "You are better than this!"

to:

- "I know that you are amazing."
- "You have a gift that no one else on this planet has."
- "Here's something to think about: How can you do what you love *and* generate the income you desire?"
- "The world is missing your greatness when you are locked behind the doors of your bedroom."
- "You are a gift."
- "I am here for you ... here to support you in your desires and goals."
- "You have shared so much with the world already. I can't wait to see what your future holds. I am cheering for you the whole way!"

As I gained clarity regarding my goals, my desires for the children also became clear. As my desires became clear, the results were completely within my control.

Here was my choice: I could set unrealistic goals and desires for another human being completely out of my control or I could set goals for myself and desires for my child that were within my control, regardless of the circumstances of my child's life.

My true desire for my child is for him to know that he is heard, valued, and loved by me and that he has purpose on this planet—unique and specific to him. Again, I am here to remind him of his greatness, especially when he needs it the most.

> "You see things; and you say 'Why?' But I dream
> things that never were; and I say 'Why not?'"
>
> —*George Bernard Shaw, Nobel Prize-winning author*

My true desire for my child is for him to know that he is heard, valued, and loved by me and that he has purpose on this planet—unique and specific to him.

What are your goals as a parent?

When we interview "geniuses" in the Genius Lab at the Everyday Genius Institute, we use a very specific and unique methodology to understand how people are thinking. The first question we always ask people when they are performing an activity is, "What are your goals in this situation?" Our behaviors always support our goals, so it's an insightful question, and we gather all sorts of information from the answer.

To make my point about goals, let's take a typical evening dinner. Is it your goal to:

- Cook your family 100% organic, locally grown, in-season food that nourishes them completely?

- Provide something relatively healthy that you can prepare in 30 minutes or less?

- Make sure that they have something to eat, and you aren't too picky about what it is so long as it tastes reasonably good?

You probably haven't consciously thought about your goals for family dinners; however, you can see that your behavior—what you do—is going to be in support of your goals. You'll do very different things if your goal is to make organic meals from scratch versus prepare something reasonably healthy in 30 minutes or less.

It was fascinating to ask Heather this question: "What are your goals as a parent?"

Heather responded, "My goals as a parent are to:

- "Be the best version of myself and stay true to myself.

- "Provide opportunities for my child to explore and feel safe emotionally and physically.

- "Acknowledge my child and hear him as much as humanly possible.

- "Provide an education, to the best of my ability, based on my child's desires and dreams.

- "Be emotionally available when my child needs me and give him independence when he doesn't need me.

- "Honor my child's vision for his life.

- "Know that my child will make decisions with which I may disagree, but trust that he will learn from them, regardless of what I think.

- "See the best in my child, even when it is hard.

- "Focus on my child's strengths and remind him of his strengths when he forgets.

- "Communicate with my child with respect, truth, and courage at all times.

- "Be everything for myself that I expect my child to be (e.g., polite and kind).

- "Be proud of myself as a parent."

Can you already imagine what kind of behavior Heather is going to exhibit as a parent in support of her goals?

Heather intuitively knows that the most important critera for a goal is that it has to be achievable by us; in other words, it has to be 100% inside our control. Otherwise, the goal is entirely out of our control and therefore impossible to achieve.

For example, I could have the following goals: "My child will graduate from high school," "My child will get into a great college," or "My child will take over the family business." These goals are ultimately outside of my control, so they don't meet the most important criteria of a goal. I could shame, guilt, or strongly encourage my child into those paths, but any feeling of control as a parent is an illusion. Could your parents ever control anything you did?

I *cannot* control whether my child graduates from high school, gets into a good college, or makes decisions with which I agree. I *can* support my child in achieving any goals he has for himself. Supporting my child's goals is inside my control.

The best thing that any parent can do is to model in themselves what they want for their children. We are natural modelers; it's built into our neurology ... literally. We have something called "mirror neurons," which mirror in our body that which we see in others. This definition explains why, when we see someone who is unhappy, our heart goes out to them. We literally feel their unhappiness in the neurology of our bodies. When we see someone get hurt, we literally cringe because we are feeling it; when we are around depressing people, we feel depressed; when we are around happy people, we feel happy. Our mirror neurons are constantly firing as we interact with others.

Mirror neurons allow us to learn a new skill by imitating. Infants and toddlers rely on it to learn how to talk and walk and eat. Mirror neurons are firing while a child is in the womb and from the moment they are born. People mistakenly believe that children aren't conscious in the womb or as infants;

> The best thing that any parent can do is to model in themselves what they want for their children.

however, their mirror neurons are firing and they are physically modeling everything through their neurology, even if their brain hasn't consciously caught up. When we get older, we rely on mirror neurons, plus our other senses and our brain, to model the behavior of others and learn new things.

If we want our child to be happy, the most powerful thing we can do is be happy ourselves. Mirror neurons allow our children to model our happiness and experience it for themselves through imitation:

- If we want our child to be a great decision maker, we would do well to model great decision making.

- If we want our child to be self-reliant, we would do well to model self-reliance.

- If we want our child to be able to speak up for themselves and have a voice, we would do well to model this behavior in our life.

- If we want our child to feel loved, then we can model feeling loved ourselves.

- If we want our children to say "please" and "thank you," we can say "please" and "thank you" every chance we get.

The key is to model anything we want for our children. When we use ourselves as a model, we give our child the chance to see a behavior in action and practice it in their life. Heather is truly a genius at this as she says, "Be everything for myself that I expect my child to be."

Throughout this book, you'll discover that Heather is constantly modeling for children. She does it through her actions and communication. You'll notice that Heather often tells children, "Well, if it were me, I would ..."

Heather models possible answers for children to try. Through her stories, she models for you, the reader, what she does in certain situations. She intuitively knows that children look to models for how to be in the world, so she is making herself the very best model she can be. She doesn't expect her children to be more than she is. She only expects herself to keep striving to be the best version of herself that she can be, and she trusts that her children will see her and do what is right for them.

Heather's goals as a parent are 100% inside of her control, and some of her goals are to model certain things for her children. Taking the idea of goals and modeling and mirror neurons, I took the opportunity to come up with a list of my goals (i.e., things I want to model with my children, nieces, nephews, and others in my life). These are goals that make me feel happy, so I can model happiness:

- Create my own destiny and follow my heart's desires.
- Seek out opportunities and experiences that will help me grow.
- Love myself completely and treat myself with respect.
- Love my body and look after it with care.
- Be in control of my emotions and choose how I feel in any given moment.
- Be kind and loving to myself and to others.
- Listen carefully to people, hear their desires, and respond in ways that support them.
- Be confident enough with myself and with my views so I can share the truth of what I think or how I feel with anyone.
- See my own genius and gifts and share them with the world.
- Make time for things and people I love and share my light with the people in this world who are important to me.

If I can be these things in my life, then I know I am doing everything I can for the children in my life. I trust that having goals for myself—things that are totally inside my control—and modeling the behaviors in support of these goals are all that really matter.

As with any goals, I am always striving to reach them. I don't reach them every moment of every day. Achieving goals is a process. For example, one goal is to love my body, so I make it a point to eat foods that nourish me, work out, and move my body in ways that feel good; yet, there are days when I eat junk food and skip the gym. I'm not perfect, but I am actively working toward each of these goals in my life.

If your parent modeled all of the behaviors on my list, what would you have thought while growing up? Reread the list and think about how your childhood would have been different. How would your child's life be different if they saw you striving to reach all of these goals—or your own goals, whatever they may be?

Stop for a moment and reflect on your parenting goals. Look back at our lists for ideas. Create a list of goals from your heart.

Review of Chapter 2: What Are Your Goals for Yourself and Desires for Your Child?

- Our goals determine our behavior. We consciously and subconsciously behave in ways that support our goals. Clearly defining our parenting goals will automatically result in parenting behaviors that support our goals.

- We can only set goals for ourselves, and they must be achievable by our own actions.

- We cannot set goals for our children because we cannot control their behavior.

- Modeling (verbally and behaviorally) is the most innate form of learning. We are powerful models for our children and can positively influence their behavior by consciously modeling it verbally or behaviorally in ourselves.

- It is not reasonable to expect our children to be more than we are willing to be ourselves.

CHAPTER 3

As a Parent, What Are You Really Responsible For?

"We have two choices: continue to blame the world for our stress or take responsibility for our own reactions and deliberately change our emotional climate."

—*Doc Childre and Howard Martin, authors of* The HeartMath Solution[1]

Ahhh ... responsibility: It's a heavy load to carry.

Since I was naïve to the responsibility of owning a preschool, it was actually a beautiful gift to me. To be clear, I never took the responsibility of owning the school lightly. I did, however, learn how to reframe the role that "responsibility" played as an owner, an educator, and a mother to the children in my life. My definition of "responsibility" drastically changed over the years.

I was instructed, mentored, and even scolded into a belief system. This system clearly mapped out expectations for parents, teachers, and caregivers and defined their specific roles in a child's development and well-being. With clear guidelines, I started the preschool believing and performing the roles that others had created.

The children were quick to correct *and* reeducate me.

While watching literally thousands of parents over the years, I have seen every style of parenting under the sun. Parenting "experts" often label parents with titles such as a "helicopter parent," an "authoritarian parent," or a "permissive parent." As you can probably guess, I'm not a big fan of labels. Growing up as the "fat" girl, I'm sure you can understand!

Here is the common denominator for every parent with whom I have participated, regardless of the assigned label: In their heart, they truly believed that they were parenting in the best interest of their child. Even when I didn't agree with their method, which was more often than not, I still felt their heart in the moment.

I often wondered if parents were following the belief system to which they were subjected over the years or if it was really how they *wanted* to parent. What if we could clearly define our role of responsibility in our child's life based on our own goals, desires, and experiences?

That's exactly what I did.

I created my list of responsibilities to my children based on my feelings and desires.

This brings me back to the "goals versus desires" discussion in *Chapter 2: What Are Your Goals for Yourself and Desires for Your Child?* I applied the same principles to this subject.

Remembering that the responsibilities had to be within my control, I created a core list or a foundation on which to build over time. Most of the core list items still remain in tact; others were lost and transformed over time, such as when a child would bust through the belief, forcing me to reevaluate my own foundation. (Occasionally we get cracks in the foundation, but they can be fixed with little disruption.)

I thought my foundation was pretty strong. The items on my list seemed reasonable, honorable, and all within "normal" expectations.

Here's my original list of responsibilities:

1. Protect my children from harm.
2. Give my children the best education.
3. Give my children all the opportunities I never had as a child.
4. Teach my children how to be nice and not hurt another's feelings.
5. Teach my children how to act in public.
6. Make decisions for my children because I know what's best.
7. Make my children happy.

This list seemed like a reasonable expectation for me. I know a lot of parents who have similar items on their list. At the time, it resonated with me and felt good.

Then, the children began to chip away at my foundation and I noticed a shift in my beliefs. It was scary because these were my core beliefs; in my mind, they could have cracks but certainly not crevasses the size of the Grand Canyon!

I was inspired to reevaluate my core responsibilities.

I asked myself these questions:

- What is my intention with this responsibility?
- Is this responsibility within my control?

When I thought about the answers, I noticed that my intention often came from a good place in my heart; however, when I asked myself if the responsibility was within my control, more interesting questions surfaced. These questions offered me the opportunity to question and reevaluate my control. The questions are simple; the challenge is about investing energy and time into the answers.

Here is my reevaluation process:

1. Protect my children from harm.

What is my intention with this responsibility?

My intention is to provide a safe environment for my children. (This feels good and is not worth changing.)

Is this responsibility within my control?

This question got me to consider and challenge my own beliefs. Am I able to protect my child from *all* harm? Will I always be there for my child? (This is where I decided to shift.)

Our playground offered the opportunity to reevaluate this belief, every day (well, it *felt* like every day). When I opened the preschool, I had super fun playground equipment, and a lot of it. Helicopters, seesaws, bikes, swings, and slides decorated the grounds like Candy Land.

As children were injured with minor cuts, scrapes, and bruises, I would reposition the equipment to accommodate their needs. If we had a more serious injury, such as those involving stitches or blood, I would move the item to the front lawn of the school as decoration. If the injury actually scared me, the item was taken to the dump. (Fortunately, only two items were in that category.)

I am so grateful that we did not experience a catastrophe! When there are 30 students on a playground at any given time, even with adequate staff in place, there was no possible way to protect every child from harm. Ultimately, I realized that the best I could do was to educate my children to be aware of their own safety, be aware and address the changes that needed to be made to the playground for overall safety, and do my best to help a child in need.

> I realized that the best I could do was to educate my children to be aware of their own safety.

Is this responsibility within my control?

Revised answer: Yes, it is within my control to provide an emotionally and physically safe environment for my children in which to engage, explore, and occasionally get hurt.

2. Give my children the best education.

What is my intention with this responsibility?

My intention is to offer amazing educational opportunities to my children. (This sounds reasonable. I will keep this!)

Is this responsibility within my control?

This question got me to consider and challenge my beliefs. What is the definition of "best" education? How do I know that *my* definition is really the "best" for my child? (A shift is coming ...)

When I was learning how to run a classroom, my mentors would guide me through the "best" way to educate preschoolers. We did everything we were supposed to do to have the children learn the essentials. During circle time, we would sit down as a group and do things like sing *Old MacDonald Had a Farm*, review the calendar and the days of the week, discuss the weather, and read books.

If you have ever had the pleasure of participating in circle time with 30 two- and three-year-olds, you would have instantly seen that there was not one way to educate each child. Some have complete attention and focus, some are looking outside, some are untying their shoes, and some are picking their nose. Whatever the distraction, I promise that some child is doing it!

I thought we were providing the best education for each child based on the guidelines the experts outlined for us. Fortunately, the children set me straight. I realized that the "best" education, regardless of age, is determined on an individual basis. Above and beyond that, each child would let me know, in many ways, what the best education was for them. If they loved reading but did not enjoy arts and crafts time, I would accommodate their specific needs as often as possible.

Is this responsibility within my control?

Revised answer: Yes, it is within my control to observe and provide the tools and opportunities to help each child be their best. Children instinctually know what is best for them, and I just need to listen and honor their feelings.

3. Give my children all the opportunities I never had as a child.

What is my intention with this responsibility?

My intention is to present the most opportunities to experience and enjoy life. (This is good stuff.)

Is this responsibility within my control?

This is within my control, but do I want to control this? This question got me to consider and challenge my beliefs. What if they don't want the opportunities that I missed as a child? Can other people provide different options for my child? (Can you feel the shift?)

My parents were not even close to being athletic. They were never really involved in any team sports, at least to my knowledge. They thought it would be best for me to play a sport in order to get exercise, learn how to be a "team player," and maybe provide them with the experience.

Well, after careful consideration and input from me, we decided on softball. It sounded like a good idea—until I got on the field. I was positioned in left field, and last on the batting list, so I'm sure you can figure out how good I was. I would hit the ball and head toward first base.

The coach would scream, *"RUN, HEATHER!"*

I would yell back, *"I AMMMMMMM!"*

I wanted to quit. I didn't like it, it wasn't fun, and the only thing I looked forward to was the pizza party at the end of the season. My parents thought they knew what was best. They thought they were offering me a great opportunity and one they never had. Unfortunately, they didn't listen to my repeated requests to quit. They said that I needed to "stick it out" and couldn't give up on my team because they depended on me. If I didn't want to play next year, they said that I didn't have to, but I was required to "give it a chance."

Had I quit, would I have let my team down when I was in left field, benched, or never able to get up to bat? By staying on the team, I let myself down. I felt worse about myself after every practice and every game. I learned that it's okay and often necessary to quit when I know in my heart that I don't like something. As a child, I knew what was best for me.

Is this responsibility within my control?

Revised answer: Yes, it is within my control to open the door to a wide variety of opportunities, allowing my child to determine what feels good and being okay with the result.

4. Teach my children how to be nice and not hurt another's feelings.

What is my intention with this responsibility?

My intention is to have my child be accepted and liked by others. (This sounds more like a goal than a desire or an intention. I can definitely clean up this intention.)

Revised answer: My intention is to allow, support, and guide my children to be the best version of themselves.

> My intention is to allow, support, and guide my children to be the best version of themselves.

Is this responsibility within my control?

This question got me to consider and challenge my beliefs. What does it mean to "be nice"? Are we really responsible for another's feelings? (This is a big shift.)

This question about responsibility took years to shift. Many times, I heard the same sentence with different endings from thousands of children.

It always began the same way: "Miss Heather, Ava hurt my feelings because ..." Then, fill in the blank with "She said I was ugly," "She won't play with me," "She won't share with me," and thousands of other words from a never-ending list.

Initially, I would ask each child to state their case, express their emotions, listen to each other, and make amends. The only problem was that it would happen again, and again, and again! It was like the movie *Groundhog Day*. It is exhausting to mediate between siblings or friends, but can you imagine doing it for an entire school? I had to learn to preserve my own sanity. I tested a number of methods, none of them achieving my desired outcome, which was peace and harmony.

One day, Sarah, a three-year old student, came to me and cried, "Kevin hurt my feelings because he took my doll from me."

I simply looked at her and said, "Is my name Kevin?"

"No."

"Who do you need to talk to?"

She looked at me and clearly stated, "You."

I simply said, "My name is not Kevin. If Kevin hurt your feelings, you need to talk to Kevin."

She looked at me, and then walked over to Kevin and actually started talking to him. I stood by to support them if they needed help communicating, but basically I stayed out of it. Success! *I was free!*

After a few months of practice from each child, they eventually learned how to communicate with each other—free from my authority and, over time, free from my support. By removing the unrealistic expectations for the children to always be nice and not hurt each other's feelings, they were actually given an opportunity to practice their communication and cooperation skills at a young age.

Is this responsibility within my control?

Revised answer: Yes, it is within my control to allow, support, and guide children to the best version of themselves. Sometimes that means me staying out of it.

5. Teach my children how to act in public.

What is my intention with this responsibility?

My intention is to help my children understand and communicate their needs and desires in any environment. (This intention feels good.)

Is this responsibility within my control?

This question got me to consider and challenge my beliefs. Maybe, when my child is small, I can have perceived control, but what happens when they outgrow me? If I control their behavior or actions in public as a small child, when will they be able to practice and master self-regulation, self-understanding, or self-discipline? (This is a challenging shift.)

I completely embraced and agreed with this responsibility for many years. I'm sure you can see the pattern over time from the previous examples; my views were altered and completely shifted. I was given the gift of children who knew what they wanted and were not afraid to do whatever it took to get their needs met. (Some would say they were "strong willed.")

Every time I was under the impression—more like *delusion*—that I could control my children's behavior or actions, they would intensify the situation to a new level. This happened every time, without fail.

True to form, the biggest, loudest, and most obnoxious outbursts would inevitably come in the middle of a prospective family while they were touring the school. It was embarrassing and humiliating, and it occurred at the worst possible time.

I would do my best to explain away the child's behavior or actions; however, one day, I just couldn't do it anymore. To be honest, I was tired of making excuses for the children. The truth is that they are new to this planet, learning what works and what doesn't, and doing their best to communicate with limited experience and resources.

We all have outbursts of anger, frustration, and sadness at one time or another. Many adults act or behave as if we haven't "practiced" communication at all. It was not an option—legally or morally—to spank, yell, criticize, or shame a child for their unwanted behavior.

> When I shifted my responsibility in my mind and my practice, I witnessed amazing benefits.

Therefore, I had to change my thought. I reframed my responsibility. My responsibility was no longer to control a behavior or action with punishment, such as a time-out. My role was to communicate my desires, listen to their desires, and work together in cooperation to get both of our needs met.

When I shifted my responsibility in my mind and my practice, I witnessed amazing benefits. I was able to tour prospective clients free from fear. The children learned how to verbalize their needs free from tantrums or outbursts, and I believed that they would be able to handle whatever came their way, with or without me.

Is this responsibility within my control?

Revised answer: Yes, it is within my control to communicate my desires, listen to their desires, and work together in cooperation to get both of our needs met.

6. **Make decisions for my children because I know what's best.**

What is my intention with this responsibility?

My intention is to guide and support my children in every way possible. (This one is true for me.)

Is this responsibility within my control?

Yes, this responsibility is within my control, but do I *want* it to be? This question got me to consider and challenge my beliefs. Does it feel good for others to make decisions for me? Did my parents make decisions for me that I could make for myself? Is it possible to benefit from the choice I made, regardless of positive or negative consequences? (This was an easy shift for me.)

> My toddlers taught me that the secret to choice was to decide what I needed and wanted in any given situation, and then offer a choice between two options with which I agreed.

It felt so good to let go of this responsibility! When I was making decisions for one child, it wasn't a big deal; when I was making decisions for 30 kids at any given time, it was incredibly exhausting and impossible.

Even beyond the task of "decision making," I quickly learned that I was taking away valuable lessons in communication and cooperation, even when I would make a decision that seemed to be in everyone's best interest.

I did not let every child in my preschool do everything they wanted to do; however, I learned to give them a choice ... *always*. When our free will is taken away, it usually shows up as an extreme primal expression of frustration or anger. There is always a choice.

My toddlers taught me that the secret to choice was to decide what I needed and wanted in any given situation, and then offer a choice between two options with which I agreed.

For example, if I wanted the children to line up outside, this is what I said:

"Okay, everyone. We are going outside and you have a choice to make. You can hop your way outside *or* you can jump your way outside. Your choice!"

It worked every time. I would get creative, mix it up, and make it fun, but there was always a choice. The added benefit was that they would often learn about consequences on their own, based on the choices they made for themselves. Again, I got out of the equation, which led to the children practicing the art of decision making at 14 months old.

Is this responsibility within my control?

Revised answer: Yes, it is within my control to give choices that will work for me and honor my children.

7. Make my children happy.

What is my intention with this responsibility?

My intention is to provide a fun, loving environment in which my children can thrive and grow. (This is what I want.)

Is this responsibility within my control?

This question got me to consider and challenge my beliefs. Is it my responsibility to make *anyone* happy? Is it even *possible*? Where is my focus on happiness best spent? Is it on others or on myself? (This requires a shift in my awareness.)

Here's an example of a recurring experience in my life: My friend calls, and she is upset, disengaged, and smack in the middle of a massive pity party. I pull all the tricks out of my bag to cheer her up, but inevitability "Debbie Downer" takes over the conversation. By the time I get off the phone, I am just as upset, depressed, and disheartened as she is. My intention is to cheer her up; unfortunately, I just go down on the sinking ship with her. How does this happen? I was feeling so good before I picked up the phone. Am I a bad friend for not being able to cheer her up?

My kids always came to the rescue with answers to my complicated questions. I would watch them in action throughout the day. For example, Jordan, who was three years old, was a great teacher and a genuinely happy spirit. She had her moments, but don't we all?

One day, Jordan was on the playground, fluttering around like a butterfly. She stopped to check in with kids who were playing in different areas, always looking for fun and happiness to add to her spirit. When she came across a sad child, she stopped, checked in with the child, and gave them an opportunity to join her in her happiness. If they didn't join her, she let them know in her own way that she didn't want to play with them.

Jordan instinctually knew that it was not her responsibility and it wouldn't serve anyone to join her friend in sadness. All she could do was lead by example by letting her happiness radiate across the playground. I love this lesson!

> Yes, it is within my control to acknowledge others' emotions, offer inspiration, and do my best not to join them in their misery.

Is this responsibility within my control?

Revised answer: Yes, it is within my control to acknowledge others' emotions, offer inspiration, and do my best not to join them in their misery. It is in my control to lead by example and let my happiness radiate across the world.

Now, my foundation is stronger than ever! I have built my core list from intention instead of control.

Here's my new and improved list of responsibilities:

1. My intention is to provide a safe environment for my children.

2. My intention is to offer amazing educational opportunities to my children.

3. My intention is to present the most opportunities to experience and enjoy life.

4. My intention is to allow, support, and guide my children to be the best version of themselves.

5. My intention is to help my children understand and communicate their needs and desires in any environment.

6. My intention is to guide and support my children in every way possible.

7. My intention is to provide a fun, loving environment in which my children can thrive and grow.

When I shifted my perspective from responsibilities rooted in control to responsibilities founded from intention, I felt a tremendous weight lifted. These were responsibilities over which I had complete control because they were within my goals and desires as a teacher and a parent. As long as I am doing my best, that's all I can do.

> "We are each responsible for our own life—
> no other person is or even can be."
>
> —Oprah Winfrey, media producer, talk-
> show host, and philanthropist

Does your child feel empowered to create their own life?

Heather has shared what she feels are her responsibilities as a parent. I also asked her the inverse of the question, "As a parent, what are you *not* responsible for?"

Heather quickly answered:

- "I am not responsible for my child's actions, especially if I perceive them as a mistake.

- "I am not responsible for rescuing them. I know that they are capable of solving all of their own problems."

As you read through this book, you'll discover a consistent pattern with Heather. In just about every interaction, she makes it a point to empower children to make their own decisions and create their own lives. She intuitively knows that making mistakes is part of the learning process. She sees her responsibility as a parent to give children opportunities to practice communication and make decisions.

Here are a few other things for which Heather feels responsible as a parent:

- "I am responsible for giving my child the chance to do it themselves and learn on their own."

- "I am responsible for giving my child the space to learn their own lessons and not remove the experiences to protect or preserve them."

- "I am responsible for creating opportunities for my child to experience the fact that they are responsible for their behavior."

Put another way, Heather feels responsible for fostering a sense of true empowerment and responsibility.

The Triangle of Disempowerment

In psychology, the "Triangle of Disempowerment" concept[2] includes three roles: the Perpetrator, the Victim, and the Rescuer. When a stressful situation arises, we often go into one of these roles.

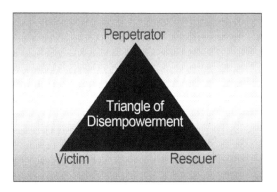

For example, if another kid bullies our daughter, we feel deeply bothered. We view the bully as the Perpetrator and our child as the Victim, and we play the role of Rescuer. The problem with this triangle is that we just end up going in circles. If we approach the bully, the bully now views us as the Perpetrator and himself as the Victim.

Here's another example: My sister was a high school volleyball coach. Parents sometimes felt that my sister wasn't playing their daughter enough in games, so they viewed their child as the Victim of my sister's coaching choices.

They "rescued" their child by talking to my sister—the Perpetrator—and telling her that she needed to play their daughter—the Victim—more. Of course, my sister felt as if the parent had become the Perpetrator and *she* was now the Victim of their demands! They all just moved to different positions on the triangle.

Our Western society is built on this disempowering frame (e.g., "We are the victims of disease," "We need to step in and rescue a nation," "The food companies are poisoning us," or "The politicians are making our lives harder.") Read the headlines in any newspaper and you will see how we are entrenched in the Triangle of Disempowerment model. We have come to believe that we need to blame others for our situation rather than take responsibility for making different choices in our lives.

We have all played the various roles in the Triangle of Disempowerment model. Read through each of these roles and think of a time when you played this role in your life. Think of how advertisers, lawyers, politicians, and our government play these roles as well.

Perpetrator: "I get to feel safe by hurting others and putting them down."

- Needs to be in control; uses verbal or physical force to stay there
- Deals with threats, new ideas, and conflict with anger to stay safe in the role of being the dominant person
- Uses blame, criticism, and attacks; vents to release stress
- Is highly judgmental of others; displays anger when others do not do what they say
- Has a strong sense of entitlement of "you owe me"; uses verbal or physical force to get it
- Has a strong need to be right and not have their authority challenged
- Finds reasons to make others wrong and scapegoats them

Victim: "I get to feel safe by being submissive."

- Deals with threats or mistreatment by "giving in" to feel safe; responds in a submissive way when others act inappropriately
- Is unable to stand up for themselves; avoids confrontation

- Believes that their needs do not count

- Can be overly sensitive, wishy washy, and unable to make and stick to decisions

- Doesn't take responsibility for their feelings

- Feeds off of the beliefs of the Perpetrator and Rescuer that they cannot take care of themselves

- Blames the Perpetrator for their problems

- Moves between "poor me" and anger; blames others

Rescuer: "I get to feel good at the expense of others' rights to take care of themselves."

- Feels they are more capable and therefore responsible for helping a "weaker" person

- Uses rescuing and enabling to connect or feel important

- Blames the Perpetrator for problems while refusing to address their own problems

- Feels guilty when not involved or helping with others' problems

- As a super caretaker, feels that they are giving their self away, which may create depression

- Has a strong sense of entitlement with the Victim (e.g., "You owe me because of all I've done for you.")

As you reflect on your experiences in each of these roles, do you feel empowered or disempowered?

When we see ourselves as the Victim (e.g., when we get a call from a nasty bill collector, when we see a boss being unfair, when our sister treats us badly, or when a neighbor upsets us), we are actually teaching our children how to be a Victim.

The more they see us feeling like Victims—or Rescuers or Perpetrators—the more they are influenced to see the world through those lenses.

Step off the Triangle of Disempowerment.

If we want our children to feel empowered, we need to shift our conscious beliefs about how to be in this world. We need to be the change we want to see in the world and realize that we have the power to create our own experience with friends, families, work, journalism, politics, and the environment. When we take responsibility for ourselves and stop blaming others, we show our children how to be in their power and do the same.

The only way to get off the triangle is to step off and stop playing the roles of Victim, Rescuer, and Perpetrator. Choose to take your power back. Choose to empower your children. Heather intuitively knows not to step on the triangle in the first place. In her model of the world, the roles of Victim, Perpetrator, and Rescuer don't exist.

Shift to the Triangle of Empowerment.

The Triangle of Empowerment model was created by David Emerald[3] as a more empowering way to view the traditional roles we play of Perpetrator, Victim, and Rescuer.

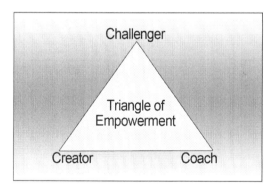

In the Triangle of Empowerment model, the roles are as follows:

- *Creator:* Someone who stops to think about what they want and about their long-term goal or vision. They are outcome oriented as opposed to problem oriented. They feel empowered to create their own reality.

- *Challenger:* Something (i.e., a person or a situation) that forces us to clarify our goals. They encourage us, through contrast, to get clearer about what we *do* want, and then focus our efforts towards moving closer to that goal.

- *Coach:* Someone who asks us questions that enable us to see the possibilities for positive action, and to focus on what we *do* want instead of what we *don't* want. They support us from the sidelines, but let us play the game.

Heather intuitively sees children as the Creators of their experiences, and she may play the role of Coach (or cheerleader, as she frequently thinks of it). In the hundreds of scenarios I have discussed with Heather, I have never once seen her play the role of "Rescuer."

It is natural for us to want to protect our children from harm, hurt, or poor choices. Take a moment and think about the responsibility of parenting. Do you want to be a Rescuer or a Coach? Do you want your child to feel like a Victim or a Creator of their experiences?

None of us wants to see ourselves as a Perpetrator, but the truth is that we have all played that role. Reread the definition of Perpetrator and then ask yourself, "Have I ever used verbal or physical force, threats, anger, blame, criticism, or judgment?"

Our current educational, business, law enforcement, and (frequently) family models are built around the idea that we need to use threats to control behavior. Here are some examples:

- "If you don't obey the law, you will go to jail."
- "If you don't perform, you will be fired."
- "If you don't do your homework, you will fail."
- "If you don't behave, you are going to get a time-out."

We rely heavily on a fear model to control the behavior we want in others. We are unconsciously playing the role of Perpetrator on the Triangle of Disempowerment. Ironically, this strategy for controlling others through fear makes us feel safe.

Fortunately, this book supports the Triangle of Empowerment model and presents a new way for us to be with our families (and with all human beings). As you learn to see the world through Heather's eyes, you will discover that, at every opportunity, she empowers her children to create their experience

> Put simply, Heather sees that her primary responsibility is to help others take full responsibility in their lives.

through choice. If their choice isn't working for them, she encourages them to choose differently. She also models how to be in her power. She provides every possible opportunity for her children to step into their power.

Put simply, Heather sees that her primary responsibility is to help others take full responsibility in their lives. As you read through this book, notice how Heather creates empowering situations in every moment.

Review of Chapter 3: As a Parent, What Are You Really Responsible For?

- We have an opportunity to define what we are and are not responsible for as parents.

- When we define our responsibilities based on a positive intention (and not on a desire for control of a specific outcome), we create a healthier and more relaxed environment for everyone.

- The Triangle of Disempowerment has the roles of Perpetrator, Victim, and Rescuer. When we play these roles, we are acting in a disempowered state.

- The Triangle of Empowerment has the roles of Challenger, Creator, and Coach. When we play these roles, we are acting in an empowered state.

CHAPTER 4

What Is Your Definition of Happiness?

"When I was five years old, my mother always told me that happiness was the key to life. When I went to school, they asked me what I wanted to be when I grew up. I wrote down 'Happy.' They told me I didn't understand the assignment, and I told them they didn't understand life."

—*John Lennon, musician and founding member of The Beatles*

It all started well.

I was a happy baby. Friends would tell my mother, "Let the baby sleep," but she would wake me up just to play with me. When I was four years old, Papa Bill designed and built a house for us in Conroe, Texas (about 40 miles north of Houston); unfortunately, it required a commute for my father that would prove to be unbearable. Eventually, my father decided to live in Houston and come home to Conroe on the weekends. After many months apart, my parents decided to move back to Houston, permanently.

This is about the time when my weight showed up. From the age of four, I was overweight. ("Overweight" is a polite way to say "obese.") Weight has been a constant theme in my life. I was raised "deep in the heart of Texas" where, at least in my experience, the expectation as a young lady was to be a cheerleader by three years old, a pageant contestant, or an athlete. (I was really good at arts and crafts!)

I was subjected to a lot of bullying throughout my school years. Remember: This was the '70s, and there were not a lot of obese children at this time, especially in my neck of the woods. I hated school—just about every minute of it. It was a dark, difficult, and stressful time in my life.

As I got older, I got bigger … and bigger. I experienced bullying every day from the moment I got on the bus, throughout the day in school, and on my bus ride home. As I got off the bus each day, I dropped my binder on the ground and took a long time to gather my papers, just to avoid walking in front of a bully who would constantly taunt me from behind when I walked from the bus stop to my home.

It was a lonely world. I had best friends, but I never seemed to fit in anywhere. I was in ballet and tap dance, so try to imagine how I felt on stage— actually, in the back, left-hand corner of the stage—in a red tutu. I didn't feel good about any attempt I made. I felt like a dumpy, fat girl who had to shop in the junior's section at seven years old.

My parents had many friends who had multiple children. (I was an only child.) I think my mom and dad would visit their friends just to have me play with other children and get me out of their hair for a few hours. I was often the oldest child in the group, so I would be declared the "babysitter." The adults would go downstairs and talk while I was upstairs with the kids. With babysitting, I found something that made me smile. I played games with the younger children, read to them, and taught them how to organize and clean up their playroom.

(I have a little OCD—not really, but kind of—when it comes to organization. I blame it on my disorganized mom. We could never find scissors or tweezers in the house, so she would buy another pair every time we were at the store. When she died, I found over 17 pairs of tweezers in various locations throughout her house!)

The parents we were visiting really appreciated me entertaining the children and, of course, cleaning the massive, ridiculous mess in the playroom. It was a win-win for everyone!

I officially started babysitting without adult supervision when I was 12 years old. I absolutely loved it. The children were always so accepting, loving, free from judgment, fun, genuine, and authentically themselves. I appreciated and admired their innocence, and wanted to return to this innocence myself. I felt happy in the presence of young children. I felt joy for the small things in life, wonder for the big things, and excitement for what the future held.

> I loved being with children. They laughed, cried, yelled, and jumped for joy.

I loved being with children. They laughed, cried, yelled, and jumped for joy. All the expressions would happen in a matter of minutes. They never waited to be happy.

I read a study that concluded, "Glee, not just laughter, in a nursery school ranges from **18.4 to 45 incidents per hour per child**."[1] In my experience, this has been true, without exception. I have never been around any adult who expresses 18 incidents per hour of glee, let alone 45 times per hour!

I pursued a career working with children. At the time, I thought I would be a kindergarten teacher. I really liked working with younger children because they offered me the closest experience to happiness on a daily basis. I worked for preschools, enrolled in child development classes, interned with Head Start programs, interned in a kindergarten class, and eventually ended up at the MGM Grand as a youth counselor. I had dreams of opening my own preschool, but I had no idea how that would happen.

For more than 10 years, I filled my life with children. One would think that I would have learned how to be happy. I thought I would have at least 10 incidents of glee every hour by that point, but I didn't.

"I'll be happy when ..."

My famous line was always, "I'll be happy when I am a size 12." A size 12 was a far journey from a size 24—literally half my size! I felt very good with my career and relationships, but the weight was literally holding me back from achieving happiness ... at least that's what I thought.

Two years ago, I experienced a major weight loss. I got down to a size 12 and—guess what? I wasn't happy! I wanted more. Then I wanted to be a size 10. I made my way to a 10 and—guess what? It wasn't enough. I was determined to be a size 8 and I made it, but I still wasn't happy. How about a 6? Would that make me happy?

Well, I never made it to a size 6; I actually went back to a size 12. For the past two years, I have spent every day looking in the mirror and asking myself, "Why isn't a size 12 good enough?" For 25 years, I waited to be a 12 and, when it finally came, I was not happy.

I am now happy to say that I am making peace with being a size 12, and I'm practicing happy expressions in the mirror on a daily basis.

I realized that I had denied myself happiness (regarding body image) for years based on the size of my clothing. What a waste of time! My parents actually reinforced this belief when they died; both were overweight for the majority of their lives.

During their last few days on this planet, they never said, "Gosh, I wish I would have lost weight to fit into a size 6!" (They did say that they wished they had taken better care of their body as well as their mind and spirit.)

> "If you wait to be happy, you will wait forever. If you are happy now you will be happy forever."
>
> —*Sally Huss, American writer and artist*

I had Sally Huss's card on my mirror for years. I never fully comprehended its profound message until a year ago.

My eyes are open. My heart is willing. The children remind me every day to be aware of happy moments. I am no longer chasing the dream of happiness ... the dream of "I'll be happy when ..."

> The children remind me every day to be aware of happy moments.

What is the source of my happiness?

My happiness comes from moments with others, by myself, and definitely with children. Happiness is unique to each individual. Things that make me happy make my husband crazy, such as riding my bicycle with my dog on the front. (I call my dog "Toto" and my husband calls me the "Crazy Dog Lady.") I am happiest on a dance floor, dancing until 5 a.m. (My husband dislikes dancing ... a lot!) My dad loved to play golf. (I thought it was a terrible sport. Hit the ball, chase it. Hit the ball, chase it. Get the ball in the hole. Do it all over again 17 more times.)

Happiness comes in different forms for everybody.

When I was nine years old, my mom decided to buy a minivan—the kind with the wood panels. I made it clear that I believed she was making a mistake. I think my exact words were, "This car is stupid, ugly, and dumb." In all fairness, we had just tested out a sports car earlier in the morning. I was shocked and horrified to learn that she was actually choosing the mini van over a sports car! My mom's boss was standing in the parking lot, and she was showing him her new van. Her boss asked me if I liked it and, of course, I told him the truth.

"It's ugly and embarrassing!"

His only response was, "That's why there is chocolate, strawberry, and vanilla!"

I never forgot that. Happiness is my choice. My happiness is not dependent on anyone's opinions, ideas, actions, or circumstances. (This concept is still a work in progress for me.)

> "I don't any longer think it's possible that any other people can hurt me. They're just giving me their observation, and I'm giving it meaning. And so I get to choose what that meaning is."
>
> –Rita, audience member in Oprah's Lifeclass

The children never asked me to make them happy.

My children always created their own happiness, and I was lucky to be able to join them in it; however, as they got older, the happiness would slowly diminish. Upon entering formal school, genuine happiness was often replaced with worry, stress, and anxiety, which led to fewer "incidents of glee" on an hour-to-hour basis.

My happiness is dependent on my awareness and focus. I focus on great experiences, people, things, and ideas I have while I am here on this planet. It is more than positive thoughts; it is a genuine attention and acknowledgement to the greatness in my life.

> I now correct myself when I say, "She didn't make me happy." I change it to, "I'm choosing to be unhappy in this moment."

I now correct myself when I say, "She didn't make me happy."

I change it to, "I'm choosing to be unhappy in this moment."

Talk about responsibility! Now I am in control of my own happiness. I choose where to put my attention. (Honestly, it's easier to blame others for my feelings than to take responsibility for my own emotions.)

When I am with a screaming child, feeling not one ounce of happiness, I remember a time when we were together in pure bliss. I hold that vision and wait until the child joins me. Sometimes I wait a *very* long time; sometimes I leave until they can join me. It never serves me or my child to join them in their unhappy moments. I hold the space. (This method actually works with my husband and friends as well!)

It doesn't mean that I am cold or disconnected from my child. I care enough about myself *and* my child to say, "I understand that you are having a difficult time right now. When you are ready, let me know how I can help. Until then, I will be in the kitchen, working on dinner. I love you, and I know that you will figure this out."

I know better now. I must do better. Happiness is my responsibility. I choose happiness, even if I have to ride in a minivan for the rest of my life.

What makes your heart sing?

Several years ago, *Time* magazine dedicated a whole issue on "The Science of Happiness."[2] Many articles summarized the latest findings about happiness research. The world's top scientists, thought leaders, and authors pontificated on the true source of happiness. One astute writer noted that Americans have a fascination—an obsession, really—with happiness unlike any other country on Earth.

The big question was, "What makes the human heart sing? Could science and research provide an answer?" The magazine was filled with interesting findings that looked at many variables:

- "Does money make us happy?" (Not really.)
- "Do pets make us happier?" (They can.)
- "Do friends make us happier?" (Definitely.)
- "Are we happier when we have a religious or spiritual practice?" (A thumbs up here.)
- "Do children bring us joy?" (Maybe not every day, but overall yes.)

... and on and on. Most of the studies looked at what *external* experiences influenced our happiness.

The results, in my opinion, were interesting but far from conclusive. What exactly is happiness? Is it different than feeling content, peaceful, joyful, connected, playful, blissful, light, cheerful, or satisfied?

For example, my job may cause me a lot of stress and frustration but, in the large scheme of things, it brings me a sense of satisfaction. Am I happy? I would offer that happiness comes with many names and ways of experiencing it. It is much simpler for me to think of happiness in simpler terms. In other words, happiness is when I "feel good" and unhappiness is when I "feel bad."

I have done deep seeking on "how to get happier" over the past 20 years. In truth, I feel as if I've only found the answer to the "happiness" question in the past year while working on this book related to children.

Heather often tells me, "Children are the real teachers—not us."

I originally argued with her, saying that I had been on this planet way longer and had a lot more wisdom about how things worked. I thought she was crazy to suggest that children had so much more to teach me than I had to teach them. However, like many of my worldviews on this subject, I realized that Heather had it right and I had it backwards. Children are the teachers, especially when it comes to learning how to be happy.

> Children are the teachers, especially when it comes to learning how to be happy.

I love the idea of finding someone who is exceptional at something, and then figuring out how they get their results. When I started thinking more about the recipe for happiness, I looked for models of pure happiness from people who were completely happy nearly all of the time.

Hands down, the Q'ero in Peru win the happiness award. They live in primitive conditions at 12,000+ feet, have no electricity, and mostly eat potatoes three meals a day, yet they are pure joy in human form. In my travels, Costa Ricans are also among the happiest people I have met. I also know several people who just emanate happiness on a daily basis. Heather is truly one of the happiest people I know.

What is the recipe for happiness?

Here's the common denominator: All of the happiest people I know have a childlike quality and a wonder for the world. I look around at the children in my life. Small children (up to the age of five or six, before we add the responsibilities of school, achievement, and life) are the happiest people on Earth. I have travelled to more than 40 countries and have experienced this to be true everywhere I have been.

What can we learn from happy people and children? What is the strategy for happiness? I have come to the same conclusion that nearly every spiritual master has reached and that every child intuitively knows: Happiness comes from within. Looking outside ourselves to our children, our jobs, our pets, money, material things, friends, or spouses cannot make us happy.

We are in control of how much happiness—how much "feel good"—we experience in our lives. (If you don't yet believe that you are in control, look at ways that you may be living inside the Triangle of Disempowerment. Step off the triangle and take your power back!)

Children intuitively do two things to experience happiness in their lives that we can model:

1. Choose "feel good" over "feel bad."

Have you ever watched small children on a playground? They move from one thing to the next, exploring everything. They spend time with things that make them feel good and move on from things that aren't fun or make them feel bad.

My four-year-old nephew is a pro at moving away from things that feel bad and toward things that feel good. At the Family Fun Center arcade, he quickly ditched the air hockey game that he didn't like—even though there was money left—and sought out and spent extra time on games that were more fun. On the jungle gym, he fluttered about, seeking friends who were fun to play with and quickly ditching those who didn't match his vibe. When I told him that it was time to go, he was super bummed because all he wanted to do was stay in a space where he was having a ball!

At home, my nephew is the same way. When his mom and I talk, he bails out to go play (or begs me to ditch the conversation and join him in a game of hide-and-go-seek). He is in constant motion, searching for things all day that are fun and feel good. When something isn't fun or doesn't feel good, he does everything in his power to escape it. Time-outs are pure torture for him, and he desperately tries to get out of the "feel bad" space and back into the "feel good" space.

We have created a world in which it's harder to bail out of things that aren't fun in any given moment; however, any spiritually enlightened master will tell you that happiness is a choice. We can't always control our external environment, but we can take our power back and choose how we experience our external world.

For example, we can choose to let our boss drive us crazy, or we can take our power back and choose to feel differently in the moment. We can choose to let our spouse upset us, or we can take our power back and choose to shift our thinking.

> Happiness comes from a place of empowerment and the realization that we have a choice in how we experience everything in our lives.

Unhappiness comes from feeling out of control in the world and the "Victim" of what others are "doing" to us. Happiness comes from a place of empowerment and the realization that we have a choice in how we experience everything in our lives. We can choose to move away from things that feel bad and move toward more things that feel good. The more "in our power" we can be, the more we can step off the Triangle of Disempowerment and take our power back, leading to more happiness. We can simply model children and choose "feel good" over "feel bad" in every moment.

So much of this book is about taking your power back and honoring what feels good to you in any situation. Heather has mastered the "feel good" strategy in every aspect of parenting. By the time you've reached the end of this book, you'll also know how to do it!

2. **Do what you want, when you want, how you want.**

Few things are sweeter than watching a child totally engrossed in an activity, having fun. The outside world has gone silent, and they are enjoying an activity for no other reason than the fun experience of exploration.

The Montessori school system—and Heather's preschool—were founded on the idea that kids are naturally curious, are natural learners, and will naturally find activities that resonate with them in the moment. Put another way, these founders know that children thrive when they are given freedom to do what they want, when they want, how they want. The more freedom a child has to experience the world in their own way, the more they will grow and seek out even more experiences.

I don't know when we lost the idea that we have the ability—the right—to do what we want, when we want, how we want, but we have lost it.

You may be thinking, "I can't just do what I want, when I want, how I want ... that's selfish! Life is not a free ride and just fun and games. You have to work hard. You have to sacrifice for what you really want. You can't play all the time because you have to support yourself."

Our culture has built up many beliefs and sayings that have become ingrained into our life (and into our parenting). We can't see that we created the limiting worldviews that are preventing us from experiencing our own happiness. After all, a belief is nothing more than a phrase we say to ourselves over and over until we believe it to be true.

We don't believe that it's possible to create a life where we get our material needs met *and* have fun, but what if we could shift that patterned thinking? What if we could find models who do what makes their soul sing *and* make a living? There are plenty of these models, and Heather is one of them.

Think about your life. When are the times that you do what you want, when you want, how you want—without caring what anybody thinks?

- Maybe you love to dress in a unique way and wear exactly what you want.

- Maybe you like to steal a few minutes and create some kind of art.

- Maybe you love to be silly with a few girlfriends on a night out or a weekend away.

- Maybe you get to choose where in town to eat on Friday nights or where in the world you'd like to go on vacation.

- Maybe you listen to your favorite music loudly in your car, or carve out "me" time at the gym or spa.

- Maybe you create something at work that is all your idea, and you have full freedom to carry it out just how you want it to be.

Take a moment and think about when and where you feel total freedom to do exactly what you want, when you want, how you want. These can be (and probably are) small moments because, in truth, life is just many small moments all strung together.

Several years ago, I decided that I wanted to shift the trajectory of my life. I wanted to take back control of my time and how I spent it. I was done working long, stressful hours in the corporate consulting world, I wanted to work for myself, and I wanted to create something unique on the planet.

Simply put, I wanted to create a life where I could do a whole lot more of what I wanted, when I wanted, how I wanted. Out of that desire and intent, I created the Everyday Genius Institute. Creating this company has been the most wonderful journey of learning, growing, and expanding in my life.

Over the past few years, I have created a totally different life than the one I had been living. In the process, I had to tune out the world (and everybody's opinion) and my critical voice (which can be very loud), and remind myself that I am in control of creating my experience and my happiness. I have the power to do what I want, when I want, how I want.

We all have this power. No matter what your current situation is, you have the power to create a different experience.

- How can you create a life where you are doing much more of what you want, when you want, how you want (without caring what anybody thinks)?
- How can you carve out more time to explore something that interests you?
- How can you break free of your obligations for a few hours a month to do something that makes your soul sing?
- How can you find a way to take a class, join a group, or pursue an interest just for the pure pleasure of it?

You don't have to start out big, unless you want to commit to what I call a "life makeover" like I did. It just requires that you put yourself first, figure out small things that make your soul sing, and commit to doing them.

For example, a couple of months ago, I felt the strangest urge to paint. I haven't painted since my fifth-grade art class, but the urge overcame me so strongly that I went down to the art store and spent about $50 in paints, brushes, and paper.

In my living room, with a towel on the floor, I randomly picked colors and moved them around on the paper in shapes that just felt right. I created all sorts of art with circles and squares and stars and lines that resembled abstract trees. If it's possible to have an orgasm of the soul, I was having one while I painted. I had no idea that something so small would bring me so much pleasure.

> When I see small children, they are in divine bliss because they are experiencing the world and really don't care what anybody thinks.

I have no plans to show these paintings to anybody. At some point, I will probably burn them in a fire ceremony and celebrate the creative force that burns inside all of us. Actually, I don't know what I will do with them, but I do know that I felt the urge to paint and I painted. It was amazing!

In reflection, the joy of painting came because neither I nor anybody else cared about the results. I did it all for *me*—all for the pure pleasure of just *doing* it. When I see small children, they are in divine bliss because they are experiencing the world and really don't care what anybody thinks.

At some point, we start teaching our children to care very much about what others think. We become obsessed about it, as indicated by our cultural obsession with manners. As if our own obsession isn't enough, marketers and advertisers thrive on (and manufacture) our fear of not belonging.

We think that we have more to teach our children than they have to teach us, but what if *they* are the ones who have it right?

- What if *we* could be more childlike and care less about what everybody thinks?

- What if *we* could do more of what we want, when we want, how we want to make us happy?

- What if *we* could play in more moments in our life?

- What would it take for each and every one of *us* to create a life where we are experiencing a lot more of what makes our heart sing?

The *Time* magazine issue looked at "The Science of Happiness." Hundreds of research experiments were conducted to discover what we need to do, own, or have to be happy. We don't have to look externally for this answer. All we really need to do, in every chance we get, is choose to follow our "feel good." All we really need to do is model the strategies of children, who do this every chance they get.

All we really need to do, in every chance we get, is choose to follow our "feel good." All we really need to do is model the strategies of children, who do this every chance they get.

Review of Chapter 4: What Is Your Definition of Happiness?

- Happiness is a choice. It comes from within and not from external factors, such as money, houses, or jobs.

- To be happy, choose "feel good" over "feel bad."

- To be happy, do what you want, when you want, how you want.

- Children are already doing everything in their power to feel happy. Our job is to recognize it and not squelch it with our beliefs about life.

PART 2

Discover the 5 Ingredients for Parenting Success

Now we're cooking!

In this section, we will reveal five main ingredients for parenting success. Heather's approach with children is a lot like a chef's approach to creating a menu at a Mexican restaurant: She loves to combine the same essential ingredients in thousands of ways.

After studying Heather and exploring hundreds of examples, I have discovered that she has a relatively small set of go-to strategies, which she has refined to perfection over the years. These strategies work with *every child, every time*. Regardless of the situation or the actual words she uses, she brings just a few essential elements to every interaction.

Heather's five ingredients for parenting success are:

1.   Choose the Energy You Bring to Every Situation (Chapter 5)

2.   Honor Your Feelings First and Then Your Child's (Chapter 6)

3.   Focus on What You *Do* Want (Chapter 7)

4.   Honor Every Choice Your Child Makes (Chapter 8)

5.   Remind Your Child of Their Greatness ... Always (Chapter 9)

I never make the mistake of confusing "simple" with "easy." These strategies are simple but, for many, are counterintuitive; as a result, they may not initially feel easy. Moving out of the deep ruts of our ingrained behavior and blazing the trail for a new set of neural pathways may take some practice.

I know you can do it!

As you read through each of the chapters in Part 2, you will notice that Heather is 100% focused on controlling herself—not her children. Many of us may categorize this idea into the "simple but not always easy" category because this is a new parenting model.

Be easy on yourself as you put on new glasses and see the world through Heather's eyes. She has wisdom accumulated over 25 years with over 30,000 kids. Use the amazing opportunity of reading this book and modeling her strategies to shortcut your own learning curve.

CHAPTER 5

Choose the Energy You Bring to Every Situation

"When your child walks in the room,
do your eyes light up?"

—*Toni Morrison, Nobel Prize-winning novelist*

It feels good to be acknowledged.

I t feels good to be appreciated and acknowledged. When my husband comes home, I do my best to greet him at the door with a smile, a kiss, and an acknowledgement of his valued presence. I didn't always do this—and honestly, I do my best—but it doesn't happen every time.

When I make the choice to stop what I am doing, acknowledge his presence, and express my love and gratitude, it feels good. It sets the vibe for the rest of the evening. We both begin the night together in a genuine space of love, regardless of the trials and tribulations of the day. I decided to make a conscious effort to greet him as a result of a combination of lessons from my little wise ones.

There is no faking it.

I had high expectations for the teachers in my preschool. As I would train them for their position, I never considered acknowledging a child's presence in a room as a "high expectation." It was a difficult concept to get across to my teachers, but eventually I figured out how to explain it, model it, and let them experience the difference for themselves.

I thought it was simple. We had a chime on the door, so we could hear when parents entered the building and when they exited. The primary responsibility for anyone within the range of the front door was to immediately greet the child first and then the parent.

The greeting had to meet certain criteria. It had to be energetic and include a warm smile, a hug, or some form of meaningful physical connection. For example, "Good morning!" would be followed by an acknowledgement such as, "We are so glad you are here today!" or "We were waiting for you!" Again, back to my intention for the children in the school: to be acknowledged, feel valued and loved, and know they matter.

There was a method to my madness.

The teachers would argue that I was a control freak. (I agree with this on many points, but this one is important.) I practiced with the teachers and they would often leave out key ingredients. Although they may have said the "script" verbatim, when they lacked the energetic attitude, gave an empty smile, or patted the child on the shoulder halfheartedly, the child would feel a difference and I would instantly feel the child's disappointment and sadness.

On difficult days, the last person I wanted to be was "Miss Heather." I had a life outside of the school. I had distractions, a wedding to plan, sick parents who needed me, a house to purchase and decorate, and my own health concerns. If I let the distractions get in the way of my "special greeting," our day would often spiral down quickly.

I made a decision. If I couldn't muster up the energy and effort to greet each child properly, I would make sure that the other teachers would do the same. If, by chance, it was 5:45 a.m. and I was alone, before the rush, I would choose to set aside the distraction in my mind and be present for them, as best as I could. I knew that it was ultimately in my best interest. It would make the next 12 hours together bearable, and most of the time even enjoyable.

Energy is not in the words I express. It's in the feelings under the words.

We use words to express *and* suppress our feelings. The energy in my body always dominates the conversation more than the words coming out of my mouth.

Energy is in my presence. It's more than what I say or do. It's a feeling that something is not right, and a gut feeling that doesn't feel good. It's also a feeling that all is well, and a gut feeling that does feels good.

As a boss, I would walk in the break room and sense the energy quickly. Sometimes it was light and fun (when the employees were talking about their weekend); sometimes it was heavy and ugly (usually if they were complaining about working late). When I call my husband, I can tell within five seconds if his day is going well or if he is struggling. When I think of my best friend, who is 2,500 miles away, she will call within minutes, starting the conversation with, "I was just thinking of you and had to call!"

Children and animals are much more sensitive to energy than we adults are. Furby, my beloved dog, knows when I am in the driveway before my husband does. He knows, without words, when I am sick, sad, happy, or mad—and so do children. (Adults also know, but we don't listen as much as children or animals do.)

> Children and animals are much more sensitive to energy than we adults are.

I use my energy to uplift and inspire, not change the other person.

It's not my job to make people happy. I want to use my energy to inspire and uplift them, allowing them to join me if and when they are ready. My happiness is not dependent on their state of being.

Our loyal puppy of 14 years—Daisy—recently passed away and my energy was low, sad, and even borderline depressed. I loved her so much and was so grateful for her presence in our lives. (I got her on a deal with my husband: If he got a big screen TV, I got a puppy.)

Our four-year-old next-door neighbor Jackson is another love of my life. (He told me that we were going to get married; I told him that he would have to ask my husband Mr. Brian first!) One day, Jackson came to the door and I did my best to greet him, as always, with energy and love. He knew that something was wrong, regardless of my words and actions, and asked me why I was sad. I explained that Daisy died.

"If you are sad, Miss Heather, just call her on the phone in heaven. Then you can talk to her and not be sad!"

After he said that, he left, but he knew I wasn't feeling much better—even though I smiled, laughed and hugged him. Within an hour, he came back with a picture frame and told me to put a picture of Daisy in it so I could remember her. After a few days, he met me in the driveway and told me how his cat Pat—yes, Pat the cat—was playing with Daisy in heaven and they were happy.

Life Lesson #1797: Children listen with their heart. They feel my energy and do everything possible to uplift and inspire me to a better place. They let me know that they are always there for me, and allow me to feel my feelings in my own time and space. They don't join me in my sadness. They don't tell me how to feel. They don't try to change me. They accept me exactly how I am and continue to be a bright light of love. They are a constant reminder that all is well.

I always have a choice.

Every situation is met with energy: energy that feels good or energy that feels bad. I have the ability to control and change my mind in any circumstance.

When I first started the preschool, I used time-out as a form of discipline (a nice way of saying "punishment") for unwanted behavior. One day, four-year-old Gavin was ready to begin his lesson for me. I put him on the step in my office for offensive behavior in class. I was pretty angry ... okay, *very* angry.

I heard the other kids say, "Miss Heather's eyes are so big and her cheeks are really red!"

I explained to Gavin why he was on the step. The explanation was in control, but the energy under the control was anger. He felt it. He fed on it. I fed it. We were in a quiet battle—no words, just anger.

> Every situation is met with energy: energy that feels good or energy that feels bad.

The battle continued. He got up; I put him back. He pouted; I reminded him of the "time" he had to spend on the step. (The professionals would say that it was handled appropriately.) Who would win?

It was an epic battle—a battle of wills.

After the 10th return to the step, he moved to the next level of communication. He was ready to get my attention in a big way. As I set him down, turned around, and walked away, he prepared to launch his weapon.

A shoe—the big, clunky, dumb-cartoon-character-kid kind of shoe—came flying through the air, hitting me squarely in the back of the head. *Perfect shot!* Gavin had an amazing throw and, as no surprise to me, actually ended up on the high school football team.

When the shoe hit my head, I had a moment of shock. Something very unsettling happens to the spirit when you're hit full force on the back of the head. As I got over the shock, the anger moved quickly to rage.

"That's IT!"

I was so angry. I knew that my options didn't allow spanking, yelling, or using force, so I immediately moved to a reactive space. Trust me, I wanted to react in a big way. How could I get my way and teach him a lesson? I was not going to let him disrespect me in this way. Then, I had an idea.

"*Aha!* I will get the duct tape!" (Stay with me. It's not as bad as it sounds.)

I got the tape and, still vibrating much anger, made sure that my words were in control.

"We wear our shoes at school. Your shoes belong on your feet, not in the air and not on my head. If you choose to throw your shoes at me, I will make sure they don't come off your feet."

Gavin was in complete shock. He didn't know what I was about to do. Then, I taped his shoes to his pants. My thoughts raced: "Ha! *Now* try and get your shoes off! That will teach you not to throw your shoes at me!"

I thought that this was a brilliant idea. I didn't yell. I didn't spank. I didn't hurt him or his feelings. I was a great teacher. *I won!*

Guess what? My behavior just intensified the anger.

Then, the worst thing happened: He lost. He was misunderstood. He gave up, and not in a good way. He was defeated and, for the rest of the day, he felt humiliated. The battle was over. We both brought the energy of anger to the situation and we both lost.

Life Lesson #437: My responsibility as a teacher, a mentor, and an adult is not to "teach" children how to behave in the classroom. My job is to model how I express my needs and desires when I am angry. My job is to calm my emotions first, and then express my desires from a space of authentic truth. I am only responsible for my emotions, actions, and energy. My job is to be aware of their energy and be conscious of what I want. If I want something different, I need to disengage and revisit the situation when we are able to communicate in a space of understanding and truth. The lesson is so much more than behavior in the classroom. How can I "teach" a child to control his behavior in the classroom if I can't control my behavior and my energy in the classroom? We are both learning. We need each other to grow, expand, and be more than we were yesterday.

How do I handle anger now?

Gavin taught me how to handle similar situations in the future. I was given the gift of practice, and eventually found a great way to check in with my energy and express my needs from authentic love. When any child demonstrates undesirable behavior, I immediately check my energy. If I am too upset to address the behavior in the moment, I let the child know how I am feeling:

"I'm really angry right now. I need to get in a better space to discuss this with you. I am going to come back in five minutes to talk to you about this."

I then take five minutes to get my energy back:

- I remind myself that this is not the end of the world.

- I remind myself how much I love this kid and how he is great in so many ways.

- I remember that this is just a moment for us to practice life.

As I calm and soothe myself into a space of lightheartedness, I am able to revisit the situation with fresh eyes. Here's what a "do over" with Gavin would look like:

I feel the impact of the shoe on my head. I immediately feel the surge of anger circulating through my body.

"Gavin, I am too angry to talk to you right now. I need five minutes to gather my thoughts and change my mind from anger to truth, so I can communicate with you. I will be back in five minutes. Count to 60 five times, and then I will be back. You are welcome to take these five minutes to gather your thoughts."

I return in five minutes and ask him to check his energy.

"Gavin, I have been able to change my energy from anger to understanding. Do you need more time before we talk? Are you able to talk from truth yet?"

He says that he is able to talk. I start the conversation and model authentic communication.

"I know you very well, Gavin. I know that you love me very much and would never hurt me on purpose. I know that you love to hug and kiss me. I know that you were so angry that you didn't know how to tell me. A shoe hitting me on the back of the head doesn't help me understand you. How can I help you find the words you need to use when you are angry? I have some ideas of what you can do when you are angry. You can ..."

I end the conversation with the authentic truth:

"You are an amazing boy, Gavin. You have so much love to give to the world. I am here to remind you of that when you forget it. Know how much you are loved and how important you are."

Life Lesson #520: I have a choice in every circumstance, in every situation, and in every moment. I can choose to meet and match the energy that others are bringing and feel terrible, or I can be in my authentic power and choose my energy to get the desired outcome that I want. I can choose to end the battle. I want to feel good. I want my child to feel good. We both deserve happiness.

Sometimes *we* create meltdowns.

A meltdown is an awesome chance to see how energy works and how we can work with it. Months before I met my husband, the responsibilities of the preschool were starting to weigh me down. My friend and I decided to go on a cruise to the Mexican Riviera, free from all responsibilities and the chance of potential clients seeing me dancing at 2 a.m. with a drink in my hand. This was going to be great! I could let my hair down, be wild, and be free (at least for seven days).

At the beginning of the cruise, we met an amazing couple with a beautiful nine-month-old girl named Samantha. We really enjoyed their company. They saw the best and worst of me on that trip. About halfway into the cruise, they asked what I did for a living and where I lived. We realized that they lived a mile away from my school and were looking for a preschool for their daughter. It was fate! A few months after the cruise, they came to the school, toured, and enrolled her.

Samantha's first day of school was difficult for everyone. She had to quickly adjust to life in "school." She was still on a bottle (a "ba-ba"), carried a blanket (a "blanky") like Linus from *Peanuts*, and put a pacifier (a "binky") in her mouth. She quickly learned that our school was a "no ba-ba, no-blanky, and no-binky territory." She cried all day; in fact, she was the first child in my school who ever cried for an *entire day*.

After the first day, she recovered and thrived. She was an amazing little girl—full of life, love, spirit, and spunk. Our families soon became friends and eventually family to each other. We often took Samantha for the weekend when her mom and dad went out of town or just wanted to spend quality time together.

Fast forward a few years: Samantha stayed at our house for the weekend and we had a great evening. She went into her room to brush her teeth and go to bed; instead, she brought out a plastic Ziploc bag with three binkies in it.

"Samantha, you don't use a binky at school or at our home. Do you need them anymore?"

She looked at the bag and quickly answered, "No."

"Well, if you don't need them anymore, do you want to throw them away?"

She looked at the bag, shrugged her shoulders, and said, "Sure!"

She marched herself to the garbage can in the kitchen and threw out all of her pacifiers with no emotion; I also didn't have any emotional attachment to this outcome. I knew that she often slept at our house without the pacifiers and didn't use them at school. She slept the rest of the weekend without any thoughts of the binkies.

> We have the power to influence each other with our unspoken words and our energy.

When her parents came to pick her up, Samantha told them in a mellow voice what she did with her binkies. Her parents were nervous but happy. They were unsure of Samantha's commitment to "no binkies." They seemed to be in disbelief.

Later that evening, I got a phone call. Samantha sensed her parents' worry when they put her to bed. They didn't know how she would do and, honestly, they didn't expect her to do very well with the transition. Samantha felt their anxiety and expressed it out loud—in the form of a meltdown—for many hours.

When I talked to Samantha's parents on the phone, they were quite upset with me. They were angry that I encouraged Samantha to throw away the binkies in the first place. They had an "emergency binky" on top of the refrigerator, ready to give it to her to stop the screaming.

Then they asked for my advice.

"Let her live with the choices she has made. Go in and remind her that this was her choice and she threw out all of her binkies."

I told them to remind Samantha how much they love her and that they were there for her. I also told them to wear earplugs because that girl can cry longer than any child I have ever met! If they could make it through the night, I knew that she would be fine. After all, the same thing happened when she came to my school. They followed my advice, buried the "emergency binky" in the trash, dealt with the screaming for one night, and lived happily ever after ... *free from binkies!*

Life Lesson #658: We have the power to influence each other with our unspoken words and our energy. If I am unattached to the outcome and clear with my feelings and my energy, I give my child the opportunity to make a choice and experience the consequences—good or bad—of the choice. All I have to do is stay in a good space, hold my child in the space, and allow them to join me when they are ready.

Food for thought: Sometimes it's all in our head.

Lunch time! Lunch in a preschool definitely required me to be in a good-energy vibe. It can go really well or spiral down quickly. What is the determining factor for success? My energy ... my attitude ... my willingness to roll with it, whatever comes my way: spaghetti in the ear, yogurt in the hair, or carrots in the nose!

I know that the parents in our school meant well for their children, always; unfortunately and more often than not, the contents of their child's lunch box did not reflect the love and effort they intended to provide. Our parents worked hard, long, intensive hours, and preparing their child's lunch was often a major inconvenience. It was also difficult for us to prepare a healthy lunch for all the kids in a timely manner every day.

My remedy was to charge a significant price for individual daily lunches, hoping to avoid having to prepare the lunches. To my surprise, some parents were willing to pay $5 per day for a lunch, just to avoid the hassle; many were not.

> I know that the parents in our school meant well for their children, always; unfortunately and more often than not, the contents of their child's lunch box did not reflect the love and effort they intended to provide.

When I went to school, my lunch box was usually filled with a sandwich, a piece of fruit, some carrots, possibly chips, and, if I were lucky, a chocolate chip cookie that my mom had made the night before (if my dad hadn't eaten the entire batch by the morning!). The children in my preschool brought lunch boxes full of items that resembled food but which had gone through many processes to get there. The ingredients were usually far from natural, including high-fructose corn syrup, modified corn starch, partially hydrogenated oil, and Red Dye #5.

To be fair, I have also served similar snack items out of habit. Now, I have done my best to avoid these ingredients as much as possible. I feel better with organic vegetables and homemade goodies. I am very fortunate to live in a community full of farmers' markets and farm-raised animals. I have seen and experienced a dramatic difference in my health when I choose foods in their natural state.

However, if I bought into our society's ideas regarding sugar and hyperactivity in children, I would have set myself up for frustration and disaster every day. My life would have been miserable for every lunch and every naptime that followed.

I had no control when a parent packed a lunch consisting of cookies, candy, a sugared "juice" drink, a fruit snack, chips, and a lunchable snack box (i.e., a box with a few pieces of processed ham, processed cheese, and crackers). I would do my best to educate the parents about a healthier lunch, but time was the dictator of quality.

Our routine was consistent. We would serve the children lunch, go potty, wash hands and faces, and then head straight down for a nap. There was no room for a certain belief regarding the effects of processed food and sugar on the kids. I had to believe and know that naptime was going to happen, regardless of sugar input.

Naptime was the only quiet time that we experienced throughout our 12-hour day. Although naptime was approximately two hours, our window of peace and quiet was usually 45 minutes. It would take time for all the children to go to sleep, and they would often start waking up before it was time to rise and shine.

Naptime was always successful; however, some days were more successful than others. We entered naptime every day, knowing that we teachers were about to get a break. We were happy, excited, and ready for everyone to go to sleep. Getting 30 children—ranging from seven months to seven years old—to sleep at the same time after a lunch filled with sugar, would be a daunting task for anyone who took on the challenge.

We all held the space for it to happen. If we wanted to have a decent break, we had to know and fully believe that each child would fall away in dreamland—at least for 45 minutes.

Naptime was an opportunity for us to recharge and fill up our cup. It was not an option to skip naptime ... *ever*! When we were sure what we wanted, and held the energy in that space, the children always conceded. Our energy was clear: We also deserved a break!

Life Lesson #593: I deserve to take care of my needs and desires. When I know and believe what I want, I carry the energy to others so they can cooperate. External factors, such as sugar and Red Dye #5, can be overpowered by the energy I bring to the situation. I need to be clear with my needs and move in the direction of that desire with a certainty of the outcome.

Shifting my energy created a shift around me.

The energy I brought to my day created the moments, the memories, and the space for love or fear. It is my responsibility to be better ... to do better, to practice, to expand and evolve into the amazing person I am. When I made the conscious effort to be in a good space when the day started, I felt better. I would still have my challenges throughout the day, but I knew that I could choose a different path.

Sometimes I made the choice to come back to my happy place; other times I stayed frustrated, angry, or annoyed. It always felt better to make the choice to move

> I soon realized that I had complete control of the classroom and the children ... not by controlling their behavior but by controlling my energy!

back to a happy space (and if I just couldn't muster up the happy vibe, I would at least move to a place of hope that the day would end soon). It took more effort and energy to move into a better place, but it always felt better to move towards happiness rather than dwell in anger or frustration.

I quickly noticed that the children reflected the energy I felt deep inside— not my words or actions. All day, every day, they sensed my feelings and displayed them for the world to see. For example, if I walked into the baby room feeling sad, every baby started to cry within minutes. If I confronted a parent regarding overdue tuition, and felt frustrated and angry, a child slapped another child across the face. If I became silly towards the end of the day, the children matched and intensified the energy in the room.

I soon realized that I had complete control of the classroom and the children ... not by controlling their behavior but by controlling my energy! I was able to shift the entire classroom by shifting my energy.

However, there's a trick: I can't fake it until I make it. The children can always see and feel through my unauthentic attempts to control. I have to make a decision—a choice. I have to change my mind. I have to step into my power to influence and inspire greatness in myself first; then, my classroom will follow my lead.

One child—Logan—taught me that words and actions will never outweigh energy... *ever*. He was from a dysfunctional home, including an emotionally young single mom, an absent dad, and an overindulgent grandma.

I always greeted Logan at the door with a smile and a happy voice, but deep inside I dreaded the idea of another day with him. He was a cute kid—loving and affectionate—and exhausting. He never stopped moving, didn't listen, and didn't get along with the other children.

Every day, I told myself, "Today will be a good day with Logan."

As soon as he entered the building, I did my best to think positively; however, within the first five minutes, my positive thoughts would go out the window. I visualized him attending another school and never returning. (The truth is not always nice, but it's the truth.)

The more I fed the energy of frustration and annoyance with Logan, the more he gave me. I practiced daily, loving and embracing Logan in my heart. More than thinking good thoughts, I actually *felt* good feelings about him.

Then, I changed my mind. Believe me, it didn't happen overnight. It took time and effort to find and then feel the energy of love and appreciation for Logan, but the shift happened.

> Children don't respond to positive thinking. They respond to authentic being.

When Logan came through the door, I felt authentic love and acceptance for him, and his energy reflected my energy. He listened more, got along with others, and eventually calmed down and avoided taking the attention deficit hyperactivity disorder medications that his doctors suggested.

Logan reminds me of Gandhi's quote: "Be the change that you wish to see in the world." As I changed my attitude and energy when Logan walked through the door, and to my surprise, he shifted his energy throughout the entire day.

Many self-help books and gurus insist on positive thinking. I don't believe in positive thinking; it doesn't work for me. I can have all positive thoughts but still be emitting feelings of fear, disappointment, frustration, resentment, and even anger.

Children don't respond to positive thinking. They respond to authentic being.

Energy is not thinking. Energy is being. Energy will always win over words or actions. It is my responsibility to check in with myself, look at what I want to change in another, abandon the effort to change another, and apply the change to myself.

The only energy I can change is my own.

"I have learned from experience that the greater part of our happiness or misery depends on our dispositions and not on our circumstances."

—*Martha Washington, First Lady of the United States*

What energy are you feeding into the system?

One day, Heather told me a story about how she flunked her high school science class. She was a straight-A student; however, she hated science and didn't think she would ever need it in her life. Heather decided not to put any energy into that class and therefore flunked it. I chuckled at this story because, on a deep and intuitive level, Heather understands one of the key principles in science: systems theory.

"Systems theory" (or "systems thinking") simply states that everything exists inside of a system and, when one element of the system changes, the whole system has to change in response. Everything exists only in relation to other things, and everything influences or is influenced by what's around it.

In the human realm, we belong to family systems, school and work systems, city and country systems, environmental systems, and so on. For example, maybe you have been at a party that is going along just fine. Then, a new guest arrives who is fun, outgoing, loud, and full of laughter and light. In the moment when this new person shows up, the whole energy of the party shifts with the addition of this new energy. One person has just shifted the dynamic of a preexisting system. At work, maybe your boss enters the room in an extremely foul mood. Unless you have the training of a Zen monk, it's pretty hard to be unaffected by your boss's highly charged negative energy.

We are part of a system at work and are influenced by all of the other elements in the system. We influence the system around us in every moment of every day. For example, Lisa has been away for a while and then comes home to her two kids. She walks into the house and it's a complete mess with toys and food everywhere. Blankets and sheets are pulled out from every closet, and there is some version of a fort (if you can call it that) in the living room.

Lisa's exhausted. She just cleaned the house yesterday. It's late, and there is still so much to do before bed. She erupts, clearly in no mood for playing.

"You have made a huge mess in my clean house! You need to clean it up this instant!"

"Mom, we were just playing!"

"I don't *care* what you were doing. *Clean it up now!"*

She storms off to the kitchen, angry to her core.

What was going on in the system before Lisa got home? Her kids' energy was playful and fun, and they were having a good time. When Lisa walked into the house, she brought the energy of frustration and anger into the system. The playful mood was over and the dominant energy in the system was now a negative one. This introduction of a negative energetic tone influenced the system. Her kids matched her energy and made a fuss at dinner and before bedtime.

Heather intuitively knows all about systems theory, which is why she is extremely aware of the energy she puts into the system. Whether she is talking one on one with her husband or child, in front of a class, or in front of a packed audience, she puts the energy into the system that drives and supports the experience she wants to have. For example, if she wants a playful energy, she puts a playful energy into the system; if she wants a calm energy, she puts a calm energy into the system; if she wants an excited energy, she puts an excited energy into the system.

What energy are you feeding into your systems?

Our goals drive our behavior.

One of Heather's goals is to model for her children ways to communicate effectively in any situation. She knows that it's important to provide a model of how to act when she is angry, so her children can see and model appropriate behavior when they are feeling angry.

For this reason (and since the experience with Gavin and the thrown shoe), Heather has a strict rule of conduct for herself that she never violates: *Never ever engage in a conversation or dialog when either party is angry, frustrated, or upset.*

She simply doesn't do it. She believes that nothing productive comes out of a situation when approached in anger or frustration. She is aware of the energy that she is feeding into the system and is conscious about what experience she wants to create. It is important for her to provide an effective communication model that her children can see and follow.

> Never ever engage in a conversation or dialog when either party is angry, frustrated, or upset.

Heather has developed strategies to quickly shift her energy from frustration and anger into love and compassion. Depending on the situation, Heather might:

- Walk away from the scene until she can pull herself together.
- Take a deep breath and, in that breath, shift her energy.
- Close her eyes and recall a picture of this child at a time when they had a loving and connected moment together, and then use that picture to remind herself that she is talking to an amazing child.

All of these techniques help Heather shift her energy, and some work faster than others. In her unwavering commitment to never engage with a child when she is emotionally charged, Heather wants to create a safe space for them and participate in effective communication. She feels that she cannot meet either of these goals when she is in a negatively charged emotional state.

Disengage from your child's charged emotional state.

Heather applies this same disengagement strategy to children. If her child is in an angry, frustrated, upset, or charged state, Heather refuses to engage with them until they have calmed down. She knows that the child is in no position to hear her when they are not in a good emotional space.

For example, if a child has cut himself, she waits until he has sufficiently calmed down before applying a Band-Aid or ointment. If a child is upset about not getting what she wants, she waits until the child has calmed down before engaging in any dialog. She simply refuses to engage in conversation when the child is not in an emotional space to hear her.

Heather will say, "I can't talk to you when you are this upset. Come talk to me when you are in a better space."

If the energy is charged in a specific location, Heather will frequently move herself and her child to a different physical space. For example, if her child is upset at something that happened in the living room, Heather will move to the hallway to discuss it. She intuitively knows that changing the physical space will break the anchor—the charge—to the emotional state. If the system contains undesirable energy harbored by Heather or her child, she disengages from the situation until the energy has calmed down.

Words communicate 7% of the message.

In the field of behavioral science, communication among people has been intensely researched. One question researchers ask is, "How important are words, voice tonality, and body language in face-to-face communication?"

Although statistics differ, one of the most commonly cited studies breaks down the importance of the various elements involved in face-to-face communication as follows:

- 7% = words, verbal communication

- 38% = voice tonality

- 55% = body language[1]

Put more simply, what we say and the words we use are the least important part of our communication with others in terms of conveying a message. Our tone of voice and body language carry far more impact in terms of what others "hear."

> ... what we say and the words we use are the least important part of our communication with others in terms of conveying a message.

Voice tonality and body language reflect how we *feel* about what we are saying. Humans are hardwired to put more emphasis on feelings than on words. Nonverbal communication is the dominant factor in face-to-face communication.

Recall a time in your childhood when your mom or dad didn't say a word but just gave you a look ... *that* look. Along with their energy, that look told you all you needed to hear. Heather's kids understand everything when she gets "big eyes" and words aren't needed. Heather didn't need a science class to intuitively understand the science of good communication.

If her energy didn't match her words when she said, "Come on, let's do it! This is going to be fun," then the words were ineffective at creating the mood she desired. Similarly, if she were angry and said, with a clenched jaw and an angry vibration, "Please stop doing that!" the child sensed that what she really meant was, "I am going to scream and lose it if you do that one more time!" The children always reacted more to her energy than to her words.

When we shift our energy, we shift our voice tone and body language automatically. Then, we become fully congruent with all three aspects of communication (i.e., verbal communication, voice tonality, and body language).

How skilled are you at shifting your energy on demand?

The more practiced we are at shifting our energy, the more we can consciously feed the desired energy into the system and create the experience we want. Zen monks spend years mastering their energy. Kids, spouses, and coworkers give us the chance every day to practice.

You can short-circuit undesirable calibrated loops.

When I was growing up, my mom's hot button was a messy kitchen. When she would leave to run an errand or work in her garden, we kids (I was one of six children) would make ourselves a little snack in the kitchen. You can imagine what a kitchen might look like after six kids made themselves a little something to eat! When my mom came home, we would all scatter. None of us wanted to be in the kitchen when she got back, mostly because none of us wanted to clean up everyone else's mess.

Then, from the far ends of our house, we would hear our mom bellowing, "I JUST CLEANED THIS KITCHEN! IT'S A MESS! GET BACK HERE AND CLEAN IT UP!" More than her words, we could feel our mom's blood boil. This happened several times a week for the 18 years that I was at home.

Behavioral scientists call this a "calibrated loop," which is a scene that repeats over and over. A trigger launches a predictable behavior, and the participants in the system all play their role and respond in a predictable way to this behavior. This "looping" behavior continues in a "calibrated" way until something shifts.

For example, when my mom walked into a messy kitchen, it set off a trigger. She would predictably get angry and yell; we would predictably ignore her; she would predictably get angrier. Then, when I was in my 30s, something shifted in the system. Now, I proactively clean the kitchen whenever I am home. I have learned how to short-circuit the loop; however, while growing up, my mom was probably the only person who could have consciously broken that loop.

We are all in calibrated loops with the people in our lives. Not all calibrated loops are negative; many are quite positive. For example, I have a routine with the waiter at my favorite local Mexican restaurant. He sees me walk up (the trigger), gives me a very big smile, and speaks to me in a super friendly tone.

"*¡Hola amiga!* It's so nice to see you again today!"

Then, I predictably say, "*¡Hola mi amigo!* It's so nice to see you too!"

He automatically gets me water with no ice and a lemon, and cheerfully brings me a menu. It's our routine and we've been doing it for years. I love going there because *mi amigo* lights up when he sees me and it feels good, so I feel good in response. Our appreciation for each other is felt beyond the pleasant words. We have created a positive calibrated loop.

Now that you are aware of energy, systems theory, and communication effectiveness, how can you consciously break free from undesired calibrated loops with your kids? How can you establish new calibrated loops that feel good?

Think about not-so-pleasant calibrated loops or some situation where you have the same charged reaction with your child every time it occurs. Maybe you have a bedtime routine that you would like to shift; maybe you'd like to react differently when your kids are fighting. You have the power to change the entire system by changing one element—*you*—in the system.

> You have the power to change the entire system by changing one element—*you*—in the system.

The goal is to interrupt the pattern and short-circuit the calibrated loop. You can consciously choose a different energy or a different reaction. When you are triggered in a calibrated loop, ask yourself these questions:

- What if I change the energy I bring to this situation? What if, for example, I consciously choose to be calm, or excited, or patient, or enthusiastic, or unwavering instead of what I am doing? (Mealtime and bedtime routines often benefit from an unwavering energy, like naptimes at Heather's school.)

- What if I choose to completely ignore this behavior and focus on something I *do* like? What if, for example, I focus on the pretty weather outside, the dog wagging its tail, the compliment I got at work, or the funny video I saw on Facebook? What if I decide, in the big scheme of things, that it's not worth it to feed negative energy into this situation?

- What if I reframe this behavior and look at it differently? What if I choose to see the positive intent behind the behavior? For example, instead of getting frustrated for the mess in the living room, what if I focus on my child's great sense of play or creativity? What if I appreciate my child's independence, such as making lunch or creating art?

- What if I take a minute to interrupt my pattern by disengaging from the situation entirely? What if I collect myself and consciously shift my energy? For example, what if I tell my child, "I need a minute," and then turn my back on the situation until I collect myself? (Physically turning your back on a scene emotionally disconnects your body from the interaction, which can be a very powerful way to reset your energy.) What if I take a five- or 15-minute break by walking into the bathroom and collecting myself?

- What if I interrupt a calibrated loop by redirecting my child's attention with diverting comments? For example, I could say, "Want to go outside and check out the new tree that the neighbor just planted?" or "I was just noticing how beautiful your eyes are in this moment."

The key is to change your response when you are triggered and do something—*anything*—that is different from your normal reaction. Put this into action in your life. When you shift your input into the system, the system will shift in response.

Create new, "feel good" calibrated loops.

Take a moment to think of some nice, good-feeling calibrated loops that you could establish in your life. Is there some routine you could implement when you say goodbye to your child when he leaves for school, when she goes to bed, when you sit down at the dinner table, or when she walks into the kitchen in the morning? How can you consciously establish small routines that set the emotional tone for the experience, like the one my waiter and I have at the restaurant?

Heather established many "feel good" calibrated loops at her school. There was a predictable greeting and a goodbye, and a predictable routine for the shift between lunch and naps. As people, we are patterned in our behavior. Take a moment to think about how you can consciously create routines that feel good to you every day.

What is the secret to becoming a kid whisperer?

Heather has a passion for children and a passion for finding what works with every child, every time.

Many people think that being a kid whisperer is attainable for a select few who are born with the special gifts of good genes and unique abilities. I believe that a kid whisperer, or any person who excels at something, is acting on their passion and keeps trying new ways of doing things until they find one that works every time.

Heather has a passion for children and a passion for finding what works with every child, every time. She has discovered that she is more effective with children when she focuses on controlling *her* energy—and not her child's—in any situation.

She doesn't expect her child to exhibit better emotions than she has. Her job is to get herself into a space where she is feeding the system with the energy and emotion she'd like to experience. If she wants the child to have fun, she gets herself into a place of having fun; if she wants to have heartfelt communication, she gets herself into an emotional space where that is possible.

A large part of Heather's effectiveness with children is her ability to control her emotions and get herself into an emotional—energetic—space that leads to the outcome she wants. She knows that her words account for less than her energy, so she is consciously aware and chooses the energy she brings to every situation with every child.

You are in control of creating the experience you desire. Take your power back.

Many parents allow their children to dictate their mood. For example, parents see a mess and they get angry, or their child won't go to bed and they become frustrated.

How do you react when ...

- ... your spouse comes home in a bad mood?
- ... someone cuts you off in traffic?
- ... your doctor doesn't give you the time of day?
- ... your neighbor complains about where you park your car?
- ... the raccoons get in your garbage?
- ... your dog pees on the furniture?
- ... your coworker drops a bomb in an email?
- ... a politician makes a decision that you don't like?
- ... your friend lies to you?

How often do you let someone *else's* behavior determine how *you* feel?

When we allow the behavior of someone else to shift our mood, we have given all of our power to them. When children (or spouses or coworkers) trigger us and cause us to feel frustrated or angry, we have allowed external forces to control us.

When this happens, we become a Victim in the Triangle of Disempowerment (see *Chapter 3: As a Parent, What Are You Really Responsible For?*). Step off the triangle and take your power back!

Take control of your own happiness. Choose how you react to events and behaviors of others in your life. Choose the energy you bring to every situation. Create the experience *you* want.

Review of Chapter 5: Choose the Energy You Bring to Every Situation

- We are all part of systems. Feed the family system with the energy you want to experience.

- Never engage in a conversation or dialog when you or your child is angry or frustrated.

- Short-circuit undesirable calibrated loops and create new, "feel good" loops.

- We hear body language and feelings more than words. Shift your energy so your voice tonality and body language are communicating what you *really* want to say.

- Take your power back and put yourself in control of how you react to behavior. Choose the energy you bring to every situation and create the experience you want.

- If you want your children to learn how to effectively handle their anger, choose wisely how you handle your anger.

See this strategy in action!

Check out the video on
Choose the Energy You Bring to Every Situation

VIDEO

VIDEO

or visit
www.raiseahappychild.com/energy

CHAPTER 6

Honor Your Feelings First and Then Your Child's

"Deep listening from the heart is one half of true communication. Speaking from the heart is the other half."

—*Sara Paddison, author and president of the Institute of HeartMath*

When it feels bad, it is bad! I trust my intuition.

One day, I was in the kitchen of my preschool, washing the lunch dishes. The other teachers were tending to the children while I was getting a jump start on the cleaning process. (The faster we cleaned, the longer break of peace and quiet we had during naptime.)

I looked out the window and noticed an older, strange-looking woman who was walking across the street. She was dressed in a long, black trench coat in the middle of a 108-degree Las Vegas summer. I had a terrible feeling in the pit of my stomach.

I thought, "I hope she doesn't come over here."

I continued to wash the dishes as I looked out the window again. She was crossing the road and heading for our building. I walked out of the kitchen at the same time the school doorbell rang.

The lunchroom was located at the front of the school, and it was full. I went to the door and, before I opened it, the entire table of children, who were facing the door and who had no idea of the woman's presence across the street, sensed danger.

All of a sudden, two children yelled from the table, "Miss Heather! *Don't open the door!* There is a bad lady at the door. Don't open it. She will *hurt* you!"

The other children joined in and begged me to leave the door closed. The children had no idea who was at the door. They didn't even know that the person was a female but said there was a "bad lady." We had a very safe school. We never had any problems in the seven years that we were there. The doors were always unlocked and welcomed anyone to come in the school; however, this was different.

I denied my feelings and, most importantly, I denied the children's natural sense of danger. My logic overrode my intuition, and all I thought was, "This is just an old, homeless lady. What could she possibly do?"

The doorbell rang again. The children warned me again, but I thought I knew what was best. (I was wrong.) I opened the door a few inches. It was enough to see her face and something in her pocket that resembled the shape of a gun. She tried to push the door open.

She said, "Come outside. I have something I need to talk to you about now."

I denied my feelings and, most importantly,
I denied the children's natural sense of danger.

At the same time, the children were screaming at me to close the door from this "bad lady."

In a very firm and determined voice, I told the woman, "Leave now. The police have been called and you will be arrested if you do not leave these premises *now*!"

I shut the door, called the police, and watched her step away from the window.

In the meantime, one of my little girls pleaded, "Miss Heather, don't go out there. That lady wants to hurt you. Don't go out there. *Please*, Miss Heather. *Don't go!*"

Because we were a school, the police arrived within minutes and searched the surrounding area. There were no signs of the woman anywhere. The children were unaware of my conversations with the police officers. When I came back inside the school, the same children approached me.

"Don't worry, Miss Heather. She is gone forever. She won't be back. We promise!"

I actually believed, trusted, and had more confidence in the children than the police.

Life Lesson #849: We are all born with a natural instinct, a gut feeling, a knowing, and a sense when something doesn't feel right. I often experience a "bad" feeling or a "red flag" early in a situation or with another person; however, as an adult, I disregard the feeling and apply logic to the situation, which proves to be a mistake. Children often sense danger without any specific visual indicators. They intuitively know when they don't want to engage. We mistake their caution and tend to label them as "shy" or even "disrespectful." I have decided to abandon the traditional lessons we teach our children regarding "stranger danger." I now offer a reminder for all the children to listen to their tummy and trust their heart. If it feels bad, trust it.

We are WiseInside.

> "At the center of your being you have the answer; you
> know who you are and you know what you want."
>
> —*Lao Tzu, ancient Chinese philosopher*

I know what is best for me. I know what I want. A voice inside my head and heart speaks loudly and clearly—if I allow it. It whispers in my ear, quietly warning me to move in one direction or the other. It can scream profanities and demand me to reroute my path immediately. Sometimes I listen; many times I don't.

I truly believe that children have a direct connection and communication with the voice inside. They listen to it. As infants, when they get a feeling of hunger, they cry; a feeling of fear, they scream; a feeling of love, they smile; a feeling of pure joy, they giggle and laugh.

Toddlers listen to the voice. They let us know when something is not working for them, often with a scream, a hit, or a bite. When a two-year-old wants a toy, they grab it. They take what they need but not because they are rude, a brat, spoiled, or uncivilized. They are clear on their desire to get what they want. They put themselves first.

I was never taught to put myself first. In fact, my mother scolded me if I didn't put a friend's needs or our family's wants before mine. It was considered rude and selfish.

My mom and dad put other people first the majority of the time. My mother would bend over backwards to help a friend, often at her own expense emotionally, physically, or financially. My father would work his friend's business so his friend could go on vacation, requiring my father to work 18 to 20 hours a day. It was my parents' choice to help a friend, but it sacrificed their well-being more often than not. My mom could be described as having a "bleeding heart" for anyone who needed help.

Ironically, my mother died from a "bleeding heart" at the age of 52; my father died at 61, also from heart problems. The two most important role models in my life both died from heart problems! Both wished that they had "taken care of themselves" better throughout their lives. I know they were speaking beyond the physical aspect of their condition.

Their experiences got me thinking, and I've asked myself many times, "What's wrong with getting what I want? What's wrong with putting me first?"

I deserve to get what I want from this experience. I came to this planet to get my desires met. I didn't come to experience what my parents want, what my friends want, what my husband wants, or even what my child wants. I came here to explore, create, and manifest *my* dreams into reality. It may seem a little—or a lot—selfish; some may even say it's because I'm an only child; however, what if we were right as toddlers?

As adults, we are constantly reminded to take care of ourselves first. If our cup is empty, we have nothing to give. Every time we fly, we are reminded to put on our oxygen mask first, and then assist our child. Mothers are encouraged to go to the spa for "me" time; dads are urged to go to the golf course to "recharge." We know what we want as a child; then, as we age, we are steered away from it, having to relearn how to get our needs met as adults.

As we grow up in our communities, we still have the intention of getting what we want; it just looks and sounds different. I learned to get what I want within the parameters of society's expectations. I learned to manipulate, pout, give the silent treatment, argue, debate, negotiate, fight for my rights, compromise, give in, or give up.

> "What's wrong with getting what I want? What's wrong with putting me first?"

When I coach parents, many "fight to be right" and say, "We are supposed to teach our children to be nice, share, be a good friend and citizen, respect and listen to adults, fit in, make us proud, and be accepted by society."

Is that true?

Is that what we really want?

Do I want my 16-year-old daughter to get in a car with her best friend who has been drinking because she wants to be a good friend, fit in, and be accepted?

- *Here's what I really want:* I want my daughter to feel confident and safe to make a decision that is best for her. I want her to be tuned into her inner compass, inner voice, and intuition, so she always acts in her own best interest, regardless of what others think or say.

Do I want my son to volunteer at the shelter because he has to satisfy his college entrance requirements?

- *Here's what I really want:* I want my son to find a way that he can use his skills and passions to serve those in need. I want him to be inspired to share his gifts with the world. I want him to volunteer because he wants to, not because he is forced or required to do so in order to get into college.

Do I want my daughter to get a bleeding ulcer just to score high on the Scholastic Aptitude Test (SAT) so I can be proud?

- *Here's what I really want:* I want my daughter to know that her worth as a human being on this planet can never be measured by a test score. I want her to know that she can have, be, or do anything she wants to do in this world, and that I am proud of her simply because she was born.

Do I want my son to *share* his car with his friend who participates in the local drag races every weekend?

- *Here's what I really want:* I want my son to make a decision to share his property with others based on his internal guidance. I want him to be clear with his boundaries and feel supported in his right to share or not share.

Do I want my eight-year-old daughter to keep a secret about her uncle, who is touching her inappropriately, because he told her to keep a secret?

- *Here's what I really want:* I want my daughter to be able to notice when something feels wrong and be able to communicate her boundaries to anyone, regardless of their age or family status. I want her to know that I believe her and will support her if she asks for help.

I want my children to stay connected to their inner voice.

I want them to be super sensitive to their feelings and understand what they mean for them in each situation. I want my children to be inspired into action, not feared by a consequence. I want them to act or do something from an intrinsic state of being. I want them to know that they are supported, trusted, and loved with every decision they make, even when—and especially if—I disagree with them.

> We steer our children away from the voice inside and replace it with our voice, our friend's voice, or the world's voice.

We steer our children away from the voice inside and replace it with our voice, our friend's voice, or the world's voice.

We honestly think, "I'm doing what's best for them," "I'm wiser because I have experienced life and its pitfalls," or "I'm just protecting her from getting hurt."

I have been guilty of this for years. It's not intentional but more habitual. I do it to friends, family, and myself. When someone tells me what I should or shouldn't do, it doesn't feel good. It actually makes me defensive, angry, frustrated, or annoyed. It feels disempowering. I feel inadequate and unable to trust my decisions or actions.

Nothing feels worse than being angry, calling a friend on the phone, and having a conversation that makes me want to throw the phone through the window. Usually, this type of conversation includes statements from my friend, such as:

- "You shouldn't feel that way."
- "You should just …."
- "That's not a nice thing to say."

- "You could …."
- "I think you are overreacting."
- "Stop being that way."
- "You're just being a brat." (Well, "brat" is not the word normally used, but you get the idea.)

I understand that my friend is doing her best to help, but the conversation is just leading me down a road on which nobody wants to travel.

It feels so much better when my friend listens, acknowledges my feelings, and gives me the time and space to figure it out and come up with a solution or remedy that feels good to me. It feels good when she helps me define my desires and reconnect with my inner voice, and allows me to create a solution in which I have a vested interest and that works for me.

I want my children to let go of what they are "supposed" to be and embrace what they "want" to be.

My niece Sophia visited us for the summer in between her freshman and sophomore year of high school. (Technically, we are not blood related. I grew up with her mother from birth and we have been best friends since. From the minute that her children were born, I was "Aunt Heather.")

Sophia and I had an amazing time with tons of shopping, museums, the zoo, manis and pedis, and lunch at our favorite restaurants. One day, we were deciding what to eat and Sophia seemed upset. Her mind was focused on an important subject, and it wasn't about what she was going to eat for lunch. The subject of school entered the conversation. She explained the requirements to get into a good college. (I wasn't even thinking of college the summer between my freshman and sophomore year. I was babysitting and shopping!)

"If I want to be successful in life, Aunt Heather, I have to get into a good college. In order to get into a good college, I have to take accelerated classes, get crazy good grades in the advanced placement courses, be involved in a team sport, pass my American College Testing (ACT) exams in the top percentile of my class, get a job, and volunteer."

Her blood pressure rose. Her face flushed and her eyes instantly teared up. A wave of anxiety came over her body, and she struggled to hold back her emotions in the restaurant.

I silently sat across from her, and gave her a chance to breathe and calm down enough to participate in a conversation. Then, I asked her the first question that came to mind.

"Why do you want to go to college?"

"I don't know. It doesn't matter. I will never be successful if I don't graduate from college. I have to get into a good school. That's all that matters."

"Is that true, Sophia? Is that *all* that matters?"

The tears streamed down her face and she cried, "Yes!"

"Well, I'm not sure that is true for me. Do you think that I am successful?"

"Oh, yes! You had a preschool, a wellness center, houses, cars, and money. You are *very* successful!"

"Sophia, do you think your Uncle Brian is successful?"

"Of course! He makes good money, has a house and cars, and he is the boss of a lot of people."

Then I gave her the zinger.

"Sophia, did you know that your Uncle Brian and I did not graduate from college?"

Her surprised look was quickly followed with confusion. She couldn't wrap her head around this concept. She had been groomed—brainwashed (with good intentions, of course)—to believe that the only way she could be successful was to obtain a college degree.

I told her about all the people in the world who had success without a degree, such as Richard Branson, Steve Jobs, and Bill Gates. We explored the definition of "success." Was it really about money, cars, and houses, or was it more important to do something we really love and something in which we have a genuine interest or talent? Was it okay to go to a specific trade school and be a dog groomer if we really enjoyed the art of grooming?

At the end of the conversation, I said, "We want you to do something that you're interested in or have a passion for. We want you to have a great experience because you want it—not because you have to have it to be successful."

Calmness washed over her body and a sense of peace filled the room. There was less pressure to perform and more emphasis on her desires for her life. The focus of our conversation shifted from college requirements to what feeds her soul, and what would make her get up in the morning and say, "I can't wait to see what *today* holds!"

> By the time her visit was over, many shifts had taken place in her spirit.

Her energy was lighter and happier—free from the burden of all she *had* to do—and replaced with the wonder of what she *wanted* to do. By the time her visit was over, many shifts had taken place in her spirit.

When she got home, her mom and dad were concerned because her new position was, "I'm not going to college ... and I'm a vegetarian." (I forgot to mention that we watched the documentary *Food Inc.,* which shows the truth of where our food comes from. They were not very happy about her announcement regarding college either!)

Her mother called me immediately and said, "What did you do to my daughter?"

We both laughed hard. (Actually, I probably laughed more than she did.)

Her parents were awesome. They didn't try and talk her out of it. They didn't argue. It was very hard for them to listen to and appreciate their 15-year-old daughter's decisions for her life. They dropped discussions about college. Sophia's father took her shopping for vegetarian food and even tried some with her. (The vegetarian thing is a difficult issue for Texans like us. We bought an entire cow from the Houston Livestock Show and Rodeo every year and put it in a freezer that outsizes their fridge.)

As time went on, an interesting turn of events happened. Sophia did not appreciate vegetarianism as much as she thought she would, and slowly added meat back into her diet. She also decided that she wanted to attend college to pursue her dreams. She ended up with amazing ACT scores, took advanced placement courses, and got great grades. She got a lifeguard job at the pool, which was perfect because she is a competitive swimmer, and is getting ready to go with her class on her dream trip to Italy in a few weeks. Sophia is heading into her senior year, ready to chase and embrace her dreams and make them a reality.

Life Lesson #1984: When I let go of what my child is "supposed" to be, it gives him the permission to explore and define what he "wants" to be. When I listen to him, allow him to decide, and stay patient and quiet enough for him to work it out, he will supersede all of my expectations. He will feel empowered to decide and supported in his decision by the people who love him the most. He reminds me to stay close to my thoughts and desires, and quiet the noise and chatter that continue to rotate outside of myself. He reminds me to stay strong in my beliefs and know that I always have the flexibility to change my mind in my beliefs. We both learn that success is defined individually. We learn to listen to ourselves and each other to make our dreams come true.

Do I just let my children have everything they want?

Yes.

I know. It may sound ridiculous. The voices in your head may be saying something like this:

- "If I let my children have what they want, I will raise stubborn, spoiled, rude, unruly, and disrespectful children."

- "We aren't supposed to get what we want. We are supposed to be the bigger person and compromise. Besides, it's not nice to our friends and family, and it looks bad to others."

HEATHER

- "If I allow my children to get what they want, I have to sacrifice, suffer, go without, be humiliated, be embarrassed, or look bad as a parent."

I found another way. I found a way to get what I want in any situation *and* a way for my child to also get what they want.

It has never felt good to compromise. When I was little, I remember my mother telling me to "come to a compromise" when I had a conflict with a friend or family member. I learned that a compromise required me to give up my needs and desires.

I resisted compromise. I fought until the other party compromised their needs. I was labeled "stubborn," "strong willed," "bull headed," and other labels too numerous to remember. (To this day, my husband will not play Monopoly with me. He says that I don't play "nice." I am too demanding and stingy with properties.)

When I decided to work with children, it was important, from the beginning, to listen to their needs and do my best to be fair. Even with my internal resistance to compromise, I made the effort to be the bigger person with the children throughout the day.

> Regardless of how I did it, I was never able to compromise with everyone's needs, especially my own.

Compromise wasn't as difficult with Maria, a three-year-old at my preschool.

When Maria woke up early from a nap, I would often say, "You can come and lie in my office, if you are quiet."

It worked for both of us—until Mason, Faith, Anna, and Joshua also woke up and wanted to come in the office and be quiet. Now, my compromise was not working for me.

Then, I would say to the child who woke up first, "If you are quiet, you can turn on the light when it is time to get up."

It never seemed fair for the other children, who were lying quietly. Regardless of how I did it, I was never able to compromise with everyone's needs, especially my own. The "if you do this, then you can do that" model seemed to be far from compromise and more like a bribe or a bartering system.

Compromise didn't work and it was not fun—especially when the children collected their energies and hit me as a united force. There was no way to compromise with 30 different personalities all day, every day. I felt as if I were bargaining and bartering 10 to 12 hours a day. It was exhausting, unsatisfying, and unrealistic. It felt like manipulation rather than communication.

Admittedly, I brought negative energy to the concept of compromise. Reading the definition of compromise confirmed my pessimistic feelings towards the concept:

> **compromise** (*n.*) a settlement in which each side gives up some demands or makes concessions[1]

I am actually thankful for the bargaining, bartering, and manipulation. Each child who offered resistance to my compromise challenged me to think outside the box. I was inspired to think harder and double-dared to find a better way. I tested my approach, changed it frequently, and finally found a word to replace compromise.

If compromise is out, what's in?

When I was getting married, a lot of people offered advice—mostly unsolicited. The common nugget of wisdom from the previous generations was, "You have to learn to compromise." Based on my history with compromise, my marriage was therefore destined for doom. (As a funny side note, we got married on June 6th—the day of World War II's D-Day invasion of Normandy!)

In the first few—okay, *several*—years of our marriage, we were not very successful at the art of compromise. I noticed that the need to compromise generally sparked from conflict. In the quest for a suitable compromise, both parties would tend to feel resentful, disempowered, slighted, out of control, or even defeated. Compromise was not an option for two people who had a strong desire for a certain outcome.

It began with a simple question from Brian: "Where do you want to go for dinner?"

Let the battle—I mean, *compromise*—begin.

"Well, I want to go to Outback Steakhouse. I'm in the mood for a filet!"

"I don't want steak, Heather. I want Chinese food."

"I don't want Chinese food. It makes me bloated. It has too much salt and MSG. I get so full, and then 30 minutes later I'm hungry again. I don't want Chinese food."

"Well, I don't want steak."

"Well, Brian, they have a teriyaki bowl at Outback. It's like Chinese food."

> We were not interested in *modifying our demands*; we were ready to battle it out.

"We *always* go to Outback. We *never* get Chinese food."

"I know because *I don't like Chinese food!*"

"*Fine* ... we will go to Outback! *Are you happy*?"

"No, because now you are mad."

"I'm not mad, Heather. I'm frustrated. Let's just *go*. I'm hungry and tired of arguing."

"Fine ... whatever ..."

Dinner was silent.

It seemed simple enough. It was only dinner, but we each had our mind set before we entered the conversation. We were not interested in *modifying our demands*; we were ready to battle it out. This time, it appeared to work in my favor; however, in the end, it didn't.

Dinner was miserable, the service was terrible, the food was mediocre at best, and it ended with my husband's final two cents: "I *told* you we should have gotten Chinese!" (The same thing would have no doubt happened at the Chinese restaurant.)

Fortunately, with time and practice, we learned to shift our communication and replace *compromise* with *cooperation*.

How do I shift from compromise to cooperation?

cooperation (*n.*) an act or instance of working or acting together for a common purpose or benefit; joint action[2]

The difference in the definition between "compromise" and "cooperation" seems miles apart:

- When I think of a *compromise* (i.e., a settlement in which each side gives up some demands or makes concessions), I automatically become defensive. I focus on the conflict and think of how to convince, manipulate, or trick my opponent—I mean my child, spouse, coworker, or friend—into adjusting to my demands. (This sounds horrible as I write it, but it is the truth.)

- When I think of *cooperation* (i.e., an act or instance of working or acting together for a common purpose or benefit), I want to focus on my desires, listen to my child's desires, and come up with a plan to get both of our needs met—together.

As I shared my ideas with parents while coaching, they often resisted the concept of cooperation. Instead, I heard statements such as:

- "I'm not here to make my child happy."
- "He can't *always* get his way."
- "I know what's best. I'm the parent. I'm the adult."
- "She is just a kid."
- "It's my way or the highway."
- "This is not up for negotiation."
- "I don't have time to explain everything, every time."
- "They should do as they're told."
- "When my children grow up, *then* they can make their own decisions."

I believe we all come to this planet with free will: the ability to choose, think, and act voluntarily without coercion. Children are not the exception; in fact, they are the rule.

So how do my husband and I now cooperate over dinner plans? We practice our cooperation skills over and over again. When we are considering dinner out, we take a moment to get clear about what we individually want and let each other know what sounds good. When we lay all our requests on the table, we look for a restaurant to accommodate each of our needs. (Fortunately, we live in the San Francisco Bay Area, which is full of restaurant options.) It is a work in progress, but it's worth it. It certainly makes the dining-out experience more pleasurable when we cooperate versus fight it out—I mean *compromise*.

Here's how we do it now:

"Hey, Brian. I'm not in the mood to cook tonight. Are you willing to go out to dinner?"

"Sure, I'm up for that. What sounds good to you?"

"Well, a big, green salad sounds good to me. What are you in the mood for?"

"I really want some good grilled salmon."

"Do you have a place in mind that would work for both of us?"

"Well, there is a new restaurant that has amazing seafood. I was talking to a coworker and told him that you hate seafood. He said that they have a great menu, with an awesome chicken Caesar salad."

"I am on board for that. Let's go!"

In this way, we both get our needs met. It just takes a little thought, preparation, and willingness to see possibilities. I actually despise seafood, but I am willing to go if I can get something that also makes me happy.

Listen to me ... I have the right to say "no"!

When I was five, I remember being at my relatives' home for a holiday celebration. As the day came to a close, we were in the kitchen, preparing to go home. We were all saying our goodbyes, giving thanks, and passing out hugs and kisses.

Then, it was my turn to give a certain family member a kiss goodbye. I vividly remember my relative standing there, waiting for his kiss. I refused (in my mind, nicely, of course).

I remember looking at my mom and saying, "I don't want to kiss him."

My mother was humiliated, embarrassed and frankly appalled. In her mind, this was not up for negotiation. I remember that her tone was firm and definite, and her face was as red as a stop sign.

> Even as a five-year-old, in my mind, it was worth the trouble to stand my ground.

Then, she said the words that always stopped me in my tracks:

"Heather Reneé, give him a kiss ... *now*."

"No, Mom, I don't want to. He kisses lots of people, and I don't want to kiss him. He is dirty."

She couldn't force me to kiss him, and I was not willing to compromise. My mother moved to the next level of anger: "Go get in the car."

Nothing could get me to kiss my relative. After a few very uncomfortable minutes for everyone involved, my mother apologized for my behavior and promised consequences to my relative for my actions.

Even as a five-year-old, in my mind, it was worth the trouble to stand my ground. Some might say that I was a spoiled, rotten brat.

Is that true?

Here's a little background to help you decide:

- I watched this family member argue and break marriage vows repeatedly.
- His wife would cry over her husband on many nights.
- I listened to phone conversations describing the "other women" in his life.

- I witnessed sadness and grief when I was in their home.

- I heard all the terrible choices that he was making regarding monogamy in his marriage.

- As young as I was, I had no desire to kiss a man who had caused so much pain to someone whom I dearly loved. I wanted to protect her and myself from everything I heard.

My mother and my relative were unaware of my observations over the years. They thought that I was not paying attention, that I didn't understand, and that I was oblivious to the situation. Although I didn't understand the specifics, I understood that he hurt her by being with other women. I didn't want to kiss a man I didn't like.

When we got in the car, my mother had calmed down and asked me a simple question: "This is not like you, Heather. What's the matter?"

I told her that I didn't like him because he was mean to my relative and that he kisses lots of gross women. (I was rephrasing overheard conversations.)

My mother looked at my father and said, "I guess we need to watch what we say."

Here's what my mother *didn't* do:

- She didn't reprimand or punish me. She just instructed me to say "No, thank you" next time.

- She didn't compromise with me.

- She didn't bribe me and say, "If you kiss him, we will get an ice cream on the way home."

- She didn't negotiate and say, "If you kiss him, you can play with paint when you get home."

- She didn't punish me and say, "If you don't kiss him, you are going to get a spanking." It wouldn't work. Honestly, she really didn't want me to kiss him if it was uncomfortable for me. (She experienced sexual abuse and was not able to say "no, thank you" to the abuser in her family.)

She didn't want me to do something that I didn't want to do; she just didn't know how to handle it in the moment. She didn't know how to handle her embarrassment. She didn't want me to be perceived as a "spoiled brat." She knew that I was an awesome child, and wanted everyone else to see my greatness.

> We both wanted to feel good about our actions and feel supported in them.

My mother, in her own way, decided to *cooperate* in a stressful moment. She decided to *work with me* by getting me out of the environment and having a conversation to get to the truth of the situation. Through this discussion, we worked for a common purpose: We both wanted to feel good about our actions and feel supported in them.

When we take the time to cool our jets, calm down, and remove ourselves from the situation, we can often experience peace. When we hold our children—and even our friends, family, and spouse—in the space of greatness and knowing, and repeat an internal dialogue of "That's not like them; that's not who they are," we can cooperate in any circumstance. We can work jointly for a common purpose.

Life Lesson #221: Children are not inherently defiant. There is often a story—a root cause—underlying our behavior. When we take the time, energy, and effort to explore the situation, the cause will often present itself. When we are busy compromising, and fighting for our demands to be met, we miss the opportunity to cooperate and work together for a common purpose or benefit. My mother knew that it was not in my nature to deny a hug or a kiss. Once she removed herself from the embarrassment, she was able to listen and hear me clearly. She was willing to cooperate with my needs and desires, even in a very stressful circumstance.

Work together for a common purpose.

I have heard parents say, "That's fine and great, but what about when I can't get my kid to go to bed? He doesn't want to cooperate. He doesn't want to go to bed, *period*. He wants to stay up and play with his toys. If it were up to him, he would *never* go to bed. I tell him to go to bed, and he says, 'Just 10 more minutes.' I say, "Okay, 10 more minutes and then it's bedtime.' We then go back and forth for another hour until I finally lose my patience and threaten him with a spanking."

Here's how cooperation looks in the same situation:

> When we cooperate, we are working together for a common purpose or benefit.

"I know you love your sleep. Sometimes I watch you sleep. You always have a big smile on your face, especially when you are asleep. I know that, when you wake up in the morning, you smile and feel refreshed from a good night's sleep. Sometimes you even fall asleep in the car when you're tired. I know that sleep is important to you. It's also important to me. I need to go to bed at 10 p.m., and I need two hours to myself before I go to bed. That means that 8 p.m. is a good time for me to put you to bed. What would you like to do before you go to bed? Would you like to tell me a story or would you rather me read you a story?"

When we cooperate, we are working together for a common purpose or benefit. Sometimes we need to remind our children of the benefits, and the proof of their experience of the benefit, when it comes to difficult situations like bedtime.

We both benefit from adequate sleep. We both need sleep. We both want sleep. That is the common purpose. It's not up for compromise to not sleep. When we are offered choices, it reminds us of our free will. It gives us the chance to practice decision making and the natural consequences of our decisions.

This concept didn't come easy.

Naptime!

Naptime was the only time in a 12-hour day that I could have 45 minutes without hearing "Miss Heather!" It was sacred. It was necessary to preserve sanity. It was *not* up for negotiation. I had to get 30 kids—from seven months to seven years—down for a nap, every day.

In the beginning, I was desperate. I was willing to compromise in any way to get my 45 minutes of silence. (Naptime was two hours; however, by the time all the children went to sleep and the early risers awoke, it ended up being 45 minutes of quiet time.)

These were my typical compromises:

- "Lie on your tummy and I will pat your back."
- "If you go to sleep, we will have popsicles for a snack."
- "Just close your eyes while this song plays."
- "If you'll be quiet, I will let you sleep in my office."
- "If you go to sleep now, I will wake you up first."

They were nice compromises; however, about 30 minutes into naptime, the compromises became demands and threats:

- "If you don't go to sleep, you are going to have to stay on your mat until everybody else gets up."
- "If you don't close your eyes, you are going to sit outside on the bench."
- "It's naptime. That means be quiet … *now*."
- "You are going to be the first one down tomorrow if you don't stop talking."

As time passed, we learned to position naptime as a benefit for all. We had the same goal and common purpose: We all needed time to recharge. A recharge for the children meant a nap; a recharge for the teachers meant a nap for the children. I learned to reposition naptime with options. For example, we gave them a choice of where they wanted to nap, whether to sleep on their tummy or back, or whether to sleep with or without a blanket.

I defined my expectations and set up choices around them.

I also made the children aware of the consequences of their choices. In other words, if they wanted to kick their legs in the air, or swing their arms across the floor and hit their sleeping friends, that told me that they "made a choice" to sleep on their tummy. (When they are on their tummy, they can't send arm and leg flares around the room.) If their choices gave them negative or positive consequences, it was none of my business. They made the choice and I honored it ... *always*.

Recently, Ronnie (one of the first children who enrolled at my preschool) and I laughed about the fact that he still can't sleep on his stomach because he had to sleep on his "tummy" every day in preschool. I reminded him that he *chose* to sleep on his tummy when he kicked his legs in the air; I just listened and honored his choice.

When I honor a child's choice—good or bad—it removes me from the equation. I am removed from blame because I just listened and followed through with a choice *they* made.

- We all want to have a choice.
- We all want to be heard.
- We all want to know that our voice matters.
- We all want to be trusted to make decisions for ourselves.
- We all want to be supported in our decisions.
- We all want to be reminded that, when we make a mistake or regret our decision, it's just practice and an opportunity to learn and grow.

Our challenge as an adult is to find ways to cooperate, so we both feel that we have a choice, that we feel heard, and that our voice matters.

My goal is to listen to my own needs first. Once I have established my needs, I can listen to my child's needs and create an outcome based in cooperation.

Cooperation is rooted in choice. It is not a compromise of demands.

Listen to the heart of the matter.

"Listen a hundred times.
Ponder a thousand times. Speak once."

—*Unknown*

When I opened my preschool, I knew that the children who would enroll were special.

When I opened my preschool, I knew that the children who would enroll were special. I had a deep understanding—more like a knowing—that they were coming into my school on purpose. They needed me, I needed them, and we would learn and grow from our experiences together.

At the beginning, "business" was a foreign concept. I attended some college courses and specialized small business classes, but they didn't prepare me for my journey. I was not experienced in business marketing and really had no plan. I was good with children and trusted that they would somehow show up. (This was definitely not the marketing plan most businesspeople would use, but it worked for me!)

I opened the doors of See World Learning Center and, on the first day, I received a phone call from a mother who was requesting information on childcare for two boys. I was rather surprised, knowing that I had not yet done any advertising or marketing. At the end of our conversation, I asked the woman where she found out about See World.

"In the classified section of the newspaper."

Interesting. I never placed an ad; actually, I never even thought about placing a classified ad for the school. Later that day, I spoke with my dad and told him the story.

"Yep, I placed the ad. That's great! It *worked*!"

I had no idea that my dad was going to place the ad, but I am so thankful that he did. You never know how things are going to work out.

The mother came to tour the school and decided to enroll both boys. Ronnie was four years old and Gavin was 16 months old. (You may remember Gavin from previous chapters. He is the center of many stories from See World.) Both boys held a special place in my heart. They were the first kids enrolled at See World—loving, fun, energetic, and honestly brilliant! Over the next few years,

I became very close to both of the boys. They had a challenging home life and often struggled to get through the experience.

One day, Ronnie—then six years old—didn't want to go outside. He refused to get in line, refused to "listen" to my requests, and eventually ran to the back of the school to hide in the toddler room.

When I came into the room, I demanded his attention and respect. I addressed the situation with my internal dialogue of anger, frustration, and annoyance. I had a classroom of children waiting to go outside and Ronnie was not cooperating. He was being defiant, unreceptive, unreasonable, and disrespectful; some would even call him a brat. I looked at Ronnie in the corner of the room and demanded that he listen to me NOW!

He said, "You are not the boss of me. I hate you! You are stupid and ugly. I hate you! I'm going to cut your head off, hang it from a tree, scream 'Dead Teacher, Dead Teacher,' and then chop you up into a bunch of pieces and eat you!" (It was extremely unsettling to visualize my head hanging from a tree and being chopped into a bunch of pieces for human consumption.)

> (It was extremely unsettling to visualize my head hanging from a tree and being chopped into a bunch of pieces for human consumption.)

My split-second response was, "I hope you are hungry because there is a lot of me to eat!"

It was not exactly a textbook response, but it was all I had in that moment. Although it would not be my response now, they were exactly the right words to snap Ronnie out of his mental state. He looked at me, confused, and wasn't sure what to say next.

Thankfully, my response snapped us both out of the situation long enough to know that this behavior was not about going outside, being disrespectful, or even eating me after chopping off my head. His words—many would say— suggested that he was in desperate need of counseling, rehabilitation, and possibly drugs.

It's a good thing that I listened to his *heart*, not his *words*. His moments of anger were expressed by hitting, yelling, and kicking, but the essence of

Ronnie—his core being and true spirit—was loving, caring, thoughtful, articulate, and considerate. Ronnie was a major teacher in this situation.

After the initial shock subsided, we began a conversation. We sat on the floor, looked each other in the eye, and listened from the *heart*, not the *head*. Ronnie confessed and told me everything that was happening at home. He was scared, confused, and worried that his life was not going to be okay. We spent the next 20 minutes listening to each other and remembering that all is well.

We are still very close to Ronnie and Gavin. Ronnie is engaged to be married at the end of the year, and he was an usher in my wedding 14 years ago. Now I will be attending his wedding ... a full-circle moment!

Life Lesson #259: Children constantly teach me to listen with my heart, not my head. They teach me to listen beyond the words that are being said out loud. I know in my heart that every child on this planet is an awesome human being. Often their words and behavior differ from the true essence of their spirit. Sometimes they are unable to communicate their fears and use destructive words and behaviors to express them to me. When I look past the behavior and beyond the words, the fear is exposed and has the potential to be acknowledged, addressed, and remedied. I am reminded to listen with my heart. I am not my words or behaviors. I remember the truth of my spirit. We are all an important part of the universe.

Listen beyond words.

Jayden came to our school when he was five years old. A close family friend referred his mother; she toured the school and enrolled him the same day. Jayden seemed eager and excited to attend See World. He bounced in the front door—smiling, happy, and ready to play.

I greeted him at the door and welcomed him with a simple question: "How are you, Jayden?"

"*Heidosoen wustousm astterdasierm oisjdenr idée lamia sowerem soerms docksee.*"

Jayden spoke a language that was foreign to our planet; however, the most amazing thing was the clarity in which he delivered his answer. He understood my question and answered it honestly and articulately, at least in his mind. We initially thought that he might have a hearing problem, a brain misfire, or a language barrier. We looked for anything to explain this condition and hoped to find a remedy quickly.

Jayden was examined and cleared by many doctors with no explanation, so we did the only thing we could do: We rolled with it. It was very interesting to give Jayden directions, have him follow them exactly, and watch him respond with what most would consider nonsense.

Perhaps the most amazing part of the story is when Jayden conversed with the other children. His friends spoke in clear, articulate English, and Jayden responded with his "out of this world" language. They understood each other ... every time! When necessary, I asked his friends to "translate" for me if I was unable to comprehend a need or want from Jayden. His friends listened with more than their ears: They understood beyond language and they were always right.

While Jayden was at my school, he never spoke a word of English or any other known language. I learned how to communicate with him but never came close to mastering the levels of communication he had with his friends. I didn't stay in touch with Jayden or his family, but I know for sure that he was here on purpose. He came to this planet to be understood, even when it didn't seem possible.

Life Lesson #750: The art of communication—to listen and be heard—doesn't require words; actually, words sometimes get in the way. Children connect to each other in spirit, and listen with an open mind and heart, free from judgment. Children don't need conventional language to get their needs and desires met. They project energy with clarity and conviction. When we are "tuned in," we can understand with ease. We don't have to speak the same language, literally or metaphorically, to understand each other. With an open mind and heart, we can hear the spirit of each other without words.

Speak up!

I was about six years old and it was the weekend—time to have fun and enjoy time with my family. However, there was one small problem: My mom had to work all day on Saturday. I had to go with her because there was no one to watch me. My mom was an accountant, and I was expected to sit quietly, color in my coloring book, or read. I was not excited because it was *soooo* boring! As an adult, I now understand that my mom was just as unenthusiastic to bring me to work as I was to go.

She was stressed, frustrated, and annoyed. When we got in the car to leave, I immediately reminded my mom how hungry I was. She was in a hurry and not in the mood. She told me that we would stop at Jack in the Box to get some hamburgers. (At the time, you could get two hamburgers for $1. What a great deal! It was easy, fast, perfect for my mom, and great for me because I *loved* their hamburgers.)

> The final straw that broke the camel's back was my last plea for no cheese.

We were almost to her work when I spotted the sign and reminded her of my growing hunger. She snapped and let me know that she "knew what she was doing." We pulled up to the drive-through window and my mom ordered two hamburgers. The attendant let my mom know that the hamburgers were not on sale, but two cheeseburgers were on sale for $1.

I cringed. I *hated* cheeseburgers. I never liked the "cheese" they put on hamburgers at any fast-food restaurant.

"I don't want cheeseburgers, Mom. I want *hamburgers.*"

The lady behind the speaker box heard me and said that the hamburgers were $.69 each. She insisted that the hamburgers were not on sale, only the cheeseburgers. (The whole time, in the back of my head, even as a six-year-old, I was wondering why it was cheaper to get cheese with the hamburger. They would save money if they just sold me the cheeseburgers without the cheese. I thought it made sense.)

The final straw that broke the camel's back was my last plea for no cheese.

"That's *enough*, Heather Reneé! You are getting cheeseburgers and you will like it. If you don't want the cheese, then pick it off. You're lucky that you are even getting Jack in the Box. I don't want to hear another *word!*"

We were waiting in line. The car was silent. I was thinking of how to get the cheese off the burger. It was impossible to scrape all the cheese off; it was always melted to the burger. I knew that I needed to keep my mouth shut and deal with it. I knew my mom's limits, and I knew I had exceeded them.

We got to the window to pay, and the attendant handed my mom the bag of burgers. As we were driving off, I opened the package and realized that there was a big problem.

> We were talking and responding to each other, but we were far from *listening*.

"Mom, my hamburgers ..."

I couldn't even finish my sentence before she interrupted.

"Heather Reneé, *what did I say*? That's *enough*! If I hear one more word about those hamburgers, I am going to throw them out the window. *Do you understand me?*"

With tears in my eyes, I replied, "... but mom ..."

She screamed louder, *"HEATHER RENEÉ!"*

I cried harder, louder, and then shouted, "There's no *meat* on my hamburger!"

My mom was angry, frustrated, and beyond description. She thought that I was just being a brat and didn't believe me. (It is hard to believe that they would forget the meat!)

"Give me that burger. If there is meat there, you are in *big* trouble!"

My mother grabbed the package out of my hand and opened it to find a slice of cheese and some secret sauce. It stopped her in her tracks—literally. She pulled the car over, apologized, and made a promise to make a great dinner for us that night.

In the moment, we both had our own agenda. We were talking and responding to each other, but we were far from *listening*. We laughed about that experience for years. From time to time, when my mom would begin to feel frustrated about something, she would say, "Don't make me go to Jack in the Box." We would instantly start laughing and the situation would be defused.

Life Lesson #137: I will have the courage to speak my truth, even if there is a risk of losing everything. I will slow down enough to fully listen to someone. I will stop and see the humor in the situation. Most of all, I will use previous "mistakes" to remind me and my child of what is important in the moment.

What is important to you when you talk with your child?

Behavioral scientists have discovered that we hold "guiding questions" in our minds as we do certain activities. These subconscious questions guide our behavior in any given situation.

For example, take a moment and put yourself back to a time and place when you were in a classroom, listening to your teacher give a lecture. Tune in, notice what guiding question is running through the back of your mind as you sit there in class, and bring that question to your conscious awareness.

You might be asking:

- "What's important to know here?"
- "When is this class going to be over?"
- "When can I check my phone or Facebook?"
- "What is the teacher going to test me on?"
- "How will this information help me in life?"

Close your eyes and notice the guiding question running through the back of your mind. How is this subconscious question directing your behavior in class?

We all operate from guiding questions in every area of our lives. We subconsciously form these questions so that we can direct our behavior toward getting what is important for us. We also use these questions as a way to organize our view of the world that supports our beliefs. Guiding questions are the ultimate filter in our experience.

Most people have never stopped to consciously consider their guiding questions and analyze how they direct behavior. In parenting, the guiding question will change based on the specific situation, but most people operate from an overall guiding question that directs their behavior with their child.

When I asked several parents about their guiding questions when they talk with their children, here are some of their answers:

- "How can I get my child to do what I want?"
- "How can I be in charge here?"
- "What does my child need to be happy?"
- "How can I make sure that I get my stuff done and my child's needs are met?"
- "How can I make sure that my child is well behaved?"

Ask any parent and they will have a different response. Stop for a moment and think about your guiding question as you talk with your child. Put yourself back in a time when you were talking with your child.

You might find it interesting to consider a time when your child wasn't listening to you. In that moment, what guiding question is running through the back of your mind? What is really important to you as you talk with your child? What is the subconscious question that is directing your behavior?

The guiding question always running through Heather's mind when she interacts with children is, "How can we both get what we want here?"

As you think about her guiding question, notice how that question is literally guiding Heather's behavior—her interactions—with every child. If this is the subconscious question running through her mind, it makes perfect sense that she is always working

> Stop for a moment and think about your guiding question as you talk with your child.

toward the goal of *both parties getting what they want*. If this were your guiding question, can you imagine how it would shape your behavior with your child? Would you do anything differently than you are doing now?

Heather makes it a priority in every interaction to listen to *her* feelings and *her child's* feelings. She wants to cooperate to honor *both* sets of desires. First, she becomes crystal clear on what she feels, wants, and desires; then, she takes the time to learn what her child feels, wants, and desires. Using both sets of information, she participates in crafting an outcome that works for both parties.

Listen to feelings and honor them.

One of Heather's main goals is to make sure that she and her children are listening to their inner voices and acting based on their intuition or feelings. It's important to her that children trust their inner voice.

- She wants her child to feel that they have a right to state what they want.

- She wants her child to feel totally in his power to tell a friend, who wants to drive her car after a few drinks, "That doesn't feel good to me. I'm going to find a different ride home."

- She wants her child to be able to tell an abusive boyfriend, "That doesn't feel good to me. I'm going to leave now."

Heather knows that it takes a lot of courage to speak our truth. She makes sure at the youngest possible age that children have a chance to practice getting in touch with their feelings and have the courage to voice them.

From the time they are born, one of Heather's convictions is to honor and validate her and her child's feelings and not override them. I've noticed that parents often override their children's feelings, wants, and desires. We can all relate to times when we (or someone we know, and maybe even our parents), have said:

- "No, you can't have that."

- "Go give Aunt Jane a kiss and say 'thank you'" [when the child doesn't want to say that].
- "Because I said so."
- "You've had enough."
- "Don't do that."
- "Be nice."
- "Share that with your sister."
- "Stop crying, whining, and being a brat."

Parents often wonder why their children make bad decisions as adults, stay in unhealthy relationships, or allow others to take advantage of them. We are all brought up in a culture that suppresses our wants, desires, and feelings in favor of an obedience model.

Obedience occurs when a person alters their behavior in response to a command from a person in authority that they feel powerless, such as a teacher, a parent, a boss, a group leader, a church leader, or an elder.

Parents often expect children to be obedient to their commands, such as "Do what I say or else" (... or else you'll lose a privilege, flunk, be grounded, or be put on medication). Do we want our children to be so conditioned to alter their behavior in response to a command from a person in authority so they feel powerless to leave a harmful situation, relationship, organization, or job?

Over the months of interviewing Heather, it was fascinating to note that she *never* used the word "no" with her kids. When you think about it, the answer "no" invalidates another person's feelings, wants, or desires:

- "No, you can't have what you want."
- "No, that's not okay to say."
- "No, you don't get to do that."

Heather is always looking to *validate*, not *invalidate*. She operates from the belief that children are just as worthy of getting what they want, are just as in touch with what they want, and have just as much wisdom inside as adults. Heather views children as *equals*, not lesser humans.

This belief may be hard to grasp, and most of us did not grow up with this seemingly radical view. We live in a culture that values obedience. All you have to do is look at our school systems, our workplaces, and our law enforcement systems to realize that this is true.

Starting in school from the age of four, we have been molded into a culture that encourages obedience above all else. When I am at the park, watching parents, most of their words are in support of some kind of obedience model. For example:

- "Don't climb up the slide like that."

- "Say you are sorry to your friend."

- "If you don't stop doing that, you won't get to play Xbox later."

By its nature, the obedience model assumes that someone is in charge and someone is subservient, such as in a boss–employee relationship or a teacher–student relationship. In this model, the person in charge feels that their desires can override the person who is subservient to them.

> Starting in school from the age of four, we have been molded into a culture that encourages obedience above all else.

Consider this:

- How many times did a teacher give you an assignment that you didn't want to do?

- How many times has your boss asked you to do something you didn't want to do?

- How many times did your parents make you do something that you didn't want to do?

- How often are you in a subservient role?

Most of our society is built around this obedience model, and we frequently live in fear of being disobedient (e.g., getting a traffic ticket, getting in trouble with the law, getting fired from our jobs, being criticized or mocked by our friends, or being scolded by our parents).

Heather does *not* see her relationship with her child in this obedience frame. She sees her relationship with her child in the same way that she would view her relationship with her good friend.

With a friend, we care about what they are feeling and what they want, and support them in how they choose to be in the world. We honor their feelings as much as we honor our own. Most of us see our friends as equals. We don't consider them—or us—in charge of the other.

When our friend wants to do something that doesn't make us feel good, we generally feel in our power to say, "No, thanks. I'm not interested in doing that with you."

> Heather always notices how she and her child *feel*.

By asking "How can we both get what we want here?" Heather is supporting her goal of helping her child to:

- Feel empowered to verbalize what she wants and desires.

- Listen to her inner voice and trust her intuition.

- Speak what she is feeling.

- Believe that she has a right to create her life and experience in her own way.

- Know that she is an important part of the universe.

Isn't that how we all would like to feel?

Heather always notices how she and her child *feel*. She looks beyond the words and notices body language and voice tone. When a child is behaving out of line or out of character, Heather intuitively knows that there is some *feeling* beneath the behavior that the child can't express in words, and she helps him find the words. Above all else, she has learned to listen to the *heart* of a child.

As you think about how you perceive children, do you share Heather's view that it's important for both of you to get what you want, or do you perceive your needs as more important than your child's? Are you operating from a *cooperation* model or an *obedience* model, or do you find yourself constantly *compromising*?

I had to shift my view over to Heather's view of children as equals, who are entitled to get what they want. I was operating from the model that I was the adult and therefore in charge of the child. The more I thought about it, the more I realized that it was a stressful model to feel *in charge* of someone—even as a boss with my employees.

When I shifted my thinking, I realized that it's a lot easier, more empowering, and more fun to be in a space where everybody feels as if they are empowered to work toward a common purpose and create their own experience. I realized that it wasn't fun to be in charge of kids, employees, or even a pet! By shifting my view, I can now create the relationships I want with the people in my life. I have shifted from being *in charge of others* to being *in charge of myself and in cooperation with others.*

I invite you to consider your model of the world. When beliefs like "I'm the parent and I'm in charge" are present, it's hard to view the world in any other way. Heather is a great model for how to view the world differently and how to honor children as equally in tune with their feelings and desires as adults. (Actually, Heather would say that children are much more in tune than adults!)

Imagine approaching every communication with your child by asking the guiding question, "How can we both get what we want here?"

As you do that, I invite you to follow Heather's recipe for ensuring that she and her child both get what they want in any situation.

How to create understanding and agreement in any situation

Use this technique any time you and your child need to reach an agreement or you want to get to the bottom of an emotionally charged situation.

Step 1: Tune in and listen to your feelings by asking yourself, "How do I *feel* about this?" If you find yourself reacting in a way that is out of character for you, look deeper at what is really beneath your behavior.

Step 2: Tune in and listen to your child's feelings by asking, "How do you *feel* about this?" Notice what feelings are beneath the behavior. If the words or behavior aren't congruent with your child when he is at his best, be a detective and ask questions that get to the bottom of the emotions. You can say, "This isn't like you. What's going on?" Validate your child's feelings using the simple words, "I hear you."

Step 3: Listen to yourself and decide what you want out of this situation first, then state what you need. Realize that you have a right to have your needs met just as much as your child does. Ask yourself, "How can we both get what we want here?" Take the time to figure out what you want first.

Step 4: Determine what your child wants and needs; verbally validate his needs. You can say, "I hear you," "I understand," or "I honor how you feel."

Step 5: Work toward a common outcome or solution in cooperation. If you need help with a solution, ask your child, "What do you suggest we do?"

Throughout this book, there are dozens of examples of how to do this in everyday situations. As you read through the stories and scenarios, notice how Heather talks with children in a way that supports her guiding question of "How can we both get what we want here?"

What happens when we force our children to exhibit good manners?

Our society has a fixation on forcing children to exhibit good manners. Heather shared her thoughts on this subject in a couple of her stories. After working with her, I have come to a place where I feel that a shift in approach on a societal level would result in a better world.

I often hang out at the park with my nieces and nephews as well as with my own family and friends with kids. Several times an hour, I hear parents tell their kids, "Say 'thank you,'" "Tell her that you are sorry," or "Answer his question, honey. He is talking to you."

When parents force their children to say certain things, the child often clams up and gets shy, or just says whatever they are being asked to say to make their parents happy with no sincerity in their words. I am pretty good at reading body language, and the clear signal from the kids is, "I don't want to be forced to say this. It doesn't feel good."

The obedience models we have built into our school and into business systems have taught us that it is acceptable for someone to override our feelings. It has become okay for someone to force us to do something that doesn't feel good. Parents prioritize their own needs of looking like a good parent with a well-behaved child over honoring their child's feelings and the fact that they may not be comfortable doing something or saying something in front of others.

> Heather strongly believes that forcing a child to do something she doesn't want to do—in the name of good manners—teaches them that their feelings are less important than being polite.

As parents, we have the unique position (and often the only place) in our children's lives to remind them that their feelings—their internal guidance system—are important. What importance do you place on your children's feelings? Would you agree that our children's feelings are more important than any manners we'd like them to demonstrate in any given moment?

Heather strongly believes that forcing a child to do something she doesn't want to do—in the name of good manners—teaches them that their feelings are less important than being polite. When we force manners, we teach our children that they must do things that make them uncomfortable. For example, when some creepy relative tries to touch them inappropriately, they don't speak up because they have become so used to obeying adults, even when it doesn't feel good.

Heather says, "I understand, first and foremost, that our children are inherently kind, caring, respectful, and loving. It is far more important to honor my child's feelings over any display of 'good manners,' even when it is embarrassing to me in a social setting.

"I remember, as a young child, feeling overwhelmed or uninspired to answer every question that was presented to me from my mother's friends, strangers at a party, or even strangers in the grocery store. I remember feeling uncomfortable kissing my relative goodbye at holiday parties. I didn't like him.

"Sometimes, I was not sorry for my words or behavior. I had the right to my feelings, and so do my children. I am not looking for my children to make me happy with their behavior or words. I am choosing to be happy, and modeling the love, care, and respect I know my child already has."

See with the eyes of the heart.

My sister prods my nephew to say "thank you" after I have given him some gift or taken him on some fun outing. She is an amazing mom and wants to remind him of good manners in social settings; however, in these moments when he is pushed, he gets shy and reluctantly utters an embarrassed and rote "thank you."

It makes us both uncomfortable. I didn't need the "thank you" to be said. The words didn't convey what I know is in his heart. I know that he loves me and is thankful for our time together by the way he smiles at me or gets really sad when I have to leave. I don't need the words because I see with his body language how he really feels, and seeing his true feelings with the eyes of my heart is far more powerful than any outward, verbal display of manners.

Review of Chapter 6: Honor Your Feelings First and Then Your Child's

- Operate from a powerful guiding question: "How can we both get what we want here?"
- Check in with yourself and honor your own feelings and desires first.
- Understand how your child is feeling. Be a detective, if necessary.
- Create an outcome where you and your child can get your needs met. If you need help with a solution, ask your child.
- Think before you decide to force your child to exhibit good manners. Instead, see with the eyes of the heart.

See this strategy in action!

Check out the video on
Honor Your Feelings First and Then Your Child's

or visit
www.raiseahappychild.com/feelings

CHAPTER 7

Focus on What You *Do* Want

"It isn't where you came from;
it's where you're going that counts."

—*Ella Fitzgerald, Grammy Award-winning jazz vocalist*

Children want, need, and appreciate boundaries … right?

When I decided to begin my journey as a teacher, many people told me to set boundaries for the children, which seemed to make sense.

I needed to:

- Make the rules.
- Set the standards.
- Create a code of conduct.

- Hold them accountable for their actions.

- Lead them.

- Be a teacher.

At the time, I thought I was so smart and progressive. Our class rules were more evolved ... *better*, or so I thought.

Here are a couple of examples of traditional rules versus my new and improved rules:

Traditional Rules	My New and Improved Rules (v1.0)
Don't run inside.	We run outside, not inside.
Don't hit your friends.	We hit the punching bag, not our friends.
Don't yell inside.	We use our inside voices inside, not our outside voices inside.
Don't be mean to your friends.	We are nice to our friends, not mean.
Don't color on the walls.	We color on paper, not on walls.

My rules sounded like "positive rules" for the classroom. Sometimes, it worked; often, it didn't. I would set a boundary, make a rule, and hope for the best. Then, Carter would break the rule over and over again. Then, Adam, Bailey, Lydia, and Cole would follow, like a domino effect. Eventually, all control was lost and almost impossible to find. The more I worked at controlling behavior, the worse it got.

I did my best to stay in control by "chasing" the bad behavior and holding them accountable for every rule they would break. They would inevitably break me. (It's much easier with one or two children versus 30 at any given time.)

I was responsible for setting the rules and in charge of enforcing them. I created consequences for each broken rule, and then followed through with said consequences for each child who broke each rule.

Impossible. Exhausting. *Miserable.*

The consequences usually included a time-out, a conversation describing my "disappointment," and some sort of retribution. It was a never-ending battle. Some days, I would pray for naptime; as soon as naptime was over, I would change my prayer for 6 p.m.

I couldn't keep up with the sheer volume of offenses that I would witness in one day and realized that something had to change ... something had to give. I couldn't keep going at that pace. I was not a police officer, a lawyer, a judge, or a jury. I wanted to have an experience with the children that I would remember with fond memories.

My instructors were right about setting boundaries, but their suggestions needed to be modified. The boundaries had to be set for *me*, not my children. I had to create boundaries that reflected what *I* wanted from my experience at See World Learning Center.

- I needed to define what was important to me.
- I had to define my boundaries as well as my "deal breakers."
- I had to take care of myself first.

The children taught me that the only person I can control is *me*. It took me a while to get there. I tested every method on the planet, and even made up my own to control their behavior; in the end, someone would always outsmart, outwit, or simply outlast me.

When I think of controlling behavior, I automatically think of a police officer whose job is to enforce a set of rules and guidelines, specific to our society. These rules are usually within reason and I usually agree with them. Unfortunately, the police officer cannot control whether I choose to speed, follow too close, play my music too loud, steal from the store, or harm another person. He can scold, reprimand, or punish my behavior, but he can't control it. I have free will.

I appreciate police officers in our community; I just don't want to be one with my children.

I did my best to stay in control by "chasing" the bad behavior and holding them accountable for every rule they would break. They would inevitably break me.

For example:

- I want my child to apologize to his friend for his behavior because he genuinely feels bad about his actions—not because I told him to say that he's sorry and that it's "the nice thing to do."

- I want my child to pay for a candy bar at the store because he understands the value of monetary exchange—not because he will be humiliated or get grounded if he steals it.

- I want my child to have the courage to fail a test and learn from the experience—not just cheat in order to pass it.

- I want my child to decide not to murder another human being because he inherently knows that murder is not an answer to a problem. I want him to make a choice based on his nature as a human being—not because he may get caught, go to jail, and get the death penalty.

These are strong examples, but they're something to think about. I often felt like a police officer in my school and it wasn't working for me; it wasn't working for the children either.

I asked myself, "What would work? What would feel good to me? How could I control my behavior and influence desired behavior in the children? What would it look like to eliminate 'classroom rules'? What would happen? Would they tie me up and hold me hostage?"

I made a bold move. I removed the classroom rules from the wall. I decided to abandon the ways that a conventional classroom was "supposed" to be managed and create a new way. (We were a different kind of school and we needed a different way.) It took years to create my boundaries and just as many years to master them, at least with the children. (I'm still working on honoring my boundaries with adults!) I took the time to decide what mattered to me.

> It was now my responsibility to control my behavior, my response, and my reaction to their behavior.

As I contemplated all the traditional dos and don'ts, I asked myself, "What am I willing to let go of? What do I want to embrace? What would work best for me?" It was no longer about me controlling the children and their behavior. It was now my responsibility to control my behavior, my response, and my reaction to their behavior. I learned that I couldn't control their behavior, but I could learn to control mine. The children gave me many opportunities to practice my boundaries ... all day ... *every day*!

When I reflect on my childhood, my mother would often set boundaries with me. She rarely set boundaries for her friends, family, or even work, but she consistently set boundaries with me. The language she would use rarely reflected what she thought I needed to do for myself; instead, and most of the time, she would declare what she needed for herself.

For example, my mom wouldn't say, "You need to go to your room for a time-out"; she would say, "I need some peace and quiet. I can't play one more game of Chutes and Ladders with you. I need a break. Go to your room or go to the living room ... go wherever you want. I just need a break."

(Hats off to my mom. She stayed at home for the first four years with an only child, who was desperate for companionship and always more than willing to drive her nuts. I often thought that she was the coolest mom for letting my friends come over and play for a really long time; I now realize that it was the easiest way to get me out of her hair for most the day. *Brilliant!*)

I clearly remember my mother asking me to do something, me not wanting to do it, and having it escalate to a verbal fistfight. I was around 10 years old and ready to stand my ground.

Then, I said one sentence that changed everything: "I HATE YOU!"

My mother's instant reaction was to slap me across the face. She had never done that before and I remember the state of shock in my body.

"How *dare* she slap me? Who does she think she *is*? She has no right to slap me. I don't care *what* I say or do, or the fact that she is my mother. She has no right to slap me across the face!" (I, of course, kept those thoughts in my head and my mouth shut.)

After my mom realized what she had done, she knew that she couldn't take it back. A calm presence came over her body and she looked at me, eye to eye. I remember the feeling I had in my body when she opened her mouth to say four words. These words stopped me in my tracks, and they have stuck with me to this day. They dictate my relationships with children, family, friends, and even work.

These are the four words that forever changed my life: "I don't deserve that."

She valued herself and knew that, deep down inside, she was a good mom. In one sentence, she laid down the law ... *her* law. She decided in the moment that she was not going to tolerate the level of disrespect I was serving. She wasn't looking for me to behave in a different way, be respectful, or change. Her small sentence actually conveyed a big message (along with her body language and tone).

The message was simple and clear: "You can say or do anything you want, but I deserve better. I am a good mother. I do my best, and that's all I can do. I deserve respect, and I am not willing to participate with you if you choose to treat me in a way that makes me uncomfortable. I am not willing to share time, space, energy, or myself with anyone who is not willing to treat me in the way that I want and deserve to be treated."

Then, she said, "I suggest that you go somewhere away from me because I am very angry, and I don't even want to look at you right now."

I gave my best effort to redeem myself, and said, "I'm *sooooo* sorry, Mom. I didn't mean it!"

"I told you what I want, Heather Reneé. I will talk to you when I am ready."

There was nothing more that I could do or say. I left the room and went to my bedroom. It seemed like days, but it was only a few hours when she came to my room to talk about the incident.

She apologized for her temper and response; I apologized for my disrespect. I truly felt bad for what I said. I knew from a young age

> I knew from a young age what a blessing my mom was in my life.

what a blessing my mom was in my life. I was my mother's world. I knew how much I was loved and valued. I knew that I had made a mistake; she knew that she had made a mistake. We both learned and never chose to communicate that way again.

Regardless of how it was delivered, my mom decided what she wanted in a relationship with me. She did what she needed to do. She knew that she was too angry in the moment to continue our conversation. She intuitively knew that she needed time to regroup and refocus on what she wanted. It took her hours, but eventually she returned to finish the conversation from a calm, inner peace that oozed from her essence.

Her attention was not on my behavior. Her focus was on how she wanted to participate in a relationship. She focused on her needs, wants, and desires. She put her oxygen mask on first.

Big lesson ... for us both!

"I know what *I* want, but how do I *make* them do it?"

It seemed like the next logical question. The children "schooled" me and reminded me again, and again, and again. I was not going to be able to "make them do anything" or control their behavior with punishments, threats, bribes, disappointment, or rewards. I never gave up hope. We had lots of time together, and I knew that I had to enjoy it to do it well and feel good at the end of the day.

I attended a continuing education class that changed my life. It was a course on the brain and our body. Generally, I am not interested in scientific data or explanations; I usually go with my gut instinct to make a decision. It's not right or wrong but just what feels good to me.

At the continuing education class, the doctor, who was presenting the data, mentioned a small area in the back of the neck—at the base of the skull—called the reticular activating system (RAS), which acts as our brain's filter. Billions of bits of information bombard us every moment, especially with our information-overload society. The RAS draws our attention to the things that we have already decided we like and warns us of any threats that are newly presented.

The doctor gave one compelling example about cars. When we get a new car, we start to notice how many of the same cars are on the road when we never noticed that many before.

When I started to date a guy who loved Jeeps, I realized that I had never experienced riding or driving in one before. A few months into the relationship, I developed a pure love for the "Jeep experience" and decided to purchase one. As soon as I got my Jeep, all I saw on the road were Jeeps! My attention, wants, and desires were focused on a Jeep. The RAS filtered the information while I was driving to bring every Jeep to my attention, and I have owned four Jeeps since then.

The doctor at the class gave another example of a sleeping mother, who hears the slightest change of breath from her child and wakes up.

I am a sound sleeper. As a child, I actually slept through a major hurricane in Texas. The trees were flying, the wind was howling, and the dogs were barking—and I was cutting Zs the entire time! All that changed when we would have the boys we frequently fostered in our home for the weekend or for extended visits. I would hear the slightest movement in their bed across the house. They would often wake up before us, tiptoe to our room, and stand over us. I would awaken from a deep sleep in seconds and my eyes would open.

The doctor's presentation made sense. Focus on what I *do* want—not what I *don't* want. It was clear. If I focus on what I don't want, my RAS will kick into full gear, filtering into my awareness and showing me exactly what I don't want.

Put another way, if I focus on what I don't what, I will start to see more of what I don't want. It doesn't matter if I focus on what I do want or what I don't want—either way, the RAS will show me my choice. This was one of the missing puzzle pieces. It was huge ... and it made perfect sense.

- If I told a child, "Don't jump off the chair," she would jump off the chair.
- If I told a child, "Don't bite your friends," I would be nursing a bite within minutes.
- If I told a child, "Don't talk to me that way," they would sass back even more.
- If I told a child, "Don't throw your food," they would announce a food fight.

- If I told a child, "Don't throw rocks on the porch," I was sweeping rocks for the next 20 minutes.

- If I told a child, "Don't color on the walls," somebody would be scrubbing the marker off the wall.

The examples are endless.

I was taught to say, "Don't do … [fill in the blank]," and changing my thinking and behavior took a while. In theory, it seems simple: Don't use the word "don't." The problem was that, the more I thought about avoiding the word "don't," the RAS brought my attention to the word "don't"!

The doctor's suggestion to my dilemma was a better approach. He said to clearly define what I *do* want, and then emotionally engage in my desires. The final step was to consistently and persistently remind my RAS what I wanted. When I focused, the RAS would do its job to search the world for information and evidence to support my desires. When I came home from the presentation, I felt equipped with a new, powerful tool to use with the children and for myself.

Success did not happen overnight; however, soon after I started practicing with the children, I was able to see immediate results. I created new rules. The only rule for the rules was that it had to focus on what we wanted. When I reviewed my old rules, I realized how close I was. I just needed to leave off the last part of every rule. I removed the words "don't" and "not" from each rule. I focused entirely on what and where they *can* do any behavior.

Here's how I started to shift the rules:

Traditional Rules	My New and Improved Rules (v2.0)
Don't run inside.	If you want to run, go outside.
Don't hit your friends.	If you are angry or frustrated, you can hit the punching bag.
Don't yell inside.	If you want to yell, you can scream outside.
Don't be mean to your friends.	If you want to play alone, just tell your friends that you need space.
Don't color on the walls.	You can color on paper for your art projects.

How do time-out, punishments, and rewards fit in with the new rules?

They don't. (Oops ... say what I *do* want.) Other methods of working with children do work. The more I focused on what I wanted, the more the need for time-outs, punishment, and rewards was eliminated. It didn't make much sense to continue using them when they didn't work all the time. The children in my center were there to educate me. We were there to share this experience and destined to learn from each other.

In order for me to move from the mindset of a time-out to a new method, I had to have a serious conversation with myself:

- I had to honestly believe, in my heart, that children are inherently pure, loving, energy beings.

- I had to accept that their behavior—regardless of how extreme, violent, repulsive, or disappointing—was not a direct reflection of *who they are* as a human being.

- In order to move forward, I could never look at a child and see them for anything other than pure light and love.

- I had to see them for *who they are*, not *what they are doing*.

That was a tall order and easier said than done; however, after years of practice, it is impossible for me to see them any other way. It's a fundamental shift in consciousness.

It is a choice.

I was recently challenged on this subject at a Character Education conference where I was selling our game called WiseTalk for Families. A well-known PhD stopped at my booth, looked at my brochures, and then proceeded to "educate me" on the topic of children's character education. He told me that we need to "teach" our children to be kind, loving, caring, compassionate, considerate, respectful, truthful, and on and on. He didn't believe, as my company name suggests, that children are born WiseInside. It was intimidating to have a PhD tell me how wrong I was; however, my position was clear. I stood strong, even though I was scared.

I simply said, "I believe that our children come to this planet as kind, loving, caring, compassionate, considerate, respectful, and truthful beings. Our job is to remind them of who they truly are when they forget or behave differently."

The PhD worked his entire life to prove his point and it was not my job to change his mind. It was my job to honor my promise to myself, and hold my promise to believe that children are inherently pure, loving, energy beings. I had to risk embarrassment, humiliation, inadequacy, and unworthiness. I had to have the courage to risk it all to speak my truth.

Honestly, it felt horrible to see children—and the world—from his point of view. It also felt like an enormous weight, a burden, and a responsibility to "teach" children how "to be" all of these qualities.

It felt better to know that they already *have* all of these qualities in them. I was reminded of my job. When children choose to behave or act in a way that is far from who they are, it is my job to remind them who they *really* are and bring them back to their truth. I see it as my job to remind children when they forget that they are pure, loving, energy beings.

The methods I learned over the years were no longer an option. A shift had to happen.

> "I believe that our children come to this planet as kind, loving, caring, compassionate, considerate, respectful, and truthful beings. Our job is to remind them of who they truly are when they forget or behave differently."

Time-out ... is for me.

Time-out was offered as the best method to use when kids were out of control or broke some rule. When I used time-outs, it was exhausting. It felt as if my entire day was about crime and punishment. I was a warden in my own school. This was not my idea of fun or what I signed up for when I started.

My office step was the "time-out" zone: a place for the children to gather their composure and think about what they did, or to remove them from a situation where they seemed to have lost their mind.

The problem was that the time-out punished me, my teachers, and the other students. My energy was focused on the child who broke the law. They would never go quietly and would rarely sit there in a state of reflection or contemplation.

This is how it usually went down:

1. I put the child in the time-out.

2. He gets up.

3. I put him back in the time-out.

4. He gets up.

5. I put him back in the time-out.

6. He gets up.

7. I put him back in the time-out.

8. He screams and gets up.

9. I put him back in the time-out.

10. He gets up, screams, and hits.

Each time I put him back on the step, he would up the ante.

John was one of the best players during a time-out. He would break a rule, usually a significant one, and be sent to the step to do his time. He didn't go willingly, ever. He would drop his body to the floor and go completely limp. As I did my best to drag him to the step, the legs would start kicking—more like flailing—all around my body.

It didn't help when his grandma would let him wear his favorite cowboy boots. Contact was always made: boot tips right to the shin bone. *Thanks, Grandma!* Eventually, I would get him to the step, but he would kick it (literally) into full gear.

I could ignore the screaming. I could ignore the name-calling. I could even tolerate the up and down, back and forth travels off the step; however, when my computer screen soared out of my office and landed on the floor, all bets were off for me.

After the initial shock of the event, and the rise of my blood pressure to levels I rarely experienced, I had to evaluate the effectiveness of the time-out. I became highly aware that the use of a time-out often escalated the frustration, anger, and annoyance in both of us. It didn't stop or even slow down undesired behavior. It was a nightmare for the child and a painful torture session for me.

I asked myself two questions:

1. What do I want?

2. How can I focus on what I want *and* feel good?

This was yet another lesson in control. The only person I can control is me. The only way to get control was to give a time-out to the only person I can control: *me.*

Teachers, parents, the children, and even I questioned this approach. It went against everything I was formally taught. It often appeared as if I were ignoring undesired behavior, dismissing it, or even letting the child get away with what some would call "murder." Actually, when I took a time-out from a situation, it taught us all a lot more than we anticipated.

For example, we had a giant sliding glass door in the main playroom of our preschool that led to the playground. We never used the door, but we always had the vertical blinds pulled back so we could get as much sunlight in the school throughout the day.

> It often appeared as if I were ignoring undesired behavior, dismissing it, or even letting the child get away with what some would call "murder."

I had awesome, creative, fun teachers on staff. One teacher had a great idea: She took a bucket full of water and our washable paints outside. She let the children paint on the window; then, when they wanted to clear the canvas, they would just wash and squeegee the window.

I was inside talking to a parent on the other side of the glass. I just happened to look out the window and witnessed Eli (four years old) literally drowning Isaac (also four years old) in the water bucket. They didn't have a love/hate relationship; it was more like a dislike/hate relationship, bitter rivals.

I learned to spare dramatics when describing the events of a day in the life of a preschool, but this was beyond dramatic. Eli was mad at Isaac, so he gritted his teeth and held Isaac's head down in the water to the bottom of the bucket. Isaac's arms were flailing, trying to do something to get out of the bucket. This all happened in a matter of seconds. I screamed through the window and ran to the door to get to the playground. As the other teachers heard my blood-curdling scream, by the time I got to the scene, another teacher had pulled Isaac out of the water and separated the two boys.

I was beyond angry. I was disgusted. I wanted more than punishment. I wanted to kick Eli out of the school.

By now, I had practiced enough to know that I was not in any frame of mind to address the situation in this moment. I had to give myself a time-out. I had to move from anger and disgust to a heart space for Eli, which takes time. I had to regroup, decide what I wanted to do, and communicate with authentic love. Again, this is hard to do when I was so mad I could "spit nails" (my Grandma Hazel's favorite line).

> I had to give myself a time-out.

I looked at Eli and said, "I am too angry to talk to you right now. I need to take a couple of minutes away. I will be back to talk to you in two minutes. Count to 60 two times and I will be back to talk to you."

Even though he was not capable of counting all the way to 60, he got the message. My energy was clear, strong, determined, and unwavering. He sat there and waited until I returned. Some might say that I put Eli in a time-out by telling him to wait for me, and it certainly could appear that way; however, the time-out was intended for me. I had to shift my energy. I would never be able to communicate from the extreme anger radiating from my body.

When I came back to talk, I was over my anger. I was ready to communicate from a place of genuine love for Eli. We took time to discuss the incident. I specifically asked Eli what he was feeling in the moment. Eli expressed his disgust for Isaac. (To be fair, Isaac often pushed many children to a place of rage and anger that they rarely experienced from anyone else.)

We discussed what Eli *can do* when he feels that anger again. When I asked Eli what he wanted to do when he feels angry, he really didn't know what his options were. I offered a couple of suggestions, looking for ones that caught his attention and gave him a sense of relief.

My typical suggestion was to "hit the punching bag when you are angry." Eli didn't seem to resonate with that idea. Then, when I suggested "throw balls in the ball pit by yourself," that was a winner in his eyes. He felt an immediate sense of self-control.

After I spoke with Eli, I wanted to give Isaac an opportunity to speak. Isaac lacked the vocabulary and social skills to express his exact feelings. I gently guided Isaac through a discussion with Eli.

"Tell Eli how you feel."

I was not looking for an apology from Eli. The purpose of the discussion was to give Isaac the opportunity to practice communicating his needs to another human being. I refrained from adding words to the conversation. I just allowed Isaac to have the space to articulate his feelings.

In the end, Isaac was able to express his feelings to Eli and clearly communicate his desires in the situation. Eli was given tools and skills to use in the future and was reminded that his behavior was not a match to his spirit— the essence of who he *really is*.

Life Lesson #920: When I take a time-out for myself, I instantly have control. I can choose to breathe, remember my child for the great spirit he truly is, and develop a plan to authentically communicate. When I feel good about my child, I can see his undesirable behavior as an unusual event, far from the truth of who he is. I remember that he is new on this planet and learning how to work with and manage his feelings. I remember that he is learning the skills to use on this planet to communicate his needs and desires. I remember that he simply needs my help to remind him that we learn from these events, and we always do better next time because we learned what to do with our anger and frustrations. I know that a time-out is for me. I am the adult. It's my job to model how to handle difficult situations with understanding and grace. The only way I can teach control is to be in control ... of myself.

No punishment is your reward.

I am cruising down the highway, minding my own business, going around 70 mph in a 55-mph zone. I hear the sirens, look in my rear-view mirror, and realize that the Highway Patrol is not happy with my choice to go a little faster than recommended. The patrol officer pulls me over and I comply with his requests: license, insurance, and registration.

Then, he asks me a very condescending question: "Do you know how fast you were going?"

I immediately think, "Of *course* I do! I have to go that fast to get to my meeting on time!"

Instead, I say, "Around 65 mph."

"No. Actually, you were going 71 in a 55 zone."

Another thought: "*Really*? You couldn't say 70? You had to say *71*?"

He issues me a ticket and warns me of all the dangers of going 71 miles per hour on this highway. He tries to scare me into being "good" and following the rules with a story of a recent fatality on the highway.

"I hope you have learned your lesson, miss."

I immediately thought, "Yep, I need to pay more attention to where you guys hide so I can slow down and avoid a ticket!"

This incident sparked a thought: Does punishment *really* work?

This ticket will not detour me from ever speeding again. The patrol officer, shaming or fearing me into not speeding, has no effect on my choice to speed in the future. I will actually look for ways to "beat the system" instead of working together.

What if we could come to an understanding? What if we were able to communicate our needs and desires to each other, respectfully, and have it result in collaboration and an understanding of what works for both parties?

For me, it feels better to leave out the punishment with any child. I want them to tell me what they need, ask me what I need, and then come to an understanding together.

You may say, "That is a great thought but not possible with a 16-year-old!"

I say that it *is* possible and actually works very well! (It works with any age, but teenagers just make the story better.)

For example, my 16-year-old son comes home very late on a Saturday night—two hours past the time he said that he would be home. I am angry but, under the feeling of anger, I am really worried that something terrible happened to him. I am sitting, waiting, and playing out the worst-case scenarios in my mind. When he finally rolls in the door, he acts as if nothing has happened.

> What if we were able to communicate our needs and desires to each other, respectfully, and have it result in collaboration and an understanding of what works for both parties?

In my angry state, my first thought is, "What can I do to him to make him suffer as much as I have suffered tonight?"

The punishments in my mind range from taking his cell phone, taking his computer, grounding him, or all of the above. I take a moment to remember my conversation with the patrol officer and instantly decide to change my approach.

As my son walks in the door, I ask him to come and sit down for a minute. The conversation sounds like this:

"First, I am glad that you are at home and safe. I am not feeling good about this situation because I thought we were on the same page when you left the house earlier. I thought we agreed that you would be home at 12 a.m. When the clock hit 12:01, I instantly started worrying that something terrible had happened."

My son interrupts and says, "Mom, I am fine. I was just late."

I continue.

"Please let me finish my thoughts and then I will hear yours. When you were late, I automatically thought that something was wrong. You are respectful, considerate, and caring, and I know that when you have run late in the past, you called. You are one of the most important people in my world. I know that you are growing into yourself and soon you will be out of this house, able to stay out as long as you want without feeling like you need to 'report' to someone. I appreciate and honor your independence. I am asking you to work with me until you do leave, so we can both feel good about our remaining time together. Do you have any suggestions about how we can both get our needs met?"

The alternative? I punish him. He is angry and resentful, and then finds a way to get around it the next time, much like my speeding story.

I look at this as an opportunity for both of us to practice *communicating what we need* and *getting both of our needs met*—free from anger, shame, or punishment. I can promise you that having an honest conversation is more effective than a punishing one. When I state clearly what I need, and ask my child to state clearly his needs, we work together to come to a solution that offers us both a feeling of respect, power, and success.

> I look at this as an opportunity for both of us to practice communicating what we need and getting both of our needs met—free from anger, shame, or punishment.

Does punishment *ever* work?

I was technically still a child when I started babysitting. I knew what it felt like to be spanked. I remember that it made me mad. I knew that it didn't change my behavior; it just fired me up even more. I remember risking being spanked for the opportunity to "get away" with something.

When I was working with children and opened the preschool, physical punishment was not a legal option. I experimented with punishment for years. I would use consequences, take away privileges, penalize behaviors, take away toys, be disappointed, guilt them into a better behavior, compare them to others, and do anything I could think of to get the behavior I was seeking.

If I took a toy away, they would cry for a minute, and then find one they liked better. They became immune to losing privileges. Guilt worked for a while, if they thought highly of me; the ones who could care less, cared less. Nothing worked consistently. Nothing worked for every child, every time.

The bigger problem was that the children didn't seem to learn anything from being punished. Even if they appeared to learn, the same behavior would often repeat itself within a short amount of time. For example:

- They relied on me to regulate, control, perceive, and monitor *their* behavior.

- They relied on me to mediate and solve the problems *they* experienced among each other.

- They looked at me as the judge, jury, and enforcer. They no longer checked in with *their* internal guidance.

- They looked to me for the answers and to "fix" it for *them*.

It was an impossible task to accomplish for 30 individuals at any given time. When I thought about it for the long term, the decisions they were making in preschool were trivial compared to the decisions they were going to be making in the future. I wanted them to be able to handle *their* lives without my constant influence.

I had to let go of punishment. It wasn't serving the children; most importantly, it wasn't serving me.

What does it look like to let go of punishment?

"In the middle of every difficulty lies opportunity."
—*Albert Einstein, Nobel Prize-winning physicist*

Fighting = punishment … *or does it?*

The preschool was a breeding ground for fights. Boy or girl, old or young, tired or wide awake, inside or outside, with each other and even against themselves, there was always a fight to be witnessed throughout the day.

I ran out of time to punish.

I ran out of energy to punish.

I ran out of patience to punish.

I ran out of ways to punish.

The stories I told myself when I would punish a child always ended with the same thoughts:

- "We are teaching them a lesson."
- "They have to suffer the consequences."
- "Commit a crime, do the time."
- "One day, they will learn."
- "It's for his own good."
- "If I don't punish him for this, he will think that he can get away with it again."
- "How will he ever learn if I don't stop him now?"
- "If we don't stop this now, it's going to get worse."

The stories I told myself always sounded responsible and honorable; however, I decided to do something different. I had to shift my thoughts. I chose to let go of the *need to punish* and replace it with the *desire to communicate*. It was easier to communicate my needs, desires, and expectations rather than patrol and punish their behaviors and actions.

Do we really have to share?

Ethan and Michael, both two years old, were notorious for their fights. They really did have a love/hate relationship. There were days when they were inseparable and others when they couldn't get far enough away from each other.

Ethan was in the Cozy Coupe toy car. Michael decided that he wanted to test the name, so he thought it was a good idea to get in the car with Ethan. Ethan was not having it—at all. He was determined to keep Michael out of the car. When Michael opened the door to get in, Ethan put on his Fred Flintstone feet and sped off before Michael could stick one leg in the car.

We teachers watched the drama for a few minutes, practicing the art of "staying out of it." The back-and-forth squabble went on for a good 20 minutes. Michael was wearing Ethan down and finally got his body in the car. (It wasn't so cozy!)

All of a sudden, Michael pushed Ethan out the other side of the car. Ethan wasn't giving up that easily and Michael wasn't going to stop. The next thing we saw was Michael driving the Cozy Coupe and Ethan's body dangling out the side, holding strong with his legs in the car. When Michael took a final turn around the sandbox, Ethan was launched out of the car and landed on the green turf. *Victory!* Michael was in charge of the Cozy Coupe and Ethan was left in the dust.

Ethan scanned the playground, looking for the closest available adult. He was sobbing and pointing at Michael, who was circling the playground like it was the Grand Prix. Ethan was doing his best to express his anger and disgust for Michael. Because they were only two years old, their vocabulary was limited; however, words were not needed. Michael was on his victory lap while Ethan was looking for redemption.

It was my turn to play and my time to practice. Typically, I would have become involved much earlier in the drama, but not this time. I would have punished Michael and taken Ethan's "side" for sure. I would have restricted Michael from the Cozy Coupe for the rest of the day.

> Typically, I would have become involved much earlier in the drama, but not this time.

Typically, I would have labeled Ethan as the Victim and Michael as the Perpetrator (read more about the Triangle of Disempowerment in *Chapter 3: As a Parent, What Are You Really Responsible For?*), but I started to question the truth of that thought because roles are often reversed. This time, Michael was the aggressor, but Ethan would often get in his licks when teachers were not around or were watching the event.

I knew that the best course of action for me was little to no action at all. When Ethan came to complain, I asked him four questions:

"Who are you mad at, Ethan?"

"Michael."

"Who do you need to talk to?"

He looked at me and said, "You."

"Is my name Michael?"

He looked confused and said, "No."

"Then who do you need to talk to?"

"Michael!"

"*Exactly!*"

> That was my cue to step in and facilitate, especially because their vocabulary was so limited.

Ethan went over to Michael and, of course, Michael was not going to give him the time of day. That was my cue to step in and facilitate, especially because their vocabulary was so limited.

I stopped the Cozy Coupe and prompted Ethan to talk to Michael. I reminded him to tell Michael what he was feeling. Ethan spilled out his guts, cried, and pointed a lot. Michael wasn't bothered at all. After Ethan was done with his rant, Michael shrugged his shoulders and started the engine again.

Ethan looked at me and, without words, said, "Are you going to let him get away with this?"

Before Michael took off, these were my words: "Wow, Michael! Ethan is really upset about losing the car. When I was watching you push Ethan out of the car, I thought, 'That's not like Michael at all. He's always such a good friend. I wonder what happened?' I know that when I push my friends out of my car, they don't want to play with me anymore. Then I get sad and wish that I would have used my words with my friend instead of pushing them out of the car."

Michael contemplated my comment for about one minute and then drove off.

Ethan looked at me and, again without words, said, "Why did you let him go? He was supposed to be in trouble. I am supposed to get the car back and make him eat my dust!"

I explained, "Ethan, when my friend does something that makes me mad, I tell them how I feel. If they don't listen or want to work it out with me, I choose not to play with them for a while. I take a break from them and find someone else I want to play with."

Ethan understood because Michael came back to play with Ethan shortly after the event, and Ethan was having fun with another friend. They were laughing and playing and would not allow Michael to join in. Of course, Michael ran to me to "fix" it because Ethan was "being mean" to him.

"Sometimes, Michael, when I am mean to my friends and push them out of a car, they don't want to play with me for the rest of the day. So I don't push my friends out of cars anymore because I really like playing with my friends."

Michael instantly knew what I was saying. He looked across the playground with sad eyes. He learned his lesson. He learned more *without* my intervention. It felt good to stay out of it. There was no need for punishment. He experienced his own punishment. My role in this was to facilitate and model my own experience so he could understand it for himself. He was two years old and he got it!

I gave both boys the opportunity to be their own authority. I allowed them to experience the natural consequences for their actions and behaviors.

It felt good to let go of the judge's robe.

It felt good to watch them have an experience *with* me—not *because* of me.

It felt good to verbally model why I don't push my own friends out of my car.

I'm not going to say that it was easy to do in the moment but, in the end, it felt better to me.

Life Lesson #596: When children are fighting or struggling with each other, it is important for me to stay out of it as much as possible (assuming no blood or weapons are involved). I need to remove myself emotionally and physically from the drama for my own sanity. It doesn't serve me or my children to engage in the chaos. It feels better to be an observer and mentor rather than a police officer and judge. When I give children the chance to work out their differences, they gain the skills they need in the future. Often, there are more lessons learned than I had anticipated. When I have patience, stay out of it, and trust the process, all is well.

Are rewards actually rewarding?

When I was about five years old, I approached my parents about an allowance. I wasn't sure what an actual allowance was, but I knew that my best friend got money from her parents for doing chores around the house, and I thought it was a great idea.

My parents didn't. They explained that I have responsibilities—not chores—in our house because I lived there. Their expectation was for me to participate in the house because I was a member of the family.

Their theory was, "We don't get paid to take care of the house. We take care of the house because we live here and want to have a nice home."

After much debate (I started young), my parents cooperated. They decided to give me $1 a week if I did "extra" things around the house. A few weeks into it, I had done a lot of "extras" (at least it seemed like a lot for a five-year-old).

My mom and dad couldn't keep track of everything I had done, so they said, "How about if we give you a dollar, and you do what you feel is right."

I never had charts, stickers, or progress reports to justify the dollar. They trusted that I would do my best. (Actually, they made out like bandits because I was an overachiever and did far more than a dollar's worth.) Eventually, my parents were over the dollar-a-week ritual.

> I never had charts, stickers, or progress reports to justify the dollar. They trusted that I would do my best.

"Let's forget the dollar. If you want money for something you need, we will discuss it in the moment and decide what's best. Will that work for you?"

I was a smart kid and agreed. I knew that a dollar wouldn't buy much. I knew that my parents were more than fair about buying me items, and I knew that I would get more if I let go of the dollar.

I never got an allowance again. As I got older and my requests were bigger, my parents offered suggestions about how to get the items I wanted. They would ask me to come up with ways they could "hire me" for a service. I was already babysitting; I just wanted more money to buy name-brand clothes that my parents were unwilling to purchase for me. I learned how to mow the lawn, so I could be hired as a landscaper for our home. I learn how to iron, so I could be hired as laundry attendant. I learned how to cook dinner, so I could be hired as a private chef.

It was the birthing of my entrepreneurial spirit and a brilliant strategy. They were completely removed. There were no charts, stickers, or money exchanged as a reward for a chore completed. I had expected responsibilities in the home, regardless. They encouraged creativity and independence to acquire any material goods that they were unwilling to purchase. They positioned each transaction as a business transaction, separate from the family. *Brilliant!* My parents allowed me to practice being an entrepreneur—even at five years old.

I have never been a big fan of a "rewards" system, most likely because my parents were not big on rewards either. They were clear about expectations— not necessarily their own, but more about expectations as a human being on this planet. In other words, they were not going to give me a sticker for cleaning my room, brushing my teeth, eating dinner, or reading a book. They did not provide charts outlining my responsibilities in the home. The thought of giving me money for good grades, being nice to a friend, or following directions would have sent them into another world.

Here's a glimpse into my parents' heads:

- "Charts are ridiculous. I am not going to waste my time monitoring her on things she needs to do to be a part of this family or a human being."

- "If she wants stickers, buy them for her or don't. Stickers are not going to determine her self-worth or self-esteem."

- "I am not going to pay our daughter for her responsibilities. I am going to honor her with my words and actions rather than with money. I want her to experience school as a place to learn and grow. I want her value as a human to be nurtured intrinsically, absent of a monetary value."

- "We brush our teeth and eat to take care of our bodies. We read a book to take care of our minds and spirit. We naturally want these things, so it's not an issue."

- "We are nice, compassionate, loving, and helpful because that's who we are as humans—not because we get paid to do it."

Owen was a student of See World Learning Center for four years. It was time for him to graduate and move on to "big school." He was excited and ready. I was still providing afterschool care for him because he only attended kindergarten half of the day. The "big school" was a big adjustment for Owen. He was actually bored and uninspired.

At our preschool:

- Children were allowed a lot of freedom.

- They were allowed to use scissors, paint, colors, and markers as long as they could hold them in their hand.

- They were given the opportunity to work out issues or problems with their friends without the teacher as a mediator.

- They were given the opportunity and space to figure out this world.

- They were trusted to make a decision and reap the benefits or suffer the natural consequences.

When Owen showed me his "rewards chart," we were both confused. The paper listed a series of actions and events. If completed, the child would be rewarded with a "treasure chest dollar," which was a fake dollar issued by the teacher and redeemable on "fun Friday." The children were instructed to complete various tasks, collect dollars, and cash them in on Friday by picking toys from a treasure chest that the teacher had at the front of the classroom.

When Owen and I went over the list, I was horrified. The list reflected actions that seemed ridiculous to associate with money:

1. Push in your chair ($1)

2. Listen to the teacher ($2)

3. Pick up the trash off the playground without being asked ($1)

4. Be nice to a friend ($1)

5. Turn in your completed homework on Friday ($1)

6. Say "please" and "thank you" ($1)

7. Play nice outside at recess ($2)

8. Eat all your lunch ($1)

9. Stand up for a friend ($1)

10. Raise your hand to speak ($2)

11. Put away your supplies ($1)

12. Be quiet during reading time ($1)

The list went on and on with five categories and over 50 ways to be rewarded.

"Miss Heather, why is my teacher giving me money to be nice and do what I do anyway? This is weird."

Owen's question stopped me in my tracks. It was exactly what I was thinking! The whole system offered a mixed message.

> I reminded Owen that it is not his job to *stand up* for a friend. It is his job to *stand by* a friend when they are in need and love them through the difficulties.

I reminded Owen that he does things like pushing in his chair, putting his supplies away, and turning in his homework because it is his responsibility as a student in the school.

I reminded Owen that he does things like being nice to friends, having great manners, and listening to the teacher because it feels good to be the best Owen he can be to himself and to others.

I reminded Owen that he picks up trash from the playground because he loves his school and wants to take care of it.

Last but not least, I reminded Owen that it is not his job to *stand up* for a friend. It is his job to *stand by* a friend when they are in need and love them through the difficulties.

"We do these things because it *feels* good, Owen. We do them because we love ourselves, our school, and each other."

Owen understood. He had four years of foundation and nothing could crack that. I didn't have to worry. He knew the reasons for his actions, regardless of the rewards being given. With all the "dollars" he accumulated throughout the week, he gave them to the other kids who didn't get them because he simply wanted to share. He wanted his friends to have the opportunity to visit the treasure chest because he knew on a deeper level that their worth and value as a human being were not determined by a fake dollar rewarded for observed actions by the teacher.

I want our children to maintain their intrinsic inspiration—not be monetarily motivated.

I want them to experience joy with their friends because it feels good—not because they were paid to do it.

What happens when the novelty of the "treasure chest" wears off? We ultimately have to keep increasing the reward. When we set up this system, we are teaching our children, "When you do this … you get that." Then, we complain that children are "entitled," "disrespectful," and "selfish." Well, *we set up the system!*

I want to acknowledge and embrace the natural tendencies with which our children come to this planet. I want them to hold these basic human traits in their heart, act from the heart, and disassociate a monetary value to the human experience.

How do I reward my children?

Here's what I do:
- I give my children every ounce of praise and appreciation I can.
- I look for every opportunity to remind them that they are amazing individuals.
- I am aware of their greatness and remind them frequently.
- I look for the behavior I want.
- I acknowledge the manners I want when I see them by saying:

- o "Thank you for saying 'thank you.'"
- o "I love it when you ask me with the word 'please.'"
- I constantly watch and look for the moments that I can say, with authenticity:
    - o "You are such a good friend!"
    - o "You always take good care of our school!"
    - o "You are so loved by your friends!"
    - o "That was an awesome throw!"
    - o "Your smile lights up the world."
    - o "You are so strong!"
    - o "You filled your belly with great food!"
    - o "I know that you are a great decision maker."
    - o "I trust you!"

> I choose to remind them of their greatness.

Many people in this world will remind us of what we lack. They will remind us what we did wrong, what we are doing wrong, or what we are about to do wrong. They will tell us that we are not good enough. They will think that they are helping us, but it actually doesn't help at all. Enough people in this world will remind my child of their shortcomings or failures.

I choose to remind them of their greatness.

> "As we express our gratitude, we must never forget that the highest appreciation is not to utter words, but to live by them."
>
> —*John F. Kennedy, 35th U.S. president*

I am committed to being a cheerleader, a coach, and a spiritual mentor for my children. I am committed to rewarding them with my love—especially when I find it difficult to do so.

I am blessed to have parents who rewarded me with their time, energy, effort, and love. I want that for every child in my life. We deserve to be loved, acknowledged, valued, and honored. I am committed to starting with the little ones … they are easier!

We are happier when there is harmony and agreement.

When Heather told me that she doesn't believe in time-outs, punishments, or rewards, I was instantly curious to learn how she guided behavior. Our parenting model, education model, business model, and even government model are based on the idea that humans need time-outs (or the adult words, such as "suspension" and "leave of absence"), punishment, and rewards to influence human behavior.

Could Heather have invented a new, revolutionary way to get results with children without using any of these techniques?

Let's start with one of Heather's most basic (and most subconscious) strategies: "My goal is to create harmony and agreement." She is always acting in support of this goal and eliminates anything that causes resistance. She has found that, when she says the word "no," it causes resistance. Time-outs, punishments, and even rewards also cause resistance.

If Heather doesn't use the word "no" with kids, what *does* she do?

Focus on what you *can* do and what you *do* want.

Heather is constantly focusing and redirecting her child's attention to what they *can* do and when or where they *can* do it. As we saw in the table describing "My New and Improved Rules (v2.0)," she redirects the child to an acceptable place to do that activity (e.g., "If you want to run, go outside" or "If you want to yell, you can scream outside").

Science backs up Heather's strategy and explains why eliminating the words "no" and "don't" are so effective. Human beings are hard-wired to think in pictures. It's how we process information, even if we aren't conscious of it.

If I were to tell you, "Don't pull on the dog's tail," what comes to mind as you process that request? If you are like most people, you just made a quick mental picture of pulling on a dog's tail.

Our minds are constantly making pictures of what we hear (very rapidly and usually subconsciously). As we process what we hear so that we can understand it, we omit the words "no" and "don't" from our mental pictures. Once we have created a mental picture of what we are hearing, our attention goes to thinking more about that picture. In this case, we think about the idea of pulling a dog's tail.

Energy flows where attention goes. Choose what you feed your energy.

A core principle of the human experience is that "energy flows where attention goes." As we create pictures in our minds all day based on the words we speak or hear, we are flowing energy to all of these pictures. We give our attention to the mental pictures and thereby create more of what we see in these pictures.

> This philosophy is counterintuitive to what we've been taught but, the more we ignore bad behavior, the less of it we get.

The trick to getting the behavior we want is to give our children a mental picture of what we *do* want and of what they *can* do. We want them to create mental pictures of what *is* okay to do, so their focus and energy go to those pictures.

This philosophy is counterintuitive to what we've been taught but, the more we ignore bad behavior, the less of it we get. This counterintuitive strategy allows Heather to get great results with children. To quote Steve Jobs, if we want something different in our life, we have to "Think Different."

The more we tell our kids, "Don't be mean," "Stop being annoying," "Don't ask me for anything at the store," or "Don't hit your sister," the more of that behavior we get. *Energy flows where attention goes.*

Where is your attention going with your children? Is it focused on what your child *can* do and what you *do* want, or is it more focused on "no," "don't," and "can't"? The challenge in focusing on what we *do* want (and ignoring what we *don't* want) is that we have all had a lifetime of experience contrary to this model. It takes some conscious shifting, like Heather did, to change our ingrained behavioral patterns.

I can appreciate the difficulty of making this shift. For example, the whole school grading model is centered on the idea that students need to be continuously assessed—measured—on how close to some preset standard of "exceptional" or "perfect" they have achieved. With every grade (unless they get 100%), students are reminded of their knowledge and skill-level shortcomings and that they are less than "perfect."

Nothing about grades ever feels good (even for straight-A students) because we are never celebrated for what we did well; we are only reminded of what we missed (according to what someone else has defined) and on what we were expected to focus.

We operate the same way with children's behavior. Our children can be wonderful 95% of the time; however, the 5% of undesirable behavior gets 95% of our attention. Is it really any wonder that, as humans, we rarely feel amazing about ourselves? Wouldn't it be wonderful if everyone in our lives completely ignored where we messed up, and just noticed and celebrated everything we did right in a day?

Wouldn't we all be happier?

Let's flip the whole model on its head.

Performance reviews on the job are another example of how ingrained we have become in believing that focusing on what "needs improvement" is a good strategy. In our society, we have developed the belief that people need job feedback to focus on where they are less than perfect and need improvement (according to someone else's opinion). We have ingrained the belief that people need to be briefly acknowledged for their strengths and widely coached on shoring up their weaknesses.

Have you ever left a performance review and felt on top of the world, as if you were totally cherished, valued, supported, and loved? Did you feel like you were an amazing human being and a huge asset to the organization? I have never walked out of a performance review and felt this way. Even when I got 17% salary increases, or was told that I was "the top performer on the team," I always felt horrible after the review.

The problem was that the high marks and praise were immediately followed by a "what needs improvement" conversation. Most of the reviewer's energy went to the small number of things that were "weaknesses" in their view in the hopes of making them strengths.

The more I focused on my "areas for growth," the more they became problems or shortcomings in my own work. *Energy flows where attention goes.* In every performance review for about eight years, I heard that my "needs improvement" area was "to slow down for others."

It took me a long time to realize that my greatest strengths are vision and speed. At the time, my bosses saw these strengths as weaknesses—that I needed to slow down to bring others along—and I believed them. I tried so hard to make them happy, but I never could because I was fighting my DNA and my nature.

What if any of my bosses had said, "Here is where we are headed as a company this year. What excites you and what can you bring to the table? What can we look forward to from you? Are there any areas where you'd like to expand?" I was already motivated. This approach would have worked so much better for both of us on the job.

This same approach also works well for parents. When kids are strong willed and spirited, instead of acknowledging the gift of how that behavior can serve them in their life, we call it a "weakness" and try to

> Wouldn't it be wonderful if everyone in our lives completely ignored where we messed up, and just noticed and celebrated everything we did right in a day?

control the behavior by labeling it and trying to correct it. This focus causes resistance in the child, and they feel defeated or push back with even stronger energy to make sure they remain who they are. Even worse, we deny their greatest gift because *we* can't see beyond it.

We can shift this approach by recognizing that we are surrounded by a model that values focusing on weaknesses or undesirable behavior.

- What if the model with which we've grown up is backwards?
- What if we flipped this model on its head?
- What if we did exactly the opposite?
- What if we took away our attention from "needs improvement" with our kids, spouse, and employees, and changed it to "acknowledge your greatness in every single moment"?

Ignore as much undesirable behavior as possible.

Heather's strategy—to ignore as much undesirable behavior as humanly possible without compromising her needs—is really a strategy of genius. She intuitively knows that the more she hovers over her children, pointing out everything they are doing that isn't appropriate, the more of that type of behavior she will get. With this method, her children will feel micromanaged and rebel in different ways until, at some point, it escalates out of control.

If Heather notices anything her child is doing that isn't exactly what she wants, she always asks herself the key question, "Can I ignore this or is it a deal breaker that I need to address?" She has very few deal breakers; instead, she spends her time modeling "feel good" instead of getting herself in a space of "feel bad." It's brilliant if you think about it. It's also a recipe for increased happiness.

My business partner and world-renowned behavioral scientist Tim Hallbom has spent decades researching human behavior. He has reached this same conclusion: People only respond to specific feedback about what they are doing well. It tells them to do more of that behavior.

Tim frequently shares a story in his seminars to illustrate the point. According to Tim, a group set out to see what would happen with children in school, based on how their parents responded to their report cards. The children brought home report cards with one A, two Bs, one C, and one D.

> People only respond to specific feedback about what they are doing well. It tells them to do more of that behavior.

- The first group of parents was directed to comment on *only* the A and not mention the other grades. They were instructed to say something like, "Wow! Great job on this A! What were you doing in this class to be so successful?"

- The second group of parents was instructed to *only* focus on the C and the D (not the A or Bs), and say something like, "What happened in these classes where you got a C and a D? Do you need some help here? Do you need to do something differently?"

- The third group of parents was instructed to comment on *all* of the report card grades. They were instructed to say something like, "Good job on the A and Bs! What happened here with the C and D?"

Guess which group of students performed significantly better on their next report card?

- The first group of students (where the parents *only* commented on the A) tended to improve *all* of their grades the next semester.

- The second group of students (where the parents *only* commented on the C and D) tended to do worse and get lower grades overall the next semester (i.e., the A and Bs became B and Cs).

- The third group of students (where the parents commented on everything) tended to get the same grades the next semester.

Energy flows where attention goes. Focus only on the As.

"I am always looking for the good, big or small, in any given situation," Heather explains. "It can be difficult to find the 'good' in two children battling it out over a toy. I have been known to say, 'Jack, you have the most amazing eyes of love. I know that you always find the love in yourself and in others. That's what makes you so special. I know that you will work this out.'

"Sometimes I struggle with the behavior and can't feel good about it at all; however, I can always find an amazing quality unique to my child—a special 'something' that melts my heart every time. If there is something going on that drives me crazy, I withdraw my attention from it and ignore it.

"For example, my friend's son started distorting his face when we would have difficult conversations. He would scrunch it and move his mouth in ways that were incredibly difficult to watch. I intuitively knew that the conversation was 'heavy' and uncomfortable for him (a conversation about the death of our dog of 14 years), and made a conscious effort to pretend that the face scrunching didn't exist. Once he understood the death process, he stopped the facial gestures."

If your parents ignored more of your behavior when you were growing up, how would you have responded? If they had noticed all of the great things about you—even the smallest things, such as doing the dishes—and acknowledged you and said "thanks" several times a day, would that have shifted your feelings about your family?

For the next two weeks, commit to ignoring as much of your child's undesirable behavior as humanly possible, and notice and comment on as much good behavior as you can. It has to be genuine, meaningful, and from your heart; otherwise, your child will notice the insincerity. Find anything positive that you can notice and share it with your child. Here are some examples:

- "Thanks, honey, for getting up on time and dressing this morning!"
- "I'm so proud of you for doing your homework all on your own."
- "Wow! Your eyes are so beautiful!"

Use this technique for getting the behavior you *do* want.

When Heather chooses to guide behavior, she always uses a consistent script (as seen in examples throughout this book and in many of the scenarios in

Part 4: Feel Like a Parenting Pro with These Proven Scripts).

This brilliant script is based in *questions*. Heather isn't telling her child to *do* anything. She is using the power of questions to get her child to *think* about the answer. When we tell our child,

Changing the strategy to the "question" approach takes a bit of practice.

"Don't do that," "Stop," or "No," we are giving them the answer rather than having them come up with it on their own.

Most parents are in the habit of telling their children what to do. It's just a lot easier to say, "Don't touch that" or "Don't do that." Changing the strategy to the "question" approach takes a bit of practice.

How to guide children's behavior

Here is Heather's step-by-step script for guiding children's behavior:

Step 1: Explain what's expected (or what's not appropriate) once. For example, you can say, "When we play outside, I need you to wear your shoes." The best strategy is to tell kids—in advance—what to expect. Let children know what *you* expect. Your goal is to get in front of something *before* it happens. Heather calls this "prepaving the experience I want to have."

Step 2: If it's important, get on eye level, make a real connection, and ask, "Do you understand?" Wait for a confirmation. If there is a situation where you expect your child to do something, make sure they hear you by getting down on their level, establishing an eye-to-eye emotional connection, and asking the question, "Do you understand?" When your child says, "Yes," it means that, in the future, she is now held accountable and responsible for upholding that understanding. By saying "Yes, I understand," your child is taking on accountability and responsibility for following through on your request. If she doesn't, come back to this moment and say, "I don't get it. You said that you understood. What happened?"

Step 3: If your child does the unwanted behavior, ask a question that requires thought and reflection so they can come up with their own answer. The goal is to have them recall their commitment or agreement to cooperate with you in the situation. For example, let's say you go outside and your child kicks his shoes off. You can say, "Where do your shoes belong when we are outside? What did we agree to before we came outside?" Now that you've explained the appropriate behavior *once*, ask your child to recall the answer every time after that. Your job of telling them is over. Now you are asking them to tell *you* what is expected. You want *them* to say, "No," not you. You want *them* to formulate the answer in their mind and give it to you. Resist the urge to tell them what to do. Have them tell *you* what they need to do through the power of your questions.

Step 4: Direct them in a way that they can do the activity. For example, ask this question: "If you want to stay outside, what do you need to do?" If they get stuck, model a possible solution that is more effective: "If it were me, I would put on my shoes so I could play outside longer. I love being outside" or "One time, when I was in this situation, I did ..." Make sure you end your statement with "... but it's totally up to you." That gives them a choice and lets them come up with a solution on their own. The goal is to have your child make a mental picture of what they *can* do. This can be accomplished with questions like, "Where *can* you jump?," "What *can* you hit?," "What *can* you say to your friend?," "What *can* you play with at this house?," or "What *can* you do to figure out your homework assignment?"

Step 5: If the undesirable behavior persists, separate the behavior from the child, and let them know that they are better than the behavior they are exhibiting. The natural reaction is to get upset and frustrated, and then threaten them with punishment when undesirable behavior continues. Squelch the urge and retrain yourself to focus on reminding your child of his greatness. For example: "I know that you are an amazing, thoughtful, and considerate boy. This isn't like you to act like this. What's going on?" Remind your child that he is amazing and this behavior is so unlike him (see *Chapter 9: Remind Your Child of Their Greatness ... Always* for the full strategy of this approach).

The steps in this script are present in many, many examples in this book. It's one of Heather's main go-to strategies. Put it into action in your life and notice how you get better and better with each new situation.

State what *you* need.

Another way that Heather focuses on what she *does* want is by utilizing the phrase, "I need you to …" Here are some examples of what many parents "command" their children to do along with examples of how Heather focuses on communicating what she needs:

Commanding / Demanding	Communicating Needs
"Stop touching the candle."	"I need your fingers to stay off the candle."
"You need to take out the trash now."	"I need you to take out the trash."
"Go wash your hands now."	"I need you to come inside and get ready for dinner."
"You'd better be home by curfew or else!"	"I need you to be home by midnight."
"Get in bed now."	"I need you to go to bed."
"You'd better knock it off!"	"I need you to use words that I can understand."
"Eat your dinner."	"I need you to decide if you want to eat your dinner or not."
"Leave me alone!"	"I need some time for myself."
"Turn off the iPad and put it away."	"I need you to put the iPad away."
"Put that glass down now. You're going to drop it and break it!"	"I need you to put the glass down."
"Stop running in the house!"	"I need you to walk in the house."
"Get dressed right now!"	"I need you to put on your clothes."
"Clean your room right now!"	"I need your room cleaned up."

As Heather says, "I am always communicating what I need. When I honor my own needs, I am modeling self-respect and self-expression. It never feels good to be *told* what to do. I respect my parents, friends, coworkers, and family when they express their needs. I want to honor their needs. I don't respond well when they tell me what I *have* to do."

When we say "I need you to ..." out loud, the words by their nature require us to be clear energetically about what we want. When we are clear with our own energy, we create the space for others to honor our needs.

Take a moment and reflect on your communication style with the people in your life. How would it be different if you changed your language to clearly state what you need? Consider how you can shift commands into "I need you to ..." statements.

> "When it comes to producing lasting change in attitudes and behavior, however, rewards, like punishment, are strikingly ineffective."

Are we punished by rewards?

Shifting our behavior to focus on what we *do* want and what children *can* do, and rethinking the idea of punishments and rewards, require some practice and a deviation from societal thinking. After working with more than 30,000 kids over 25 years, Heather has figured out that punishment and rewards don't work, and many psychologists have reached the same conclusion through their studies.

Alfie Kohn really rocked the world with his book, *Punished by Rewards.*[1] He explains why rewards systems at home, in school, and in the workplace just don't work for long-term behavioral change; however, they can work for short-term compliance or control.

In his *Harvard Business Review* article, "Why Incentive Plans Cannot Work,"[2] Kohn says:

> "Do rewards work? The answer depends on what we mean by 'work.' Research suggests that, by and large, rewards succeed at securing one thing only: temporary compliance. When it comes to producing lasting change in attitudes and behavior, however, rewards, like punishment, are strikingly ineffective. Once the rewards run

out, people revert to their old behaviors. Studies show that offering incentives for losing weight, quitting smoking, using seat belts, or (in the case of children) acting generously is not only less effective than other strategies but often proves worse than doing nothing at all. Incentives, a version of what psychologists call extrinsic motivators, do not alter the attitudes that underlie our behaviors. They do not create an enduring commitment to any value or action. Rather, incentives merely—and temporarily—change what we do.

"Punishment and rewards are two sides of the same coin. Rewards have a punitive effect because they, like outright punishment, are manipulative. 'Do this and you'll get that' is not really very different from 'Do this or here's what will happen to you.'"

If you notice that punishment and rewards are not working for long-term behavioral change in your family, you would be experiencing what scientists have discovered: *Punishment and rewards really don't work for anyone.*

If I don't give time-outs or punishments, what do I do instead?

If time-outs, punishments, and rewards are not effective, then what is the model? What would work better and create more happiness? Take several pages out of this book and model Heather.

For example, explore how you *can*:

- Create a relationship based on mutual trust and respect by operating with the guiding question, "How can we *both* get what we want here?"

- Eliminate the obedience model and focus on controlling the only thing you really can control: *you.*

- Ignore behavior that you *don't* want and focus on behavior that you *do* want.

- Explain to children what they *can* do and direct them to where they *can* do it. Take a moment to explain to the child how he *can* appropriately express himself in any situation.

- Squelch the desire to immediately punish. Take the time to become emotionally centered and in a space of love, and then discover the underlying feelings causing the behavior. For example, if the point of punishment is to teach a lesson, wouldn't it be more effective to teach a child how he can better express himself when he feels frustrated, angry, or challenged in some way? Get yourself into a space where you can have this conversation.

These are a few examples of things you *can* do that are more effective than time-outs or punishments. We will present even more alternatives to time-outs and punishments in *Chapter 8: Honor Every Choice Your Child Makes* and *Chapter 9: Remind Your Child of Their Greatness … Always.*

Ask "How can I help you?" instead of "What's wrong?"

Another technique parents can use to guide behavior is to change the question they ask when their child is upset. When a child is hurt, crying, upset from a fight, or complaining, most people intuitively ask, "What's wrong?," "What's the matter?," or "What happened?" Heather believes that these questions keep the child's energy and their focus in the past and on the negative emotion. She intuitively wants to get to a "feel good" space as quickly as possible.

> Another technique parents can use to shift behavior is to change the question they ask when their child is upset.

Heather says, "We are so programmed to ask 'What happened?' when someone is upset. This question keeps us stuck in the drama and stuck in the victim mode. When I am upset and someone asks me, 'How can I help you?,' I immediately focus my attention on what I need in the moment, and what I need to get out of my funk and feel good.

"When I dig deeper into my child's problem, what I am really doing is gathering information on what happened so *I* can help create a solution for them. But the truth is, I might not have the best solution; moreover, I don't want the responsibility of having to fix my child's problems. I would rather empower my child to check in with their *own* needs and ask for help when they need it, especially when they are upset. I want them to learn how to ask for a hug, space to work it out, a Band-Aid, or wisdom."

When a child is upset, Heather asks a very different question. She first empathizes with the upset child by saying, "Oh, baby, I know." and then asks, "How can I help you?" or "What do you need from me?" This approach guides the child to consider what *they* need to feel better in the moment.

The next time your child is crying or upset, practice empathizing with the emotion and then ask, "How can I help you?"

Consciously create harmony and agreement.

Raising a happy child (and being happy too) is about creating more moments of harmony and agreement. This is exactly what Heather strives to do every day with every child. To increase the harmony and agreement in your life, I invite you shift your thinking and put into action some of what's been presented here.

Learning anything new often takes practice. Shifting decades of our behavior and thinking can take time. Be easy on yourself and celebrate the fact that you tried something new, even if you don't get the result you want in that moment. Do it again, maybe with a twist next time. You'll get it, and you'll notice that your happiness will improve dramatically.

> "Happiness cannot be traveled to, owned, earned, worn or consumed. Happiness is the spiritual experience of living every minute with love, grace, and gratitude."
> —*Denis Waitley, motivational speaker and writer*

Review of Chapter 7: Focus on What You *Do* Want

- Make it a goal to create harmony and agreement in your interactions.
- Energy flows where attention goes. Choose what you feed your energy.

- Shift your attention away from what "needs improvement" with your kids, spouse, and employees, and change it to "acknowledge your greatness in every single moment I can."

- Ignore as much undesirable behavior as possible and just focus on the deal breakers.

- Use the technique for getting the behavior you *do* want. Explain once, ask a question that gets *them* (and not you) to say "no," and redirect the behavior to where they *can* do it.

- Rather than issue a command, instead say, "I need you to ..."

- Shift your approach of punishment (and rewards) by focusing on the desired outcome, which is to help your child learn how to express himself appropriately in any situation.

See this strategy in action!

Check out the video on
Focus on What You Do *Want*

V I D E O   V I D E O

or visit
www.raiseahappychild.com/focus

Honor Every Choice
Your Child Makes

"Tell me and I'll forget; show me and I may
remember; involve me and I'll understand."

—*Chinese proverb*

I trust the children.

O ur school had an open kitchen. A "safety gate" was installed to keep the children out; however, as I reminded the children how smart they were, they lived up to it and figured out the gate immediately. I was so surprised because it was a difficult lock, even for the adults! I knew that I needed to educate each child on the dangers of the kitchen without instilling fear in them or simply demanding that they do what they were told "because I said so."

179

When a new child enrolled in See World, I took them on a tour to become acquainted with each room, let them know where to go potty (*very* important), and make them aware of our school's expectations. On the tour, we would make our way through the school, ending at the kitchen door. The most dangerous place in our school was the kitchen, and the gas stove was easily accessible once they made it through the safety gate.

I wanted each child to *experience* the heat from the stove. I wanted them to remember *why* the stove was to be used by adults or with adult supervision (we allowed our children to cook on the stove with our help). Altered for each child, based on age and ability to understand me, this was the typical speech:

> I wanted each child to *experience* the heat from the stove.

"Stoves can get very hot. Right now, it is off. When I turn it on, it will get very hot. Adults need to turn stoves on and off. We have had more experience with stoves and, until you have more experience with a stove, I need you to work with an adult to cook.

"Now, I am going to turn on the stove. See the flame? That is fire. It is hot. We need to pay attention to take care of ourselves. I want you to feel how hot it is. I am going to hold your hand high up to feel the heat. Then you will know how hot it is."

I would then take their hands and hold them over the fire. Sometimes they were reluctant because they had been told by others not to do this. Even though they had been told, it never detoured them from touching the stove!

"Do you feel how hot that is? Remember that we are not even touching the metal plate. It is so hot already. Do you think it would hurt if we touched the metal plate? Do you think it is a good idea to touch the stove without an adult? When can you touch a stove?"

After this dialogue exchange, the children *never* touched the stove. We would often just leave the door open to the kitchen—not because we were irresponsible but because we trusted the children. We knew that they *completely* understood how it felt to touch the stove, and we never had a negative incident in the kitchen with *any* child. I didn't have safety locks on the cabinets. When they understood the expectations and *why,* they were compliant. We had hundreds of children who were clear on the expectations, understood the natural consequences, and made their own decision to avoid a hospital visit.

Skeptics say that we were lucky. I say we honestly trusted that every child had the ability to make a decision in his own best interest when properly educated and informed. I wanted the children to avoid the stove because they knew they had the potential for injury. I wanted them to make an informed decision for themselves, especially when I am not paying attention, unaware, or somewhere else.

When their hand hovered over the heat, asking questions and taking away the mystery of the stove, the children were no longer full of wonder for the "forbidden stove" or interested in being burned. Their curiosity was satisfied and they made a decision to stay away based on their experience of the heat on their hand. When they are given the information and experience, they are capable of making a decision in their best interest.

Who is in control?

control (*v.*) to exercise authority over; direct; command[1]

Growing up, I knew who was in control: my mom—or at least she appeared to be. My mom was very emotional, demonstrative, and never ran out of ways to express her feelings. She yelled, threw things, slammed doors, cursed like a truck driver, and clearly made us aware of her anger, frustration, or disgust. She cried (a lot) when she was sad, happy, or mad. She also gave her heart and soul to every friend who came into her life. She went above and beyond the call of duty, *always*. She was full of fire, wonder, and passion. Most of all, she smothered me with love, affection, appreciation, and warmth to always let me know how much she loved me.

My father was logical, contemplative, and extremely reserved with his expression of emotions. He never spoke an ill word about anyone, *ever*. I never heard my father use foul language. Without shedding a tear, I watched him carry Papa Bill's casket. The first time I ever saw my father cry was when my mother left home and asked for a divorce; the last time I saw my father cry was when he was in hospice and told me how much he was going to miss me.

> The first time I ever saw my father cry was when my mother left home and asked for a divorce; the last time I saw my father cry was when he was in hospice and told me how much he was going to miss me.

They were extreme opposites. I really appreciate the demonstrations of both ends of the spectrum. They both gave me the opportunity to see the natural consequences from each perspective.

When I was around seven years old, my mother came home from work and I could sense her energy as soon as she walked in the door. She was frustrated from the day and already past the point of exhaustion to begin the night. She struggled with working *out* of the home and then coming home to work *in* the home—not an uncommon mothers' struggle for balance. My father had the *Leave It to Beaver* approach where the woman prepared the food and took care of the home. (It was a bonus if the woman also worked and brought home a check!)

On this evening, my mom prepared dinner—casserole surprise, which consisted of leftover ingredients from the week's previous dinners in one dish ... *disgusting!* I complained (a lot). My father was numb to my complaints and would eat anything my mother put in front of him; if he didn't like it, the cure-all was ketchup.

After dinner, my father got up, left the table, and went back to his office to "work" (i.e., he watched *Star Trek*). I left the dinner table to do my homework. This was the last straw that broke the camel's back. My mom was left with all the dinner dishes and a lack of appreciation from both of us. (To be fair, I really appreciated my mom but not her casserole.)

All of a sudden, my mom yelled, "Well, that's fine! If no one wants to help with the dishes, I guess I will do them myself. Don't worry, I will do them. You both just do what you need to do!"

Crash! One dish hit the floor and shattered; another dish hit the floor with record speed. By the time my father and I made it back into the kitchen, five dishes were shattered in pieces on the floor. My father told her to stop and she refused.

"No! Y'all want me to do the dishes, so I am *doing the dishes!*"

My father grabbed her and pinned her against the wall. He wasn't angry, at least not outwardly. His intention was to stop the insanity. He held her there until she calmed down.

He said two words: *"That's enough!"*

Eventually she calmed down, and it ended with a tremendous amount of tears. She was exhausted, not sure how to ask for what she needed, and completely out of control emotionally, physically, and spiritually. She would give and give until she had nothing left to give. Now, as an adult, a wife, and a mother for many children, I totally understand her frustration.

My father's next sentence was, "All you have to do is ask."

Well, that set my mom off again.

"I shouldn't *have* to ask! You should both just *help!*"

My father, in his controlled voice, responded, "We don't know what you need or want unless you tell us. You always clean up. How do we know you wanted something different today?"

The fact that I remember this event 30 years later reflects the profound effect it had on my life on many levels:

- I learned about control.

- I learned about setting clear expectations for myself.

- I learned to speak up for what I want and need, even if it is different than what I was taught.

My father showed control in many ways. He stopped her from destroying all of our dishes and gave her the space to figure out the real issue. He helped her gather her emotions and define what she wanted, and gave her the dialogue to describe her needs to us.

It was easy to see how my father's behavior was in control; it was more challenging to see how my mother taught me *about* control. Outwardly, she appeared to be completely out of control; actually, she was able to gain control of the situation quickly. It was effective and memorable. She was angry. She felt that she was doing everything. She felt unsupported and unappreciated. She got our attention … *fast*.

This experience was a gift. I learned that shock value often plays a big role in control. Both of my parents demonstrated control in their own way. There was no right or wrong. They gave me the chance to witness both and decide which one felt better for me. Most of all, I learned that there are many ways to gain control of a situation, but the quickest path is to *check in with myself, decide what I want, and ask for it.*

What can I control?

- I can't control events, but I can control how I respond to them.

- I can't control how someone treats me, but I can control if I participate.

- I can't control another's happiness, but I can choose my happiness.

- I can't control another's decisions, but I can influence them by sharing my experience.

- I can't control another's perception of me, but I can set clear intentions when I am interacting with another.

- I can't control if someone believes me, but I can believe in myself and know that my light is shining brightly.

Who can I control?

The only person I can control is *me*. I am in control of my perceptions, my words, my actions, my decisions, and my life.

After many years of working diligently to control the children, I gave up. I didn't have the strength or the stamina to fight anymore. I didn't *appear* to be out of control with the children, but appearances are often deceiving. I had to *practice* control, and they gave me every opportunity to do so.

The more I "controlled" the classroom, the more they learned to "control" the classroom in their own way:

- From shoes to computer screens, objects would be launched in my direction (practice control: *control my reaction*).

- Words that hurt to words that scar would be screamed at me (practice control: *control my words in response*).

- I was hit, kicked, spit on, pinched, bit, slapped, and bruised (practice control: *control my hands from talking for me*).

I thought that I could control Gavin; after all, I was bigger than he was. He may have been a child, but he was strong in every way, physically and mentally. I thought that the best way to handle and control his outbursts would be to physically restrain him.

> I learned that there are many ways to gain control of a situation, but the quickest path is to *check in with myself, decide what I want, and ask for it.*

I didn't come to this conclusion initially. I did my best to exercise my control and he would trump it by following me throughout the school, hitting and kicking. It felt as if I had no choice. I was at the end of my rope. I was exhausted and tired of being kicked emotionally and physically.

I took him to my office, sat on the floor, plopped him in my lap, crossed his legs and put mine over his, crossed his arms across his chest, and held them until he calmed down.

He didn't calm down; it got worse. He bent over and bit a chunk out of my arm. He used his nails to scratch wherever he could reach. The battle raged on. Some would say that he had behavioral problems or needed to be on medication.

After 30 minutes, we were both worn down, beyond tired, and further from understanding each other than when we started. It became more about winning and losing. If I outlasted him, I was the winner and in control; if he outlasted me, and his actions resulted in a phone call home to come and get him, he was the winner and in control. It was a false sense of control for both of us (practice control: *define what control looked like for me*).

If I wanted to teach the children to "control" their behavior, I had to get out of the way. I had to be an example of what control looked like. I opted to go towards my father's example more than my mom's—not because it was easier but because it was legal!

Here are some examples of our dialogue:

- When the children got mad and screamed, "I HATE YOU," I would respond with a simple, "Wow! That's too bad because I really like *you*!" and then walk away.

- When they yelled, "YOU ARE STUPID," I would respond, "I'm sorry you feel that way," and then walk away.

- When they shouted, "I'M NOT GOING TO BE YOUR FRIEND," I would respond, "Oh, man, I really like *you* as a friend," and then walk away.

I gave up the futile battle to "make them" respect me, listen to me, or even love me. I decided to respect myself. I decided to listen to my instincts, inner voice, and wisdom. I decided to love myself enough to participate and engage— or not. I knew in my heart that I had a choice in every moment. I could choose to let their behavior hurt me or inspire me to think outside of the box and grow in each moment.

> "Between stimulus and response, there is a space. In that space lies our freedom and power to choose our response. In our response lies our growth and freedom."
>
> —*Viktor E. Frankl, Austrian neurologist, psychiatrist, and Holocaust survivor*

After 25 years and thousands of children, I rarely get knocked off my game. I rarely, if ever, lose my control with children. I have graduated to adults now. I practice often—sometimes with success but often without. I am doing my best to apply the same principle in my life when a police officer pulls me over, my husband comes home in a bad mood, my friend is depressed, when I don't get a delivery on time, when my neighbor is complaining about my fence, when I am overcharged for a sandwich, and even when my dog pees on the furniture.

I am working on control—my control—and how I respond and react to every situation that comes my way.

Practice control ... *always.*

Give them what they want ... control.

> "Parents don't want their children to make the wrong
> decisions, so they don't allow them to make the decision.
> And then the child becomes dependent, and the parent
> resents that, and it gets off into a blameful thing early
> on. If you are encouraging children to do all that they
> can do—and not squelching the natural eagerness
> that is within them, so that they can shine and thrive
> and show you and themselves how good they are at
> adapting to the physical experience—everyone wins."
>
> —*Esther Hicks, inspirational speaker and best-selling author*

The concept of giving children control is scary and against everything I was ever taught: "I am the adult. I must be in charge. I know what's best for us all. I know better. *I must be in control!*"

What if this is not true—at least in the way we perceive it or in the way our children perceive it?

choice (*n.*) the right, power, or chance to choose; option[2]

In my mind, choice is a human right. It goes hand in hand with free will. It doesn't feel good when my choice, or free will, is taken away (or appears to be taken away). I want to have a say. I want to have a choice. I want to know that I have control over my life and my destiny. I am empowered when I have a choice.

Children feel the same way.

They want the opportunity to make a choice. Contrary to our beliefs (and often their responses), they *want* to learn from their choices. They want to succeed. They want to fail. They want to experience as much of this world as possible, as quickly as possible.

As I was working through control issues and embracing the art of choice, questions would pop up in my mind and out of my clients' mouths. Our questions were legitimate. It didn't seem possible for *both* of us to have a choice. Either I was right or my child was right (time to practice: *put my words and thoughts to the test*).

Here are the questions:

1. *"How can I give them a choice when there is no choice?"*

2. *"Why do they even need to have a choice?"*

3. *"What if I don't like the choice they make?"*

4. *"How can I be in control of myself if I give all the power—choice—to my child?"*

Now, let's look at each question in depth:

1. *"How can I give them a choice when there is no choice?"*

I was coaching a mother who said, "Heather, there is no choice for my daughter. She is two years old and not allowed to walk in the street without holding my hand. She has no choice."

I responded, "That depends on how you look at the situation."

I understood this mother's concern. I actually agreed with and appreciated her point ... *and* there was a choice for her daughter. I am always looking for the opportunity to offer choices when there appears to be none available.

The first part of the mother's challenge was to be clear: She didn't want her child in the street by herself. *Great!* Half the dilemma was solved. Then, knowing what she wanted, and what would work for her, she could offer a choice to her daughter.

The next step was to find two options that would work for her child and herself. Because her daughter was two years old, it was somewhat easy to present the options.

I suggested that she say to her daughter, "You can hold my right hand or my left hand when we go in the street. Which one do you want to hold? It's your choice."

This approach worked for the following reasons:

- The mother decided what she wanted first. Her energy was clear and unwavering.

- When she was clear, her daughter didn't question going in the street without holding hands.

- The mother offered two choices to her daughter, which would work for the mother first.

- The daughter, at two years old, felt empowered. She felt capable and able to make a decision *and* get her way.

> The children sense and read my energy. They know if there is wiggle room.

My experience has been very similar to the mother I was coaching. The only time it doesn't work for me is when I am unclear, uncertain, or feeling guilty for wanting what I want. The children sense and read my energy. They know if there is wiggle room.

2. *"Why do they even need to have a choice?"*

I get it. There are enough things to think about and do in a day. The last thing I wanted to do was create and offer choices for 30 children every day, all day.

I didn't understand or fully appreciate the value of learning how to make decisions at a young age until I started offering choices to one- and two-year-old children. I didn't realize that I was actually giving the children a chance to practice early; then, when the decisions were far more impactful and important later in their lives, they would have years of data on which to reflect and consequently make an informed decision. They would also have the confidence to make the hard choices in the future. The simple decisions gave them courage, strength, and trust in their own power and wisdom. Every decision brought them closer to understanding the natural consequences of their choices.

They also had less hesitation in their decision-making process. I know that the more I hesitate making a decision, the harder it is to make that decision.

When the children made a choice, and then get upset with the result, I gently reminded them, "This was *your* choice. The good news is that you can always make *another* choice next time."

I was released from all blame and responsibility, and would say, "I didn't choose this. If it were my choice, I would have chosen differently."

Benji was a very smart four-year-old in my preschool. If there were any loopholes in my system or theories, he would find them. He was the best child on which to test new ideas and concepts. He would let me know in an instant if it was going to work (or not). When I first started using choices in the classroom, it worked well and I thought it was bulletproof; however, Benji let me know that it wasn't. He taught me how to make a slight modification so it would work—even with him.

> I was released from all blame and responsibility ...

We were on the playground, and Benji thought it would be a great idea to go up the slide when Claire was coming down the slide. An accident was imminent.

"Benji," I said, "you have a choice. You can go down the slide or get off the slide."

He froze, halfway up the slide. In the meantime, Claire was holding on to the side of the slide to avoid kicking Benji in the face.

"Benji, make your choice."

Again, no response.

By now, Claire was crying because she couldn't hold on anymore and didn't want to hurt Benji.

"Benji, you can go down the slide or get off the slide. I am going to give you three counts to decide. If you stay where you are, then I will know that your decision is for me to take you off the slide. Do you understand?"

Benji was up for the challenge and stayed put. After I counted to three, I didn't say anything. I removed him from the slide and thought that I would carry on with my day, but he wasn't going to let me off that easy.

He threw himself on the ground, screaming, "*You didn't let me make my choice!*"

I let him get the anger out for about 10 minutes and didn't say anything. After the fit subsided, I reminded him, free from emotion, that *he* made the choice to get off the slide.

"No, I *didn't*," he insisted.

I repeated the part of the script that he forgot.

"I said that I was going to give you three counts to decide. When you stayed on the slide, it told me that your decision was for me to take you off the slide. You chose to get off the slide. I was just listening to your choice. You can always make a different choice next time."

Life Lesson #849: I always have a choice. When I avoid choosing, I am actually still making a choice. I know that if I don't make a choice for myself, I invite and empower others to make decisions for me. My choices lead me to valuable lessons in life. When I see each choice I make as an opportunity for growth, I can free myself from shame, blame, guilt, and frustration. I always have an opportunity to make a different choice next time.

---

3.   *"What if I don't like the choice they make?"*

It's not possible. I create the choices based on what I want. I give two choices based on what will work for me. I design the choices. If I don't like a choice my child makes, it is *my* problem, not theirs. I am very careful. I choose wisely. I look for choices that I can live with. Actually, I want to blame the children when I offer lousy choices, but I can't. I am responsible for defining the available choices.

Lunchtime, which was right before naptime, was hectic and crazy. The teachers knew that, if we made it through lunch, we would have a window of peace during naptime. One day, as lunch was wrapping up, we were working to get all the children clean and down for a nap. I was busy getting the children on their mats, patting their backs, and waiting patiently for all to fall into a deep slumber.

Leon, a four-year-old who despised naptime, had something else in mind. He was the last to come in for a nap. By this time, most of the children were out like a light. This is typically when I would help with the cleaning so we would all be able to enjoy a break.

I was cleaning the tables when I heard, "*Ouch*, Leon! *Stop it*! Miss Heather!"

Leon decided to play "whack a mole" with the sleeping children. He went from mat to mat, hitting each child on the head until they woke up. I was beyond angry. He was jeopardizing my break, which was the only quiet I had all day, and of course hitting the other children.

Before I had a chance to think, I blurted out, "Leon, you can choose to get on your mat or sleep in my office. It's your choice."

The other teachers looked at me with fear and I was kicking myself. Why did I offer such a stupid choice? I knew that he wasn't going to lie on his mat. He would rather be in my office, listening to us and staying awake. Of course, he chose my office.

For the remainder of naptime, I had Leon at my feet, moving, twitching, and making sounds—anything to disturb my teachers and me.

No break that day for anyone!

Life Lesson #903: It is not in my best interest to give a choice to my child when I am frustrated or irritated. I need to take a breath and think about the possible consequences of the choices I offer. I need to be clear with my desires and find choices to support my desired outcome in each situation. I am responsible for my choices and the good or bad consequences that may come from them.

---

4. *"How can I be in control of myself if I give all the power—choice—to my child?"*

"You've always had the power, my
dear. You've had it all along."

—*Glinda the Good Witch, from The Wizard of Oz*

I was not a fan of *The Wizard of Oz*, but it was one of my mother's favorite all-time movies. Every year, they would feature this movie on a major broadcasting channel, and every year I would go to my room for the night. I didn't like the flying monkeys. I didn't like the Wicked Witch. I didn't like the guy behind the curtain. I just didn't like the movie.

However, I believe that Glinda the Good Witch had it right: We always have the power. We have had it all along.

Children know that they have the power.

Children know that the power is within; however, as we get older, we are bombarded with information and input that tell us something different. We begin to lose faith. We lose a core, fundamental belief in our own power.

My intention is to nurture and expand the power that lies in each and every child. I want them to experience the power of choice at a young age. I want them to remember that they always have a choice. I want them to be empowered, be inspired by the power, and inspire others to do the same.

> My intention is to nurture and expand the power that lies in each and every child.

The only way I have found to succeed with my intentions is to remain constant in my own power. I see myself as a lighthouse, shining brightly, guiding and serving those I can see and many I can't. It is my responsibility to take care of my lighthouse—to constantly check in, do required maintenance, and shine brightly.

I am in control of my power. I have a choice. As I embrace and accept my own power, I can share it with others without losing anything. In fact, the stronger I get, the longer and brighter my light shines to serve others.

Sometimes I can't be "fixed." I just have to move through the experience.

I didn't *want* to be a mother; I just *knew* that I was a mother. I didn't know that I would be a mother to so many, but I knew that being a mother was my destiny.

Four months after I married Brian, we found out that we were pregnant. It was such a surprise and a blessing. We couldn't believe that we were able to get pregnant so fast! We were ecstatic.

I immediately went to the doctor, who said that all was well. Time passed and my routine appointment rolled around. We didn't know that this visit would include an ultrasound, so Brian stayed at work and I went on my own. When the doctor began the ultrasound, she had a noticeable look of concern. After a few moments, she turned off the monitor and asked me to meet her in her office. I knew it wasn't good.

The doctor told me that I was going to have a miscarriage. The baby had no heartbeat. There was not going to be a baby. She told me that I wasn't that far along and assured me that I wouldn't suffer any pain when I actually miscarried. She said it would be like a piece of raw hamburger meat coming out of me. (Those were her exact words. She missed the class on proper bedside manner with her patients.)

I was in shock. I was so worried about getting pregnant before I was married that it never dawned on me to be worried about keeping a pregnancy once I was married.

> I didn't know that I would be a mother to so many, but I knew that being a mother was my destiny.

A few days later, it was Christmas Eve—the night I thought that I was dying. Apparently, I was further along than my doctor thought. I was hemorrhaging for more than four hours before I finally decided to go to the hospital. Once there, I found out that I was experiencing contractions and my body was struggling to make it through the process.

The emergency room doctors decided to ask my doctor to come in on Christmas morning. She arrived—beyond angry—and said that she was missing her children opening their presents. She wanted to hurry up and take care of this so she could go back home. (Like I said, she had the bedside manner of a troll.)

I ended up in surgery, which was the first time I was ever in a hospital bed. The surgery was successful and the doctor was able to go home. All was well—except for me. It was Christmas morning, I lost my baby, I had surgery, and I was devastated.

My family came over in the evening to help me, support me, and love me through this tragedy. They wanted to fix it. They wanted to make it better. The only problem was that this couldn't be fixed. It had to be felt, processed, and accepted, which takes time.

They were uncomfortable. They were not sure what to say or how to say it, so nobody said anything about the miscarriage. It was Christmas as usual. The plan was to act as if nothing had happened and enjoy the holiday. Have dinner and open presents.

Everyone thought it was going well until I opened a present from Grandma Hazel: maternity clothes. My poor grandma was mortified and tried to fill the air with words of comfort.

"You can still wear them or save them for next time."

It didn't work. I lost it. I was hysterical. I was done.

Life Lesson #439: The ones we often hold as an authority in our lives—like a doctor—are not always right or compassionate. My doctor was not qualified to diagnose the amount of physical, emotional, mental, and spiritual pain I experienced having a miscarriage. Everyone seemed to have the same idea: Fix it. The doctor wanted to fix it with surgery, my father wanted to fix it with laughter and jokes, my grandma wanted to fix it with gifts, my friends wanted to fix it by visiting, my husband wanted to fix it by not talking about it, and my mom wanted to fix it by celebrating Christmas. They all had great intentions and did their best to fix the painful situation, but it couldn't be fixed. It had to be experienced in its entirety. I had to process the experience. I had to feel it for myself. I had to accept it in my own time and space. When I went back to the preschool and told the children about the miscarriage, they didn't try to fix it. They felt it, processed it, accepted it, and moved on (much quicker than I did). I followed their lead and did exactly the same thing.

Children don't want to be fixed. They are not broken and they know it.

Children often let us know that they want to move through the process. They want to feel the pain and gather information from the experience. After doing this, they are ready to accept it and move on.

The miscarriage opened a door to a new way of thinking. I decided to let go of the need to fix a problem or situation with the children and instead embrace the opportunity to support each child while they were moving through a painful process.

Whenever I felt the desire to fix something, this is what I would say to the children instead: "I love you. I can't change it or fix it, but I am here if you need anything. I know you will get through this. I believe in you."

"Fixing it" is not exclusive to times when my child is in pain. It applies to any time they are in a situation to which I feel I have the solution. *That's big!*

I am officially out of the "fix it" business, which includes fights and arguments between siblings or friends, hurt feelings, boo boos, bad grades, and even mistakes.

I moved from a mediator to a facilitator.

A "mediator" settles disputes between parties; a "facilitator" leads discussions to help every one move forward with ease. For me, it feels better to be a facilitator. Being a mediator is too much work and drama.

It has been a difficult process. My husband calls me "Nosey Rosie," so you can imagine how difficult it was to learn to stay out of it; however, it feels freeing to be out of the muck. It feels good to be on the outside—watching the process unfold, learning from their conversations, learning from the children how to move on quickly from a dramatic event, and learning how to forgive and let go of the resentment that often lingers. It feels good to let them "work it out." Then, when I am called to facilitate, I do just that: I facilitate a discussion to move us all forward with ease.

As I mentioned earlier, it took time for the children to adjust to life without a mediator, especially because most of the children were accustomed to being mediated at home. When I started the preschool, I was definitely a mediator. It felt like the right thing to do at the time. I was trained by many to mediate. After all, I was the teacher—the adult—who was in charge of the classroom. I was responsible. That was my job. When a fight would break out, Miss Heather came to the rescue.

> A "mediator" settles disputes between parties; a "facilitator" leads discussions to help every one move forward with ease.

Ella and Lilly were best friends—sometimes. Lilly was a strong personality and very demanding. Ella was softer spoken and often willing to play Lilly's way. They were both around three years old when, one day, Ella had enough. She clearly told Lilly that she was ugly, mean, and stupid and didn't want to be her friend anymore. Lilly lost her mind. She was devastated. She couldn't believe that her best friend would turn on her.

Lilly came to me, tears streaming down her eyes.

"Miss Heather, Ella hurt my feelings. She said that she doesn't want to be my friend anymore. She said that I was mean, ugly, and stupid. She said that she doesn't want to play with me anymore."

Playing the role of the mediator, I immediately asked Ella to come over and resolve the situation. With both girls face to face, I started to lecture Ella.

"Ella, you hurt Lilly's feelings. It's not nice to say mean things to our friends. Lilly is your friend, right?"

"No. She is mean to me, and I don't want to play with her anymore."

Lilly interjected, "That's not true! I wasn't mean to her."

Both stood strong in their position.

"Ella, you and Lilly have been friends for a long time, and sometimes we say things that we don't mean. Why don't you both hug and go play."

Lilly smiled and dove into Ella's arms, and Ella reluctantly threw her arms around Lilly. Then, Ella did her best to avoid Lilly for the rest of the day. It seems like a successful interaction, but was it really successful?

Here's what I have realized about this situation:

- Their argument had nothing to do with me. They were better served if I stayed out of it. It would give them the opportunity to practice communication and social skills, and reap the rewards or suffer the natural consequences for their words and actions.

- Ella may have had reason to say mean things to Lilly. I wasn't there and maybe that is the only way Ella could get relief from Lilly. Again, Ella would experience the natural consequences of her words if I stayed out of it.

- When I affirmed that Ella hurt Lilly's feelings, I affirmed the idea that Ella had control of Lilly's feelings, which is not true.

- By telling Ella that "sometimes we say things that we don't mean," I completely disregarded Ella's truth in that moment. She did mean those things. She was mad. When I told her that her feelings were not true, it taught Ella to disregard her inner wisdom.

- The suggestion to "hug it out" seemed innocent enough, but it didn't help. Ella didn't want to hug Lilly; in fact, it just made it worse. Ella moved from annoyance with Lilly to disgust.

> Their argument had nothing to do with me. They were better served if I stayed out of it.

I decided to change my approach. I played the role of facilitator, and the same situation had a completely different result.

Lilly came to me crying, and I simply said, "Lilly, I am not Ella. If you have a problem with Ella, go talk to her."

Lilly ran back to Ella. Ella wouldn't have anything to do with her.

Lilly ran back to me and said, "Ella is being mean to me. She won't listen to me, and she won't be my friend."

I moved closer in the vicinity of Ella, so she could hear my response. (She was listening anyway, and watching what I was going to do, but I wanted her to be able to hear my response clearly.)

I said loudly and clearly to Lilly, "Wow, that's not like Ella! She is always a great friend. Well, if my friend said that I was mean and ugly, and refused to play with me or talk to me, I would go find another friend to play with. I would find a friend who wants to play with me and wants to have a good time. That's what I would do. I have faith in both of you. I know that you guys will work this out!"

This method was uncomfortable at first. Of course, I wanted them to get along. I wanted them to be friends. I wanted them to say nice things to each other. I wanted them to play "nicely." I wanted peace and harmony in my school.

Over time, I have learned that I am not always the avenue for my children's learning. We attract people into our lives who give us the opportunity to learn how to communicate, cooperate, and practice life skills. When I stay out of the drama, allow space for growth, and offer wisdom from my experiences, I give them the space to learn from each other.

Was playing the role of a facilitator a successful interaction? *Absolutely!*

- Lilly felt supported and guided by me in the moment. She was aware that I was not going to make Ella like her or fix the situation.

- Ella felt supported by hearing me say, "That's not like Ella! She is always a great friend."

- Ella was given permission to work this out and experience the natural consequence to the words she chose to say to Lilly. (Later that day, Ella wanted to play with Lilly again and Lilly was busy with someone else, which was a natural consequence of Ella's actions.)

- I didn't tell Lilly what to do. I offered her wisdom from my experiences and shared them with her. Notice that there were no "you shoulds" in the response. Instead, I verbally modeled a way that I would handle the situation if I were in it.

- At the end, I reinforced my belief in both of them. There were no sides to take. Even if I perceived one to be "right" and one to be "wrong," I reinforced the belief in both of them by saying, "I know that you guys will work this out!"

"Be silent, if you choose; but when it is necessary, speak—
and speak in such a way that people will remember it."

—*Wolfgang Amadeus Mozart, classical composer*

Life Lesson #670: The children have taught me over the years that it feels better to be in control of my feelings, my actions, and my words. It feels better to experience the natural consequence of my actions than to have someone tell me what I should feel or do in the situation. Saying "sorry" is overrated. It doesn't count when I am not really sorry (at least not sorry in the moment). It doesn't feel good to hug someone when I am angry or irritated with them. When I am allowed space, time, and support, I can arrive at my own solution to the problem. It feels good to be supported, not directed.

How can I replace control with influence?

"We can teach from our experience,
but we cannot teach experience."

—*Sasha Azevedo, actress and model*

Knowing that the only person I *can* control is me, it makes the journey of working with and raising children so much easier. It is freeing. It feels good to not feel responsible for every experience, every lesson, every emotion, and every action that another human being experiences.

With that said, I still *want* to participate and engage in a meaningful relationship with my children. I want to share my innate wisdom as well as the wisdom I have learned on this planet. I want to share my experiences—not dictate theirs. I want to be a shining, bright light: stable, clear, energetic, loving, and *alive.*

The best way I have found to be the parent, the teacher, and the caregiver that I want to be is to shift from control to influence. I influence children—and hopefully adults—by the power of example. My influence is not always what I would like it to be; it is a work in progress. I do my best to influence the children's lives by modeling behavior, actions, and words that I would like them to use.

For example:

- Instead of demanding a "thank you," I say "thank you" every chance I get.

- Instead of demanding an apology, I apologize when I make a mistake.

- Instead of demanding respect, I give respect to them.

> The best way I have found to be the parent, the teacher, and the caregiver that I want to be is to shift from control to influence.

Often, and in times of struggle or conflict, my modeling has not been enough of an influence for my child. I have to remind myself that I am a big influence but certainly not the *only* one.

I also remind myself that my child has his own life to live. He has his own journey. He has his own wisdom, both innately and what he's gathered along his path in life. He will find ways to learn and process life that hopefully will be better than my ways.

I am from "Deep in the Heart of Texas." When I was growing up, children were always introduced to adults with a "Miss" or a "Mister" in front of their first name. We would refer to my mom and dad's friends as "Miss Sandy" or "Mr. Billy"; if they were a very close friend of the family, they would often be referred to as "Uncle" or "Auntie." As I recall, we were never forced to say "Miss" or "Mister"; it was just modeled by our parents. They believed that they had a good reason, which was to show respect for your elders.

If we ever "slipped up" and called an adult by their first name, there was only a moment of correction. In other words, if I said, "Hi, Billy," my mom would simply say, "Excuse me. 'Mr. Billy,' please."

I carried on this "tradition" throughout my life. When I refer to myself or another adult to a child, I always add the "Miss" or "Mister." I was, am, and always will be "Miss Heather."

I now live in northern California. My experience in both states— food, environment, attitudes, and political beliefs—has been extreme opposites. I am not interested in right or wrong. I just want to live the best life I can. I want to feel good and love where I am, regardless of the physical location.

My experience in California has been very different regarding how adults are introduced to children. The children call the adults by their first name only. Honestly, the first time I was introduced to a friend's child as "Heather," I was shocked. It was uncomfortable and unsettling. I do not share the same reasons for using "Miss" or "Mister" as I was taught as a child. I am not interested in demanding respect for our elders. I believe that we can only respect others when we first respect ourselves.

> I am not interested in demanding respect for our elders. I believe that we can only respect others when we first respect ourselves.

It's difficult to articulate why children calling me by my first name didn't feel good to me. I did my best to explain my feelings to my husband, and the only explanation I had was that I call my friends by their first name but not my parents' friends. Again, each person is different; there are no right or wrong answers. I can only say what feels good to me and honor it.

So far, my quest to have the children address adults as "Miss" or "Mister" has been unsuccessful in California (there's always hope!); consequently, I am continually introduced as "Heather." I have done my best to get over it, evolve, adapt to my surroundings, and change my mind. Even so, it still makes me cringe.

Enter my beloved four-year-old neighbor Jackson. When he was introduced, he called everyone by his or her first name. Brian (who is fine with just "Brian") and I have spent hours on the subject. I feel better about "Mr. Brian." We disagree and have agreed to disagree.

> "Often, to say nothing is more powerful
> than having to say something."
>
> —*Amir Zoghi, speaker on self-awareness and human potential*

I decided to conduct a little experiment to see how the power of influence works, and I started with Jackson. In every interaction and conversation with him, I would refer to myself as "Miss Heather" and my husband as "Mr. Brian." My experiment was not to change Jackson by correcting his behavior. I wanted to only be a model. I wanted to see if I could influence him with my actions and words, regardless of his actions and words. A few months went by (we don't see him every day), and Jackson was at our house. Brian was playing with both of us and then it happened: Jackson autocorrected his words.

"Brian ... I mean Mr. Brian ... can you play puppets with me?"

I looked at Brian and he shook his head. We both laughed.

The interesting twist to this story is that I was not only influencing Jackson but, little did I know, I was influencing his mother, brother, and grandma. They all now refer to us as "Miss Heather" and "Mister Brian."

My intention was not to change Jackson or his family. My intention was to honor how I felt and do what felt good to me, regardless of everyone's opinion on the matter, including my husband. Brian was concerned that it would be confusing for Jackson. I knew that Jackson would adapt. We all do.

Life Lesson #2037: I have a choice. I can choose to accept or reject the "social norms" we have in our society. I have the right and responsibility to honor my feelings. I now know that I don't have to force someone to do anything to me or for me; I just have to stand in the space of knowing, believing, and being what I want others to be to me. I can influence others by having the courage to act on and honor the feelings and desires I have for myself. It's my choice to change or embrace traditions. It's my choice to be different.

> "It is not our purpose to become each other;
> it is to recognize each other, to learn to see the
> other and honor him for what he is: each the
> other's opposite and complement."
>
> *—Hermann Hesse, German–Swiss Nobel
> Prize-winning author in literature*

Geniuses aren't conventional.

Heather and I probably own over 100 books on parenting. In looking through nearly all of these books, I've noticed that the conventional wisdom in parenting around control and choice can be summed up by the following statements:

- Give your children some control—through choice—but let them know that you are still the boss.

- "If you are going to get into [a control battle], win at all costs." (This is actually a direct quote from one of the most popular parenting books out there.)[3]

- If your child is out of control, punish them by giving them a time-out, removing a privilege, taking away a toy, or grounding them, to teach them that this behavior is not acceptable.

- If your child disobeys you, let them know that you are the boss through some form of discipline. They need to learn the consequences of being disobedient.

If you've reached this chapter, you can already guess how Heather feels about the above conventional parenting wisdom! These approaches create resistance; Heather is all about eliminating resistance, and creating harmony and agreement while still getting her and her child's needs met.

The way in which Heather thinks about control is the key to her success. She believes that control is rooted deeply in the concept of choice. Control is not about having her child "do what I say" but rather "I'm just here to honor every single choice you make. You are in charge." It's a very interesting twist to conventional thinking. By always honoring the child's choice, Heather is more in control than if she viewed her role as "the boss."

Stop for a moment and think about your children:

- Do you feel that you are only a good parent if your child obeys you and does what you say?

- What if you shifted your thinking to Heather's model?

- What if you reframed your idea of good parenting from "I want my child to do what I say" to "I honor every single choice my child makes"?

- What comes up for you as you try on this way of thinking?

Give your child the opportunity to practice decision making.

One of Heather's key goals is to give her child every possible opportunity to practice making decisions. Starting from the youngest age and moving through life, Heather wants her child to know that:

- He has a choice about what he experiences in life—always.

- There are natural consequences to every choice she makes.

- If he doesn't like the consequences, he can choose differently next time.

With her goal in mind, Heather constantly reminds her children of their ability to choose for themselves. She gives them many chances to practice choice and experience the consequences of that choice, going way beyond, "Do you want a hotdog or a hamburger?"

For Heather, this idea of choice is a foundation to her philosophy about children and life. It's about making sure that she and her children feel empowered to create their own life, and empowered to make different choices if they aren't experiencing what they want in their life. As you read through many of the examples and scenarios in this book, you'll discover that choice is always present.

How to offer choices to your children

I am always amazed at how quickly Heather comes up with choices for kids. With practice, you'll become just as good. Here is her process for offering choices:

Step 1: Get clear on what you want first. Get to a space where your energy is clear and unwavering.

Step 2: Come up with two decent choices where you can get what you want and your child can get what he wants.

Step 3: Present the choice and let your child decide.

Step 4: Honor whatever option your child chooses (even if you regret one of the choices you presented).

Step 5: If your child won't choose from the options you have presented, then state, "When you decide to ignore your choices, it tells me that your choice is for me to choose for you. You have two minutes [or another timeframe] to decide." If you make the choice for your child, remind him that this experience is because of a choice he made (i.e., his choice was to not choose; therefore, he was telling you to decide for him).

Present a choice inside of every experience.

Heather finds ways of providing a choice, even when it appears that there is none. Frequently, she will state what is happening and then provide a choice within that activity.

> Heather finds ways of providing a choice, even when it appears that there is none.

For example, she will say, "We are going outside. Do you want to wear your tennis shoes or your flip flops?"

By offering these choices, Heather is asking herself, "We are doing this activity. How can I give my child a choice about *how* we do it?"

Here are some other examples of how to use this effective approach around a choice:

- "It's bedtime! Do you want to tell me a story or do you want me to read you one?"

- It's bath time! Do you want to take a quick bath or take some time to play with your toys in the tub?"

- "Good morning! Do you want to wear your Batman or your Spiderman shirt to school today?"

- "It's time to pick a school. Do you want to go to X school or Y school?"

Choice *always* exists, even when the choices aren't outwardly presented.

Every behavior that a child displays is an opportunity for Heather to notice what the child is saying and to honor the child's choice, even if the choice hasn't been verbally offered. Heather sees that every behavior a child exhibits is actually a choice that the child is making.

For example, my 16-month-old nephew started to throw his food on the floor when he was in his high chair—*a fantastic mess!* Telling him, "No, don't do that," wasn't working. I called Heather and this was her suggestion:

"If he throws his food, that action tells me he is done eating. His choice is to be done with lunch. Just say, 'When you throw your food, that tells me you are done. I honor your choice. All done.' Then, take him out of his high chair regardless of how much he has had to eat. He'll learn."

"What if he goes hungry and then whines later?"

"I would tell him, 'I'm sorry that you are hungry. When I'm hungry, I eat my food, not throw it. If it were me, I would have eaten my food.' Then, let him go hungry until the next meal. He'll learn."

I said, "He is only 16 months old. He can't understand that."

"He understands. Trust me."

Heather wants children to know that they always have a choice and that every choice has a consequence. The genius of this approach is that the child doesn't view Heather as someone who has authority over them. They view her as someone who just listened and honored the choice *they* made. Heather has framed it so the child can't get upset with her—*ever*. They can only be upset with the choice they made. It's really brilliant and accomplishes so much, so simply!

"I'm honoring every child's choice, every time," Heather explains. "I don't have to establish a choice for a choice to exist. I pay equal, if not more, attention to choices that present themselves through behavior that a child is exhibiting. I want every child to know that I am listening to them in every way. I want them to be aware that their body language, actions, and words are all telling me a story. I want them to fine-tune how they communicate with me, so they are able to articulate and express themselves clearly to the world. I want them to experience the natural consequences of their communication."

> Heather wants children to know that they always have a choice and that every choice has a consequence.

Here are some situations that Heather shared. All she had to do was notice what a child was communicating through their behavior to honor the choice:

- *Playing with or throwing food:* "When you play with or throw food, it tells me that you are done. I honor your choice. No problem. All done."

- *Hitting a friend:* "That's not like you at all. When you hit your friend, it tells me that you are not interested in playing together anymore. I honor your choice. Go find someone else to play with or play by yourself. It's your choice."

- *Throwing a toy:* "Wow! When you throw your toy at me, it tells me that you don't want to play with that toy anymore. I honor your choice. I will put it away for the night."

- *Throwing a temper tantrum:* "When you are screaming this loudly and I can't understand you, it tells me that you want time to yourself. I will be in my room when you are ready to talk."

- *Behaving undesirably at the playground:* "When you [fill in the blank, such as throw sand, continue to hurt a friend, don't stay inside certain boundaries], it tells me that you are done playing. I hear you. Let's go."

- *Doing something unsafe:* "You know how to use scissors. When you run with them, it tells me that you don't want to cut with them. Go ahead and put them away."

- *Making a mess in their bedroom:* "That's interesting. I thought you liked your toys. When you leave them on the ground to be stepped on and broken, it tells me that you really don't want them. I hear you. Let's get a garbage bag and throw them away."

Heather says, "The key to this approach is following through. In other words, when I say, 'It tells me that …,' I need to be very careful about what I choose to say in that moment. I know that I need to be prepared to do what I say I am going to do. This is where trust is built. If I am not willing to throw away all the toys on the floor of my child's room, then I would never suggest getting a trash bag."

It's about communication, not punishment or manipulation.

The verbal pattern that Heather uses is, "When you do X, that tells me Y." She uses that language to tell children what their behavior is communicating to her. It's important to emphasize that she is not using this verbal pattern as a form of punishment or manipulation.

She is using it as a way to tell her child, "I hear you. Your actions are speaking for you, and this is what your actions are communicating to me."

I've heard many parents say, "If you keep doing X, then we are going to do Y." The parent notices some behavior and then threatens a punishment if it persists. For example:

- "If you keep running around the pool, we are going to leave!"
- "If you keep whining, you are going to go to the car."

- "If you don't stop throwing that, I am going to take it away."

This verbal pattern of "If you ..., then I ..." puts the parent in a position of creating a law and then enforcing a punishment if it is broken. The child then feels like the parent has power over them, which creates resentment and resistance. Heather's verbal strategy results in the child feeling in control of the choices they make around their behavior and knowing that they can make a different choice next time.

> Heather's verbal strategy results in the child feeling in control of the choices they make around their behavior and knowing that they can make a different choice next time.

In her *Positive Parenting Solutions* blog, Amy McCready describes how to use the "WHEN-THEN" routine: "WHEN your room is clean [which means I can see your entire floor and the horizontal surfaces are clear of clutter], THEN you can have your TV time, or THEN you can join us for dinner."[4]

McCready also states, "Creating a WHEN-THEN routine in which the room must be cleaned before a more enjoyable part of the routine occurs creates a natural incentive. If you follow a WHEN-THEN routine every single day there's no need to fuss or fight about it. As my mother-in-law says, it's the law. It's just the way we do things around here. That's called 'letting the routine be the boss' so you don't have to be."[5]

Here's Heather's feeling about this routine: "If I embrace the WHEN-THEN suggestion, I am silently manipulating the actions that I want him to do to make me feel good. It's just a nicer way of saying, 'If you do this, then you get that.' It's back to the rewards model. It puts me in a boss and enforcer role, and those aren't roles I want to play. It's so much easier to state simply what I need, such as, 'I need you to clean your room.'"

Here's an example of how Heather handles a typical conversation with her child using the "When you do or say X, that tells me Y" routine. This scenario describes Sara, who is working on an art project but is not getting it done.

"Sara, I guess you are done with the paints. Let's put them away and clean up."

"*Noooooooo!* I'm not done. I'm still painting."

"Well, that's interesting. When you leave the art table and don't work on your painting, it tells me that you are done. I'm just honoring your choice. When you want to work on your art, it's a good idea to stay at the table. Next time, you'll know."

Notice how Heather has put the child in control and yet remains in control herself.

As another example, Heather's child is playing with his food at a restaurant and she is on a tight schedule.

"It's time to go, Brad. Let's go."

"But I'm not done with my dinner!"

"When you play with your food and don't eat it, it tells me that your belly must be full. Let's go."

"But I am still hungry and want it."

"When you are hungry, Brad, you eat all your food. Playing with your food and not eating it tells me that you are done. Next time, you'll know. Let's go."

Children (and adults) learn to make good decisions by having the chance to decide what happens to them every day—not by following someone else's directions or commands. The goal is to remind the child that he is in control of his life and we parents are just here to notice their behavior and honor their choices. There can be no resistance in this model because, the way it is framed, the child has to take responsibility for their choices and experience the consequences.

The conversation in this model ends with, "The good news is that, if you don't like this outcome, you can choose differently next time."

Honor choices ... always.

Parents weaken their effectiveness in their children's eyes by *not* consistently honoring choices or by using choices as a way to threaten them.

For example, "You are making a mess with those paints. Be more careful or we are going to put them away!" When the child still makes a mess, the parent repeats, "What did I say? Do you want to keep painting or put them away?"

Heather will simply explain it once. Then, the next time she notices the behavior, she honors their choice … always. There is no "second chance."

She would simply say, "Oh, I see that you are using the paints on things other than your painting, which tells me that it's time to put them away. All done."

When parents aren't consistent with honoring choices—or give their children a second chance—it's confusing to the child. Heather wants children to feel that their choice is *always* honored, *every time.* She wants them to know that there is a consequence to every choice. She wants to be trustworthy to the child. When she offers a choice, she honors it the first time ... always.

> When parents aren't consistent with honoring choices—or give their children a second chance—it's confusing to the child.

If the child doesn't like the consequences or whines, Heather simply says, "I hear you. If it were me, I would have chosen differently. You made this choice. The good news is that you can choose differently next time."

This is a good line to commit to memory!

With this short response, notice how Heather:

- Acknowledges that she hears the child, which builds rapport: "I hear you."
- Models with her words a different choice that the child can make next time: "If it were me, I would have chosen differently."
- Lets them know that they are having this "undesirable experience" based on a choice *they* made: "You made this choice."
- Lets them know that they have the power to have a different experience by making a different choice: "The good news is that you can choose differently next time."

At no time does Heather put herself in a position of "doing something to" or "having power over" her children. Remember Heather's view of the world with children: "I'm just here to honor every single choice you make. You are in charge."

Stop for a moment and consider the following two frames of mind:

1. "I want my child to do what I say."

2. "I honor every choice my child makes, every time. They are in charge of creating their experience."

How do you feel with these two different outlooks?

For me, the first frame of mind feels like a lot of pressure—like I need to be the boss. I get into a posture where I need to control my child's behavior. When I try on the second outlook, I feel much more relaxed. I feel like I just need to notice what my child is doing and honor their choice. The second one seems much easier and more fun.

What do you notice?

When parents put themselves in a position of control *over* their child, it calls the Triangle of Disempowerment into play (see *Chapter 3: As a Parent, What Are You Really Responsible For?*). The child feels like a Victim of the demands of a Perpetrator (their parents) or of something their parents did to them. The choice framework from which Heather operates is about empowerment. It's about giving the child ample opportunity to understand that he is the Creator of his own reality and fully empowered in life.

What is *our* behavior communicating to our children?

Our children's behavior is always communicating something to us; however, have you stopped to consider what *our* behavior is communication to our children? Words aren't necessary for communication. Our children are listening to us and watching our behavior.

I heard a recent news story,[6] which went viral, about a 15-year-old high school girl in Texas, who was getting swatted (i.e., spanked on the bottom with a paddle) by a male vice principal and getting very bruised. She was in trouble for letting a friend copy her homework. It was against the rules for a male to swat a female student. (Only females could swat other females.)

> Do we want our children to believe that it's okay for people to physically hit others?

The girl's mother told the media, "When a man hits a girl, he is telling all of the other boys in the school that it's okay for men to hit girls, and it's not okay."[7]

In my opinion, that was only part of what was being communicated. In 2012, 19 states still allow corporal punishment in schools.[8] Put another way, in 38% of our country, it is legal for teachers and administrators to hit children.[9]

What is our behavior communicating to our children? Do we want our children to believe that it's okay for people to physically hit others? It's as if we are saying, "It's okay for people to hit you until you turn 18. Then, it's not okay for people to hit you because it's violence or abuse."

If that's what we are saying, then we are also saying, "We can exert any kind of obedience measures we want until you turn 18. Then, we expect you to be a solid member of society who treats others with fairness and respect."

Heather and I had a long conversation on this point. As a kid whisperer, I asked her how children "hear" behavior from adults. She said that this is what kids hear:

- "When I get punished, it tells me that I can't be trusted to make a mistake and learn on my own."

- "When my mom forces me to do things that make me feel uncomfortable, it tells me that my feelings don't matter."

- "When my grandma forces me to say I'm sorry when I am not, it tells me to deny my own truth."

- "When my dad tells me to toughen up, it tells me that I am not enough."

- "When I get yelled at, and mean or hurtful words are said, it tells me that it's okay to communicate like that with others."

- "When I hear adults talk about other people disrespectfully, I learn how to gossip and blame others for my mood."

- "When I am told to shut up or be quiet, it tells me that my voice doesn't matter."

- "When I am told to share when I don't want to, it tells me to deny my own feelings."

- "When I hear my parents complain about me, I hear that I am a bad person and I hurt them."

- "When I ask, 'Why?' and am answered, 'Because I told you to,' it tells me that I can't understand."

- "When I read my mom's Facebook rant about me, I hear that I am a mistake."

- "When I am told what to do, I hear that I am not capable."

- "When I am told that I should do something, it tells me that I am not capable of making a choice."

- "When I am told to sit in a chair for three minutes in a time-out, it tells me that I am not worth the time to explain the problem."

To sum it up:

- "When you tell me that I am a bad boy, I cry—not because I am mad at you or myself but because I know in my heart that it is not true. I am still connected to my true spirit. I am confused because I know in my heart that I am a good boy, but I trust you more than anyone on this planet, and I believe you and disconnect from my own truth. I disconnect from my light and my source. Instead of my light shining, it becomes dim and eventually turns off."

Children hear and internalize more information than we realize. Our behavior communicates a lot to our children.

What do we want to be saying?

Experience is the only true teacher.

Any great teacher will tell you, "Words don't teach. Experience teaches." Think about your life. Where did you learn more about how to do your job: in a classroom or on the job? How about parenting? Have you learned more from a book or from the actual experience you have with your children?

Life experience is the only way any of us learns anything. We might get insight, knowledge, or new ideas from outside references but, until we have our own experience with it, it's all just theory. Our experiences and what we've learned from them are our most powerful teachers.

We can't bear to watch our child suffer from a bad choice, so we often make the choice for them. By doing this, have we really done them a service by helping them avoid pain? The more affluent we become in our society, the more available resources we have to protect our children. The more fear we have about things (e.g., safety, bad manners, college entrance, jobs, and the economy), the more motivated we are as parents to make sure that our child is successful at all costs.

> We can't bear to watch our child suffer from a bad choice, so we often make the choice for them. By doing this, have we really done them a service by helping them avoid pain?

For example, we stand up for them when their coach doesn't play them enough, when their teacher flunks them in class, or when someone says harsh words to them at school. We think that we are doing them a favor by paving the way as best as we can with all of our resources; however, are we really just standing in the Rescuer role on the Triangle of Disempowerment? Aren't we denying them a chance to make their choices and have their experiences, regardless of the pain and suffering that may come from them?

Although this desire to reduce the pain our child experiences is rooted in positive intent, it's really quite selfish. I realize that "selfish" is a harsh word, but take a moment to think about it. We can't bear to see people we love suffer, so we intervene with the belief that we are helping. What we are really doing is putting *our* need to feel okay over our *child's* need to have experiences, learn from them, and grow.

When we deny our children harsh experiences, such as flunking a test or getting into a fight, we also deny their critical learning moments. The wise parent knows that experience is the only teacher and allows their child to have as many experiences as possible. Experience happens because we make a choice and then experience the consequences (good or bad) of that choice. The more experiences, the more we learn, and the wiser we become.

As children get older, the choices and the consequences get bigger. I recently gave a keynote talk to parents who homeschool their children.

One parent said, "My seven-year-old son hates doing the required worksheets for school. [The state requires homeschooled kids to complete mandatory worksheets and tests.] What should I do?"

My response was, "Well, would you rather your child learn at age seven about what happens when he doesn't complete the required work—or at age 17?"

The parent didn't want her seven-year-old son to "fail" in school over some silly worksheets that neither of them wanted to do.

Then, I said, "You have a choice. If you disagree with the worksheets, then maybe you would benefit from another educational option. The one you and your son signed up for has required worksheets. If that doesn't work for you, then you are free to choose another option."

We often feel like "Victims" with no choice, but we *all* have a choice, in every moment.

"What did you learn from that?"

Many years ago, I heard a speaker talk about the greatest gift his parents ever gave him:

"My parents were wonderful parents. They never got upset with me or scolded me or expressed disappointment in me. Instead, after every experience in my life, they asked me a question. It was the same question, whether I fell down the stairs and got hurt, didn't make the baseball team, lost my money through a hole in my pocket, or had a broken heart over a girlfriend.

"The question they asked me was, 'So what did you learn from that?'

"Into my adult years, I realize what a gift they gave me. I realize that I don't see life in terms of failures or setbacks. I just see every experience as a chance to learn and grow.

"When I ended up in a job I hated, I just asked myself, 'So what did I learn from this?' Then, I deciphered the lesson and moved on with a new insight about myself to the next job where I was happier.

"The gift was so simple and so profound in my life. It's hard to imagine how one question has shaped my whole outlook on life."

Review of Chapter 8: Honor Every Choice Your Child Makes

- Choice always exists, in every moment of every day.
- Give your child lots of opportunities to practice decision making.
- Present choices with which you are comfortable and always honor the choice.
- Present choices within an experience that is not up for choice, such as going to the store or going to bed.
- Honor your children's choice, always and the first time.
- Honor the choice implicit in their behavior by saying, "When you do X, that tells me Y. I hear you."
- Be aware of what our behavior is communicating to our children. When they see us do things, it communicates a lot to them.
- Experience is the only true teacher. Let your child experience the natural consequence of every choice, even if it's hard to watch.

See this strategy in action!

Check out the video on
Honor Every Choice Your Child Makes

V I D E O

V I D E O

or visit
www.raiseahappychild.com/choice

CHAPTER 9

Remind Your Child of Their Greatness ... Always

"What a man thinks of himself, that is what determines, or rather indicates, his fate."

—*Henry David Thoreau, American author and poet*

We can all own our greatness.

Over the years, I have noticed a common trend among the majority of my friends, family, and society. We are busy working to prove our worthiness. We often begin our sentences with, "I'll be happy when I have more, work harder, be more." It's never enough. Enough people in this world tell me everything that I am not and, truthfully, I do a good job all by myself. I am bombarded daily with the notion that I am not enough.

For example:

- The doctor says that my test results are not good enough.
- My friend says that I'm not there for them enough.
- My children say that I don't pay enough attention to them.
- My dog barks at me for not feeding him enough.
- My job says that I'm not working hard enough.
- My bank account says that I don't have enough money.
- The media ... well, there are too many ways to list how I am not enough according to them.

In the moment, it's easy to agree; however, there's something unexplainable, like a feeling at the core of my being, which says that *what they are saying is not true.* Then, I shift to anger.

- It's easy to be angry at a friend for something they "did" to me.
- It's easy to be angry at my husband when he lets the trash overflow and spill on the floor, waiting for me to take it out.
- It's easy to be angry at my dog when he pees on his bed every day.
- It's easy to be angry at the DMV worker who is not interested in my story.
- It's easy to be angry at my child for coloring on the wall with permanent markers.
- It's easy to be angry with my child when he says that he hates me.
- It's easy to be angry at my teenager for coming home past curfew.
- It's easy to be angry at the guy who cuts me off in traffic.

In the moment, it's easy to justify my anger, but something doesn't feel right. A feeling at the core of my being says that I am not really angry at the media, my friends, my husband, my kids, or my dog.

I am angry at myself. I know better. I am choosing each experience. I have free will. Even if I can't control the circumstances, I have control over my mind. When I focus, I can change my mind about any circumstance. I can purposely shift my energy to a better feeling space.

Most of all, I need to remember that *I am enough.*

As I look into the eyes of my children, I am committed to being the force in their lives that constantly reminds them that *they are enough.* When they are young, it's not a problem. They know that they are enough; in fact, they know that they are *more* than enough. They know their value. They know that they are here on purpose. They know that they matter. Then, things change when we start shaming them to believe differently, and punishing and throwing guilt at them to be different.

I recently went to a friend's house and her five-year-old daughter Kimberly was in the living room. When I came in, I immediately acknowledged Kimberly and told her how beautiful she was today.

> As I look into the eyes of my children, I am committed to being the force in their lives that constantly reminds them that *they are enough.*

She said, "Yep!"

I told her how bright her smile was today.

"Yep!"

I told her that she did a great job picking out her clothes.

"Yep!"

I told her that she was an amazing little girl.

"Yep!"

She never disagreed. As I gave her all of these compliments, I was curious how many times she would respond this way. Sure enough, every response included a big smile and "Yep!"

However, if I had said, "You need to say 'thank you' and not 'yep.' That's rude. You need to be polite when people say nice things to you. Now, say you're sorry and say 'thank you,'" Kimberly would believe differently. To add insult to injury, we usually follow up—out of shear embarrassment with the other adults—with, "I'm so *sorry*! I don't know *where* she gets that from!"

As soon as an art project is completed, the first words out of a three-year-old's mouth are, "Look how pretty my picture is. *Look!* It's so pretty. I did a good job!"

However, if we had said, "Well, it's good, but you could have colored that a little nicer. You are getting bigger now. You are going to school soon, and you need to do better," they would believe differently. They believe us.

When I was in a hurry at the preschool, I would often help the children put away their sleeping mats after naptime. They would all say the same thing: "I can do it. I can do it all by myself. *I can do it, Miss Heather!*"

> It takes time—especially with children who refuse to believe us—but eventually it happens to every one of them. They believe us when we say that they are not enough.

However, if I had said, "I know, but I am in a hurry and I can do it faster. Let me do it. You're not moving fast enough. Quit lollygagging around," they would believe me, always.

It takes time—especially with children who refuse to believe us—but eventually it happens to every one of them. They believe us when we say that they are not enough.

I have a different view and choose to see it differently. For example, when I gave five-year-old Kimberly all of those compliments, she beamed with happiness and pride. She never intended to be perceived as rude, impolite, or disrespectful. She believes in herself. She knows that she is worthy of every compliment—and then some! She is teaching us to love every part of our being. She is teaching us to agree with our greatness. *She is teaching us that we are enough.*

The three-year-old who is completing the art project is living in the moment and not thinking of school. He believes that his art is amazing. He's not looking for input; he's looking for acknowledgement. He is searching to affirm his beliefs about himself. He is reminding us to be proud of our accomplishments and share them with the world in a big way. *He is teaching us that we are enough.*

In my preschool, the children wanted to take the responsibility of putting away their own mats. They wanted to affirm that they were capable of the task. They wanted to know that they could do anything they put their mind to. They are teaching us to believe in ourselves, even when others don't have the time. They are teaching us to stand up for ourselves. *They are teaching us that we are capable and enough.*

It takes courage, persistence, and strength to see and act differently. It's hard to remember, but there is a space in my heart that remembers I am enough. I want my children to remember. I want them to feel good about their life. I want them to keep the feeling of greatness alive and easily accessible. I want them to remember, especially when the world tells them that they are not enough. I want them to know that it's simply not true. I want their response to be, "I'm sorry you feel that way."

I choose to replace "Why can't you be like ..." with "There is no one else like you on this planet. You are a unique and special gift to everyone you meet. The world would not be the same without you here. We are all thankful to have you in our lives."

> "Be who you are and say what you feel,
> because those who mind don't matter and
> those who matter don't mind."
>
> —Dr. Seuss, American author and cartoonist

I want my child to know, in their heart, that I refuse to define them by their actions, behaviors, words, grades, accomplishments, or even failures. I choose to see them for exactly what they are: a pure spirit, full of life and love, who came to Earth to experience, expand, and be the light that shines brightly, even in the darkest times. I want them to know that my love and belief in their greatness is unwavering. I honor their greatness. I appreciate their greatness. As I remind them of their greatness, I am instantly reminded of my own greatness as well.

Leave the labels out of it.

> "Remember always that you not only have the right to
> be an individual, you have an obligation to be one."
>
> —Eleanor Roosevelt, First Lady of the
> United States, author, and speaker

Our parents meant well. They were doing their best to show us how proud they were of our accomplishments and attributes, but sometimes they missed the mark.

For example, Grace and I have been best friends since we were born—almost 40 years ago. Our parents, who were also treasured friends, raced Corvettes together. As infants, Grace and I would go to the races with our parents and they would leave us in a playpen in the back of an old Chevy Suburban. (Everyone at the races would take the responsibility of looking after us.)

As we got older, our parents were proud of us for different reasons. Grace was the "pretty, little, quiet one" and I was the "loud, big, smart one" (my perception). My parents would always comment how cute, adorable, and quiet Grace was; Grace's parents would comment on how smart I was (leaving out "big" and "loud"). Consequently, I mostly got straight As in school and Grace didn't do so well; Grace always looked adorable and I ... well ... didn't.

Even though it was never said (at least to me), there was an energy that could be felt a mile away and a feeling that we both had: "Why can't I be like *her*?"

(As a side note, I always thought that Grace was so much smarter than I was, even though her grades in school didn't reflect that. When I was five or six years old, spending the night at her house, I took a bath and put on my panties backwards ... *again!* It was a terrible problem that I had forever—or so it felt. As I went into her room, I was still trying to put them on. She asked me what was wrong and I told her that I couldn't figure out how to put on my panties the right way, every time. Grace didn't laugh or make fun of me for being stupid, but said, "Oh, that's easy. You just lay them on the floor and look for the half circles. Lift them up, turn them around, and put them on." She demonstrated the sequence and that was it! I forever knew how to put on my panties. It made no sense to call me the "smart one" when I thought that she was much smarter than I was. She knew how to put on panties!)

Even though the intention was coming from a good space, it still didn't feel good or help either one of us to assign a label of any kind.

> Our parents meant well. They were doing their best to show us how proud they were of our accomplishments and attributes, but sometimes they missed the mark.

It's a challenge to leave out labels. With my experience and history, I still struggle with this concept—not because I disagree with it, but because it is a habitual behavior. When someone shows us specific characteristics, we tend to hold on to the prevalent ones to describe them in the future. It feels normal.

Unfortunately, when our children are coming into this experience, they are exploring, experimenting, and adapting to their environment. What may appear to be their nature or a true characteristic has the ability to quickly shift and morph into something completely different.

I graduated from "labeling" children in stages. When I labeled a child out loud, it always came from a good intention. I did my best to highlight their strengths as much as possible; however, the labels I had in my mind were not always from good intentions.

Here are some of the labels I assigned out loud:

- "Julian is the fastest runner in the school!"
- "Natalie is the only one who finishes her projects!"
- "Ian is our rough and tough boy in the school!"

These labels were not necessarily harmful, but they set a pace. They also set up a standard that each child had to attain and against which the others had to measure themselves.

Here are some labels in my mind, which were not the best:

- "Logan is the kid who never stops. He drives us all crazy!"
- "Mason is enough to drive me to drink!"
- "Kevin is the one who always causes some trouble."

Although the labels in my mind were never spoken, their energy was present and prevalent. Because I had those labels assigned in my mind, my attention was always focused on the same thing with each child. The RAS was back (see *Chapter 7: Focus on What You Do Want*). Unconsciously, I was always looking for proof to make the labels true. The boys never let me down. They provided proof all day, every day.

I let go of the labels in my mind compared to the labels I said out loud, switching them with ease and minimal effort. Here are some examples of "before" and "after":

Before: "Julian is the fastest runner in the school."

After: "Julian runs so fast!"

Before: "Natalie is the only one who ever finishes her projects!"

After: "Natalie loves her projects!"

Before: "Ian is our rough and tough boy in the school!"

After: "Ian takes a lickin' and keeps on tickin'!"

I still wanted to honor each child for their uniqueness and efforts, but I had to omit the idea that they were the only one capable of these things in the school *and* leave it out of the conversation when I was actually describing the child. It was far more difficult and time consuming to let go of the labels in my mind compared to the labels out loud.

I had to train myself to use a new way of being with the children. It took time—*lots* of time—and, truthfully, I didn't master this behavior with children until a few years ago. It proved to be a bigger challenge than I had anticipated.

When Logan would run away from me, go crazy in the classroom, disregard any instruction, or completely ignore me, I would immediately go to the label that I assigned him in my head: "Logan is the kid who never stops. He drives us all crazy!" The more I acknowledged the label, the worse his behavior became.

> It was far more difficult and time consuming to let go of the labels in my mind compared to the labels out loud.

As I focused on changing *my* mind, and letting go of the label for Logan, I noticed a shift. When I replaced the old label with a new one—"Logan has amazing gifts to offer"—the more my attention would focus on the amazing gifts that Logan brought to our school and to our lives. In truth, I never completely replaced the label in my head about Logan. I did, however, do it enough to experience more good days than bad days with him.

Life Lesson #843: Labels didn't feel good to me as a child and they don't feel good to me as an adult. When someone else has a label for me, it is his or her perception and not necessarily my truth. Our behaviors and actions do not define us; they are just a piece of our experience on this planet in this moment. I can honor the children in my life by acknowledging their talents and unique characteristics without assigning a label to define *who they are* as a human being.

Own the lesson and appreciate it.

"It is better to live your own destiny imperfectly than to live an imitation of somebody else's life with perfection."

—*The Bhagavad Gita, ancient Dharmic scripture*

If I was "learning a lesson" while growing up, it usually didn't end well for me. There was rarely a positive spin to learning a lesson. The message was often sent by an aggravated adult with a sarcastic, condescending tone, delivered with different words but all meaning the same thing: "You screwed up. Don't do it again."

Here are some ways that "lessons" were presented to me as a child:

- "You should learn your lesson."
- "Haven't you learned your lesson yet?"
- "That ought to teach you a lesson or two."
- "How many times does it take for you to learn your lesson?"

lesson (*n.*) a useful piece of practical wisdom acquired by experience[1]

I wanted to see lessons as children see them: gifts and not consequences, mistakes, or failures. The above definition resonated with my spirit and just feels good to me. There are no limits to the lesson. The lesson is not defined as good or bad. It just is.

When I make a mistake ("learn a lesson"), I need to know that the mistake doesn't define me. I need to know that the mistake is simply an opportunity to gather wisdom through an experience, whether it is perceived as good or bad. I need to know that the experience doesn't make me a good or bad person. It is simply data to remind me what I need to do in the future to have a similar or a dramatically different experience.

I can't and do not want to prevent or control lessons. That is the joy of life: learning, growing, and being. When I let go of the idea that lessons indicate my worth, intelligence, or value, I can see them for exactly what they are: *wisdom acquired from experience.* When I let go of the idea that a lesson is a strong indicator of a mistake, I give myself permission to experience the event without judgment towards others or myself.

> When I make a mistake ("learn a lesson"), I need to know that the mistake doesn't define me.

In most cases, this is easier said than done.

One night, my mom was cooking dinner. She had a long, hectic, exhausting day at work and the last thing she wanted to do was cook. When I checked on dinner, I noticed spaghetti in the pot. I have never been a fan of spaghetti; I will eat it, but it certainly is not a dish I would ever choose.

My natural reaction was, "Oh, man. Not *spaghetti!*"

My mom did her best to ignore me. As she was stirring the sauce, I noticed that it was a sauce I really hated. It had big chunks of onions and I despise onions.

"Not *that* sauce! It has big onions in it! *Yuck!*"

There was a strange calmness in my mother's reply: "Pick them out if you don't like them."

I thought, "*Really,* Mom? Pick them out? That's *impossible!*"

I didn't dare say it out loud. I could sense her energy. It was telling me to stop talking. I listened.

Unfortunately, my father was not aware of our conversation. He walked in the kitchen, looked at the pot, and spoke his mind: "Really? *Spaghetti* for dinner? We just *had* spaghetti."

Hold on tight ... here we go.

Mom screamed, "That's *it*! Both of you don't want it? *Fine*! Figure out your own dinner. I'M *DONE*!"

She took the pot of spaghetti and threw it against the wall. Until then, I didn't know that spaghetti sauce had the potential to travel such a far distance. From the ceiling, to the refrigerator, to the floor, spaghetti sauce covered everything—even us.

My mother left the kitchen, saying a few final words: "... and *both* of you can clean it up!"

I looked at my dad and said, "Thanks a lot, Dad!"

He just looked at me and shook his head, and we cleaned up the mess. We didn't eat dinner that night; when we moved out of the house six years later, there were still sauce stains on the ceiling.

There are so many lessons to be learned from this experience. When I look at it through judgmental eyes, it's either right or wrong. I can easily say:

- I was ungrateful. I was a spoiled brat. I should be thankful for any food. There are starving children in the world. I could have been helping.

- My father was ungrateful. He should have been helping my mother in the kitchen. She works just as hard as he does. He could do his fair share.

- My mother was being unreasonable. She let her emotions and exhaustion get in the way. She didn't have to scream. She certainly didn't have to throw the pot and make a huge mess. Maybe she should be on medication for her temper.

The problem with seeing this experience through these eyes of judgment is that it places blame, anger, frustration, guilt, and hopelessness as the attention of the lesson, and it doesn't feel good. It doesn't help any of us learn from it. It's not productive ... and the judgment statements are not true.

Here is the truth:

- I was an extremely thoughtful and awesome child. I went above and beyond to help my mom. I was just disappointed that we were having spaghetti and not sure how to convey my disappointment with clarity. Being thankful for food was never an issue.

- My father was an incredibly grateful husband. He appreciated everything that my mom did for him. He wasn't always expressive about his appreciation, but he honestly felt it in the bottom of his heart. He never intended to hurt my mom or be disrespectful.

- My mom did her best, always. She provided and cared for us more than herself. It was not her intention to scream or throw the pot. She didn't know how to control her emotions and express her frustration without the energy behind it. She suppressed her needs for too long and then erupted. She loved us and didn't know how to ask for help.

When I look at the experience through the eyes of truth, I realize that we are all here to learn. It's our job to see the best in ourselves first, and then see the best in others who are participating in the event. When I look at the situation from the viewpoint of truth, I feel compassion, understanding, and love. I take it for what it was: *wisdom acquired from experience.*

What was my lesson?

- I was young enough to see the truth of who my mom was.

- I knew that she loved us both.

- I knew that she was tired and needed help.

- Most of all, I learned to listen to my gut. I could sense her anger and frustration from the energy she was emitting. I learned to give her space and stay away until the smoke cleared.

We never outgrow lessons. They come to us all day, every day. Every experience I have gives me the opportunity to grow and expand. Every experience offers me the chance to get to know myself better. Every experience allows me to take another step towards or away from my dreams.

I always have a choice.

"I've missed more than 9,000 shots in my career. I've lost almost 300 games. 26 times, I've been trusted to take the game winning shot and missed. I've failed over and over and over again in my life. And that is why I succeed."

—*Michael Jordan, professional basketball player*

Life Lesson #539: When I see each lesson as an opportunity to gain wisdom, I free myself and anyone else from blame. I can look at the experience with the eyes of truth and hold the participants in a space of knowing. I know that their behavior does not define them as a human being. I know that they are amazing people, learning from me and with me. I can leave the experience with wisdom, understanding, and compassion for all involved. I can feel good about each lesson because I am learning and growing from every experience. When I see the lesson through the eyes of truth, I give others and myself permission to "screw up" and feel good about it.

Hold the space and believe.

"Promise me you will always remember: You're braver than you believe and stronger than you seem, and smarter than you think."

—*Christopher Robin to Pooh*

When I started to work with children, I made a commitment to myself and to all the future children with whom I would eventually come in contact:

- I promised to do my best.
- I promised to remind them of their greatness.

- I promised to hold space for them to be their best self, even if I had to wait a long time.

- I promised to do this especially when it was easier for me to be angry. Win or lose, I wanted to be on the sidelines, cheering them on, believing in them, and reminding them of their greatness ... *always*.

Although I am not a sports fan, I appreciate cheerleaders' role in each sport. (Secretly, I always wanted to be a cheerleader; little did I know that I would be one. It just looked different.)

Cheerleaders never stop when their team is losing. Cheerleaders are all about rallying the energy around the situation, seeing only the possibilities, and cheering loud and clear and out to the world. They never give up hope, especially when it seems hopeless. Even if the team loses, cheerleaders are smiling, reminding us that there is always another game.

> Cheerleaders are all about rallying the energy around the situation, seeing only the possibilities, and cheering loud and clear and out to the world.

It's easy to do when the children give me something to cheer about; it's much harder when my own dreams, goals, desires, anger, frustration, annoyance, or ego get in the way. It's still a work in progress when I apply the same principles to family, friends, and the DMV worker.

"Holding space" for the children has many meanings:

- Holding space *physically* can look like this: I am patiently waiting for them to put away their own mat and reminding them of their greatness by saying, "You can put away your mat all by yourself! How fast can you go? Wow! I *knew* you were amazing!"

- Holding space *mentally* can look like this: "When you yelled at me, I couldn't believe it. It's not like you at all. I am going to go to my room and give you some space to work through this. I know that you will figure it out. I will be in my room when you are ready."

- Holding space *spiritually* can look like this: "I'm not sure exactly how you are feeling right now, but I will share something with you. Once I had a boyfriend who cheated on me and we broke up. I know how it feels to be cheated on. I'm not sure if you are feeling the same way I did, but it took some time for me to process it. I'm sorry that you are going through this. I know that you will get through it. I am willing to help in any way. I am here for you. I love you. I am proud of you. You are a gift to this world and to me."

Here's a great example of all three meanings of "holding space":

When Jackson was at our house on July 4th, we decided to make some chocolate chip cookies. We got out the stepstool and he was in business. (Making chocolate chip cookies in a freshly cleaned kitchen definitely offers an exercise in holding space.)

All was going well and Jackson was doing a great job. The recipe called for two bowls: one for the dry mix (flour, baking soda, and salt) and one for the wet mix (butter, white sugar, and brown sugar). We mixed the dry ingredients and only a small amount of flour spilled on the floor. *(No problem.)*

The wet ingredients were next—Jackson's favorite. He was purposely getting it all over his hand so he would be able to lick it off. *(Hold space.)*

Just as I was going over to the sink to clean the spoon, I looked back and saw Jackson take a spatula full of the dry mix and shove it into his mouth. *(Hold space.)*

He immediately looked at me with big eyes. Before I could get a word out, Jackson opened his mouth just enough for a "puff" of the flour mix to fill the air, which was very funny—like Puff, the Magic Dragon. *(Hold space.)*

After we rinsed his mouth out several times, we went back to mix the dry with the wet ingredients. Jackson poured the dry mix, completely missing the bowl, with half on the counter and half on the floor. *(Hold space.)*

We scooped the mix off the floor and counter, and decided to use it anyway. Then it was time to mix the batter together. Jackson took control of the mixer, which he had never used before, so he was unaware of the consequences of pulling the mixer out of the batter at full speed. Batter officially covered the entire kitchen. *(Hold space.)*

We gathered as much batter as possible. We rolled the dough together and put it in the oven. When we brought the cookies to the party later, Jackson announced to everyone, "We made these cookies. They are perfect. They are so yummy. You guys are so lucky to have them." *(Hold space.)*

I was the first to speak: "We were a good team! You are a great baker and we are all lucky to be eating these amazing cookies. Thanks so much for sharing your cookies. That's just like you!" *(Hold space.)*

I was doing fine until the batter covered my stainless steel appliances, my floor, my cabinets, my hair, and even my dog.

I had to focus. I had to see this as an experience to remember forever. I had to remember that the only intention Jackson had was to make amazing cookies. He was doing his best and it was my job to cheer him on. It was my job to change my mind, in the moment, about a clean kitchen.

> The moment I truly let go of the frustration of a filthy kitchen, I had permission to see it for what it was ... *a really good time!*

The moment I truly let go of the frustration of a filthy kitchen, I had permission to see it for what it was ... *a really good time!*

Life Lesson #4759: When children give me the opportunity to practice "holding space," I have a chance to see the world from their eyes for a moment. I can see what is really important. I can replace anger and frustration with a "feel good" moment. I can be in control of my emotions and of myself. I can have fun. I can be proud. I can remember that I am enough. I am here on purpose. My life has meaning and I matter.

"I always prefer to believe the best of everybody; it saves so much trouble."

—*Rudyard Kipling, Nobel Prize-winning author for literature*

Feel the wonder and marvel in it.

"Instructions for living a life: Pay attention.
Be astonished. Tell about it."

—*Mary Oliver, Pulitzer Prize-winning poet*

One of the most valuable lessons I have learned from every child is that they avoid joining me in a feeling that doesn't feel good to them. They refuse to join me—and stay with me—in anger, frustration, or depression. They will acknowledge me but never join me. They tend to acknowledge it and resist it, acknowledge it and ignore it, or acknowledge it and simply leave it.

I have noticed that, the younger the child, the more true this lesson proves to be. They will naturally walk up to a friend who is crying and ask if they are okay. When the child doesn't respond or keeps crying, the concerned child will shrug their shoulders and walk away.

This behavior is very interesting to watch, over and over again. It is the same with every child, every gender, and every ethnicity. They are all genuinely concerned; however, if the other party is not willing to see the situation another way, they simply walk away and never feel guilty. They never feel the need to fix the other person. The concerned child allows the angry, upset child to feel his feelings and figure it out.

At first, I bought into the idea that we needed to teach our children compassion, care, and responsibility for another's feelings; I now know differently. I know that these qualities are already in us and I don't have to teach them.

As an adult, I have the potential and ability to stay in anger, frustration, or depression for a very long, long, long time. (I am still working on anger towards a family member from years ago.) The children with whom I have worked can hold anger for minutes, sometimes hours, but never for days or years.

Samantha was on the playground, having a great time with Blake. He told her that he didn't want to play with her anymore. She begged, but he said no.

She started to cry and he decided that he was not going to participate. She followed him for five minutes, pacing the playground. I was watching carefully to see how this was going to turn out.

Finally, Samantha gave up and ran to me to tell me all about it. She was in the "ugly cry," with snot dripping in her mouth, big tears, and a bright red face. I listened but, before I could say anything, she looked past me and noticed a butterfly.

Samantha screamed, "Miss Heather! Did you see the *butterfly*?" She ran over to Blake screaming, "Blake! There's a butterfly!"

Blake and Samantha were on a butterfly hunt for the rest of the time that we were outside.

Life Lesson #6: I have the right to say that I don't want to play with someone. If I throw a fit or get depressed, I don't expect or hope that people will join me. If I am aware, the universe will show me another way to look at things. I have a choice. I can find a way to snap out of it and be with it for minutes or hours, instead of days or years. When I marvel in and appreciate the wonder that surrounds me, it all seems to work out in the end.

In our society, it is challenging to feel the wonder of the world. As I work on the deadline for this book, I struggle with the feeling of wonder when I am at my computer for 12 to 16 hours a day. However, the universe, in all its wisdom, never disappoints me. I am blessed to live next to a greenbelt full of wildlife. Every day that I have "locked" myself in my office, I look out my window and see a family of deer eating in my backyard. I often stare out the window and thank them for coming to visit. They add wonder to my world.

I am also blessed to have an amazing sidekick: my dog Furby. He was Grandma Hazel's dog and, when she passed away, my mom took him; then, after my mom passed away, Furby came to live with us. He was a feral farm dog, who is now living a mile from the ocean. He is my buddy, my companion, and a true friend.

Furby is almost 14 years old, so he sleeps an average of 22 hours a day. He stays by my side throughout the night, without hesitation. The other day, he went outside and was gone much longer than normal. When I checked on him, he was in the grass with his eyes closed, smelling the air. The next time Furby went out, I went with him. We sat in the quiet, listening to the wind, feeling the breeze on our faces, feeling the sun warming our bones, and taking it all in. We marveled in the wonder together.

Life Lesson #5932: When I watch how others marvel in the wonders of the world, I am given the opportunity to test it out for myself. If I focus, I can feel magic in the air.

"There are two ways of spreading light:
To be the candle or the mirror that reflects it."

—*Edith Wharton, Pulitzer Prize-winning novelist*

See beyond the behavior and remember the love.

"There is more hunger for love and appreciation in this world than for bread."

—*Mother Teresa, Nobel Peace Prize winner*

Heather lights up when she is around children. Nothing makes her happier than being in their presence and they feel her love. When we are in the presence of someone, and can *feel* how much they love us and how much joy we bring them, we want to match their energy and become as great as they believe us to be.

Heather has dropped the labels with kids and has trained herself to focus on their special gifts. She has found a way to see beyond behavior, find that beautiful soul inside every child, and remind herself—and them—that they are amazing beings who are here on purpose. She does this especially when a child is acting in a way that is undesirable. Most parents focus on addressing the undesirable behavior; Heather uses a totally different tactic by ignoring the behavior and focusing on how amazing the child is at a soul level.

In all of my interviews with Heather, I can count hundreds of times when she said, "I just hold them in their greatness."

"Heather, what would you do if your child was being a total pill?"

"I hold them in their greatness."

"What would you do if your kid came home with four Fs on their report card?"

"I hold them in their greatness."

"What would you do if your child was upset because other kids said some really hurtful words?"

"I hold them in their greatness."

It took me a while to figure out exactly what she meant by this. When I am around kids, coworkers, or people at a coffee shop, and I see them doing something I really don't like, I do not think to "hold them in their greatness" at that moment. I immediately think of how they need to correct their behavior.

One day, I asked Heather to relive a scenario where she "held a child in her greatness" and I tracked her eye movements. Many people don't realize this, but our eyes are the windows into our minds.

"Eye movement tracking" is an important technique that we use at the Everyday Genius Institute when we want to understand how someone is thinking and what is happening in their minds. When we move our eyes, it's as if we are accessing files in our brain.

With eye movement tracking, we slow down eye movements and notice the tiny micromovements. For each micro eye movement, we then analyze what the person is literally "seeing" in their mind. Many of our most interesting discoveries on how geniuses think come from slowing down and unpacking the split second of their eye movements.

When I tracked Heather's eye movements, I figured out exactly what she does to "hold a child in their greatness"—and it all made sense! In a nanosecond, her eyes darted to four distinct places. Each place was a step in her mental process when she was interacting with a child.

> Many of our most interesting discoveries on how geniuses think come from slowing down and unpacking the split second of their eye movements.

How to remind your child of their greatness (even when it's hard)

In just about every challenging situation with a child—whether they are being rude, fighting with a sibling, making a mess, experiencing a meltdown, complaining that a friend has been unkind, or coming home with an F on their report card—Heather does the same thing every time in her mind:

Step 1: Notice the undesirable behavior and immediately ask, "Is this something I can let go, or do I need to address it?" Heather says, "I really do my best to ignore most things and give my child the space to figure it out on their own. If I see undesirable, deal-breaker behavior, I address it. If I see that my child could really use some cheerleading, I address it."

Step 2: Instantly recall a situation where your child was behaving completely opposite of what he is doing now and get in a place of feeling love. Heather says, "I remember a specific moment when my child was at his best. For example, I remember a time when I saw him being great with a friend, and I recall his light and smile. As I hold that image of him at his best, most loving self, in my mind and in my heart I know that my child is love, and this behavior or reaction is not who he is. It is important for me to remember this, so I can approach him in a loving state."

Step 3: Ask, "How can I connect with my child? How can we hear each other and both get what we need from this situation?" Heather adds, "Now that I am in a good emotional state, I recall a specific time that I connected with my child when we both heard each other and communicated well. I bring up that time in my mind's eye. I remember what I did in a previous situation when we connected. To me, 'connecting' means putting aside my anger or frustration—or putting away my need to fix something—and looking at each other, eye to eye, and connecting heart to heart."

Step 4: Repeat that past connection strategy in this moment, get into rapport with the child, and then communicate. Heather explains, "Sometimes I remember a time we connected after a moment of silence. Sometimes I remember a time we connected when I held him. Sometimes I remember a time we connected when I got on his eye level. I repeat the same thing I did in the past in this moment and really connect. Depending on the situation, I might state something I need, ask what my child needs, or model a possible better behavior. For example, I might say, 'If it were me, I would ...' I then remind him of his greatness and his ability to solve this issue on his own. I might say, 'I know that you are amazing ...' and frequently end with, 'I believe in you!'"

Heather is so practiced at this strategy that she does it in a nanosecond in her mind. For those of us who are still learning, all it takes is a little practice.

I love the timing of the universe. As I am writing this chapter, I am spending the week at a friend's house, babysitting her beautiful and amazing 13-year-old daughter Kayla; however, like many 13-year-olds, she isn't great about cleaning up after herself.

After a few days of hurricane-level mess in the kitchen after every meal and snack, I kept thinking, "Wow! She is really a slob and just expects me to clean up after her!"

I got more and more worked up and, after a couple of days, I was totally annoyed. It wasn't a deal breaker yet, but I could sense it moving in that direction ... *quickly*. I decided to try Heather's strategy and changed my thinking.

"Kayla takes care of making her bed, washing her sheets, and doing her own laundry," I thought. "I know that she loves this house. I know that she appreciates me being here for the week. She is an amazing and special light on this planet."

After a single day of remembering how amazing this girl is, I shifted my energy around the subject. I went from feeling annoyed to feeling grateful, and the rest of the week was much more fun and relaxing for me. Guess what? By the end of the week, I noticed that she was making more of an effort to pick up after herself in the kitchen, and I didn't utter a word about it.

It just happened!

Shift your thoughts and notice how the energy shifts.

Heather asks herself, "How can I connect with my child?"

When we shift our thoughts, it shifts our energy; when we shift our energy, the dynamic in the system has to shift (see the discussion of systems theory in *Chapter 5: Choose the Energy You Bring to Every Situation*).

I asked Heather to create a list of common thoughts that parents have about their children and suggestions about how they can reframe them. As you read this list, notice that Heather begins the process of reframing by thinking about specific examples of when the child behaved in a way that was *opposite* from what they were doing now. Then, she comes up with more general thoughts that remind her how amazing and loving the child is. She considers what gifts are present in the behavior or how that behavior might help them (or her) in life.

When Heather sees her child doing something undesirable, she thinks, "This behavior is not a reflection of who my child *really* is. How can I remember my child in his best light? How can I shift my focus and energy so I can get into a loving place?"

You may be thinking, "If I'm just nice to them all the time, what will they learn?"

The answer is: *effective communication skills.*

- They are learning that they can hear and be heard when they connect in a space of love.

- You are learning that it feels infinitely better to be with your children in this space.
- Both of you are learning that you can feel happier a lot more often.

Reframe common thoughts about children.

I've included many examples so you can get some practice with this strategy. As you read through each of the examples, you will get better and better at this reframing technique, and you'll soon be as fast as Heather!

Initial reaction: "Quinn is so thoughtless! She is selfish and doesn't care about anyone around her!"

Reframe: "Quinn was so thoughtful when she sent her grandma a get-well card. I know that Quinn is an amazing person who loves her friends and loves this family."

Initial reaction: "Rachel is a spoiled brat. She keeps asking for more and more, and thinks that I am here to give her everything she wants."

Reframe: "Rachel often thanks me for being her mom. I know that Rachel is an amazing dreamer who thinks bigger and bigger all the time! She also reminds me to think bigger for myself."

Initial reaction: "Sophia is mean to her friends, and can say and do really cruel things."

Reframe: "I know how kind Sophia is with many of her friends. I know that Sophia is an amazing human and cares about the people in her life. I know that she is doing her best to figure out how to be in the world, and I trust her to have the experiences she needs in order to grow."

Initial reaction: "Joseph never listens to me! He just does what he wants all the time."

Reframe: "Joseph often listens to me, especially when I tell him that I love him. He is working out how to get his needs met in various situations.

TARYN

I know that, when I listen to him, I am quietly modeling how to listen to others and cooperate."

Initial reaction: "Jesse will not learn to use the potty. He refuses. He is so stubborn!"

Reframe: "Jesse is a quick learner. He is obviously not ready to use the potty and unsure how to communicate his needs with me in the moment. I know that it has served me to be stubborn at times in my own life. I trust that the timing is off and he will eventually be able to use the potty."

> When Heather sees her child doing something undesirable, she thinks, "This behavior is not a reflection of who my child really is. How can I remember my child in his best light? How can I shift my focus and energy so I can get into a loving place?"

Initial reaction: "Sarah says the most embarrassing things in public! She is so unpredictable and random."

Reframe: "I love how Sarah is able to be herself in public. She owns her greatness, regardless of what others think. I know that her feelings are far more important than others' opinions."

Initial reaction: "Amanda never comes home on time. She completely disregards my authority!"

Reframe: "Amanda is a respectful and considerate child. She texts me when she arrives and then leaves every destination. She is testing the boundaries of curfew to make sure that she can trust me. She is making sure that I will honor my word with her. She is giving me practice to honor myself."

Initial reaction: "John needs to get a job. He needs to learn responsibility. He's just being lazy."

Reframe: "John handles the responsibility of babysitting his little brother after school every day. He does a fantastic job! I trust that he will get a job in his own time, and I am committed to being clear with my financial responsibilities to him. I know that a job does not determine John's worth."

Initial reaction: "Alex only wants junk food. He is such a picky eater!"

Reframe: "Alex loves carrots. When he is exposed to different foods and watches us enjoy those foods, he is inspired to test them out for himself. I love that Alex makes and owns his decisions. I know that my job is to provide the best foods I can to support him in every way. I know that he will always eat plenty of foods that support his body, mind, and spirit."

Initial reaction: "MacKenzie pushes my buttons all the time. Her goal is to aggravate and irritate me."

Reframe: "Every night, MacKenzie comes into my room, before bedtime, and cuddles with me. She loves me and I love her. MacKenzie has the ability to see when I am off my game, and lets me know, in her own way, that I need to be clear with my wants and desires in the moment. She helps me focus."

Initial reaction: "James never follows the rules in the classroom. He doesn't respect his teacher."

Reframe: "James has had great feedback from many of his teachers. I know that James offers respect more often than not. I know that I need to create a space for communication and initiate a dialogue to understand what is going on in his classroom."

Initial reaction: "Melissa is such a bad little girl. She bites her friends and doesn't even say that she's sorry."

Reframe: "Melissa is so full of love and passion. I know that she is learning how to communicate. When she can't find the words to express her anger and chooses to bite, I know that saying sorry is not an indication of comprehension or understanding in the moment. I know that both children are learning valuable lessons in the moment. I know that Melissa will figure it out!"

Initial reaction: "Sherry is such a drama queen! She makes a mountain out of a molehill every time."

Reframe: "Sherry has a great stage presence. I'm not sure exactly how this is going to work out for her, but I know that she will use this to create all her dreams. I know that she has witnessed and copied my behavior and drama more than I desire. It is my job to be the best example of 'letting go' of the small things that bother me."

Initial reaction: "Megan doesn't apply herself. She is not trying hard enough. She is such a procrastinator!"

Reframe: "Megan has been successful with many obstacles that have come her way. When she is involved in projects that she loves, she works diligently until she has achieved success. I know that we all work differently. I honor her approach, even when I don't agree with it, and know that her greatest lessons will be learned from her experiences."

Initial reaction: "Billy never accepts what I say. He is so argumentative and always disagrees with me."

Reframe: "Billy listens to my stories every night. He is a great listener. He is learning the art of cooperation and practicing with me to master it. I can appreciate his gift. Who knows? Maybe he will pick a career that requires the 'natural art of debate' he has already. I need to work on my communication skills and remember to stay true to my word, always."

Initial reaction: "Jennifer disregards everyone's opinion. She is so arrogant. She needs to learn to be humble."

Reframe: "Jennifer is a great questioner of life. She wants to know the 'why.' If she is not satisfied, she will continue on her quest until she is satisfied. I know that Jennifer is a kind, loving spirit. I know that she is searching for her truth, and I honor her mission. I know that she will find the perfect people to resonate with and explore the world in ways that I have never imagined."

Initial reaction: "Susan has such a bad temper. She has a meltdown every time she doesn't get her way."

Reframe: "I am really thankful that Susan has the ability to express her feelings. I would rather hear them out loud than have her shove them down and pretend that the anger doesn't exist. I need to remember to give her space and allow her to move through the feeling. I need to foster communication when we are both calm. I am really glad that Susan has such strong desires to get what she wants in life. She will be a great leader."

Initial reaction: "Alec is so conceited! He thinks that he is better than everyone else. Who does he think he is?"

Reframe: "I know the truth about Alec. I have seen him befriend the most unpopular child in school while enduring teasing from the other children. I know that Alec is just working on his own self-worth and self-esteem. I know that the best plan of action is to continue affirming the best qualities in Alec every chance I get."

Initial reaction: "Patrick is such a control freak. He has to have it his way or it's the highway!"

Reframe: "I honor Patrick. He is clear on his goals and desires in life. He is determined to lead his own life and be the captain of his own ship. I appreciate Patrick for his clarity and willingness to stand up for his beliefs, even if he is standing alone."

Initial reaction: "Tammy is so shy. She will never make it in the real world unless she speaks up!"

Reframe: "I know that Tammy will succeed in life. I know that she has to stay true to her nature and herself. I know that there are times when Tammy is loud and clear with her wants and desires. I know that she is great, just the way she is. She often teaches me the value of silence."

Initial reaction: "Carla is such a flake. She never gets her homework done."

Reframe: "Carla is the best dog sitter on the block. She is on time and responsible. I know that Carla will work out her homework schedule on her own. I know that she will experience the natural consequences of her choice without my participation. I love that she has started her own business and know that she will be successful in life, regardless of her homework status."

Initial reaction: "Tom is such a grump when he wakes up. He is such a whiney crybaby."

Reframe: "Tom has a smile that lights up the room. He is always the life of the party. I know that it takes him a little longer to get in the groove for the day. I honor his feelings and give him the space to find his smile in his own time. I know that I can remain happy, even if my child appears to be unhappy."

Initial reaction: "Rene is such a perfectionist. She has to have her hair perfect before we leave the house. She is such a pain to get ready!"

Reframe: "I love Rene's attention to detail. She always puts her best effort into everything she does. I love that she honors herself enough to care how she feels before she leaves her home. She reminds me to do and be my best, daily."

Initial reaction: "Mike needs to learn some manners. He never says 'please' or 'thank you.' It is so embarrassing!"

Reframe: "I know that Mike is incredibly thankful. I trust that he will learn how to express his appreciation in his own way. I know that the only action I can take is to be the best model of appreciation in his life. I start with appreciating him, exactly the way he is."

Initial reaction: "Donna is such a scatterbrain. She needs to learn to focus and pay attention!"

Reframe: "Donna is a big thinker. I know that her mind is always going. She has the unique ability to multitask in ways I can only imagine. She is focusing her attention in ways that I can't even comprehend. I honor her process and do my best to focus and pay attention to her greatness."

Initial reaction: "Tyler's attitude is terrible. He needs to knock it off."

Reframe: "Tyler is often working on his self-expression. I know that he is an amazing student and that he is practicing his self-expression in a safe place: at home. I know that the only thing I can do is take responsibility for myself and choose whether to participate. I have a choice, always. I know that Tyler will work this out."

Feel the love and connect.

Can you imagine what it would feel like as a child to have someone hold an image of you at your best, and then address you with that image in mind and with a feeling of total love for you?

Can you imagine what it would feel like as an adult? For example, when you came in late for work, your boss said, "It's not like you to come in late. Did something go wrong this morning? Is everything okay?"

Would that feel differently than, "You are late! You need to be here on time! Work starts at 8:30 a.m."

Which one feels better? In which scenario do you want to be on time more often?

Reframing the initial frustrated thought is the first part of the "How to Remind Your Child of Their Greatness" strategy. The second part is to recall a time when you have successfully connected with your child; then, repeat that same strategy from the past in this moment.

> Can you imagine what it would feel like as a child to have someone hold an image of you at your best, and then address you with that image in mind and with a feeling of total love for you?

Maybe you looked into your child's eyes with love. Maybe you had a moment of silence together before you started talking. Maybe you touched your child in a loving way. The goal is to create an energetic connection *before* addressing your child. Then, once you have connected, you can both hear each other and get what you want out of the situation.

The reason kids listen to Heather is that she makes sure they are listening before she talks. Can you imagine how much more effective your parent (or boss or spouse) would be if they looked into your eyes and had a positive energetic connection with you (using the first part of the "How to Remind Your Child of their Greatness" strategy to get in a space of love) before they addressed you?

It sure beats yelling across the house, "Go clean your room!" or "Stop doing that!"

I believe that the difference is Heather's simple guiding question to herself: "How can I connect with my child in this moment?" It drives her entire strategy. It drives *how* she talks with the child in a way that the child can hear. She gets herself in a good emotional state where she can connect with the child by remembering a time when the child was great. This step puts her in a place of love so, when she talks with the child, the child feels her love and wants to listen. Contrast that with what many people do: assume a position of authority and then tell their child in a stern voice that they need to change their behavior.

Over the years, Heather has built up a huge catalog of examples from which to draw regarding how to connect with children and what to say in any given moment. Now that you know this strategy, you will be consciously drawing on your own catalog of examples of loving moments and times when you successfully connected with your child.

For specific examples of the "How to Remind Your Child of Their Greatness" strategy in action, check out our blog post:
http://raiseahappychild.com/behavior

We meet people's expectations about us.

Over the years, many psychology studies have tried to determine how much of success or greatness is "nature" versus "nurture." In every study of which I am aware, it has been proven that people perform dramatically better when the person leading believes in the greatness of the people with whom they are working.

In one well-known study,[2] teachers were led to believe that certain students (selected at random) were likely to show signs of a spurt in intellectual growth and development based on their intelligence quotient—IQ—test scores. In other words, teachers were led to believe that some of their students were going to make a big jump in learning and development over the next several months.

The results were startling. At the end of the year, these "gifted" students showed significantly greater gains in intellectual growth than those in the control group. Put another way, the power of positive expectation had a very real impact on how the children performed.

When a teacher believes that a child is going to behave in a certain way, the child lives up to that expectation. In reality, the "signs" from the test scores had nothing to do with the students' success. The students made huge leaps in learning because the teacher expected they would.

Wouldn't it be great if we didn't need test scores to believe in the capabilities of a child?

We are hardwired to want to push ourselves beyond our current ability when people believe in us. For example, when someone says, "I believe in you," it gives us the courage we need to do the thing that pushes us just a little bit beyond our comfort zone. It makes us feel good that someone we respect trusts us to create an outcome for ourselves.

If we want our children to be happy and amazing people, we need to hold the energetic space in our bodies that they *are* amazing and that they *are* capable. Simply put, we need to keep reminding ourselves of our children's greatness, especially when it's hard. In those moments when our child is being anything *but* great, we need to remember it most, so they can also remember it. It all starts with us, as parents, kicking off the process to remember their greatness.

I've had the privilege of studying the healing strategies of the renowned Q'ero shamanic healers from the high Andes in Peru. Being in the presence of these shamans is like being in the presence of the most unbelievable light and joy, and their healing power is immense. They believe that a large part of their job as healers is to hold a very clear and strong vision of the sick person as *already healed*. By holding this vision of the patient in an already healed state, they shift the momentum of the sickness.

If you were to ask them how they get such miraculous healing results, they would tell you, "I set my intent to heal and see the client as healed. Then I engage in a ceremony where this healing can unfold."

In our Western mind, we think that this is impossible; however, it is *exactly* this strategy that makes great healers (e.g., shamans, doctors, therapists, coaches, and teachers) so great. The Q'ero shamans of Peru are particularly skilled at holding their patients in a clear visual state of already being healed, and they hold the space in a healing session for the patient to live up to their expectation.

Heather uses the same strategy and holds an image of her child in their greatness.

Separate undesirable behavior from the person.

Heather is very careful to separate undesirable behavior from the innate goodness of the child. In her mind, the child is always amazing. If the child is exhibiting undesirable behavior in the moment, she lets the child know that she is genuinely puzzled by this display.

Notice these examples of how many parents label their children in frustration and what Heather would say instead:

- "You are so stubborn!" versus "Wow, this behavior isn't like you. What's going on?"

- "You are such a drama queen!" versus "Wow, this behavior isn't like you. What's going on?"

- "You are so slow!" versus "Wow, this behavior isn't like you. What's going on?"

- "You are so demanding!" versus "Wow, this behavior isn't like you. What's going on?"

When many parents see very undesirable behavior, they say in an exasperated tone, "What are you *doing*? You know better than *that*!" It's a strategy based in shaming the child into exhibiting better behavior.

Heather takes a different approach and responds to undesirable behavior in a genuinely curious tone by saying, "Wow, this behavior isn't like you. What's going on?" With this simple response, Heather accomplishes so much at once:

- She separates the undesirable behavior from the child.

- She reminds her child of their greatness.

- She listens to her child, realizing that there must be some good reason for this undesirable behavior to manifest.

- She feeds a frustrated emotional space with love.

When we label a person, they tend to live up to the label; conversely, when we look at the behavior, it is just a fleeting moment in time and they have the chance to demonstrate something different in the future. The behavior doesn't define them or who they are as a person.

Heather only separates the behavior from the child if it's undesirable behavior. She links good behavior with the person if it's something she is praising. Using this positive praise, she makes it part of who they are as a person and affirms what she knows about the child. For example, she would say:

- "You are such a good cleaner."
- "You are such a great student."
- "You are so funny."
- "You are a great decision maker."
- "You are such a good friend."

Heather is very careful not to project her ideas of what the child must be thinking. She would never say, "You must be so proud of yourself!" Remember: Heather's goal is to help kids listen to their own feelings, so she would never assume that they are feeling a certain way or project a perceived feeling onto them. Instead, she would say what she is feeling, such as, "I am so proud of you. I knew you could do it!"

Some might say that this strategy causes children to look to her for approval. Heather's philosophy is that she is acknowledging their greatness in every moment she can, and validating what she knows to be true about that child.

Many parenting books talk about "helicopter parents," "lenient parents," or "drill sergeant parents." I have never heard Heather refer to parents like this. She would not put a label on parents any more than she would put a label on children. She knows that, when we get labeled, we live up to the expectations of the label. When it's an undesirable label, we just get more of the undesirable behavior.

Hold the space for your children to be the best version of themselves.

"My job as a parent is to be my child's cheerleader," Heather explains, "to cheer him on with what he wants to have, what he wants to explore, what he wants to experience, what he wants to know, and what he wants to be. The cheerleader never stops when you're losing. The cheerleader never says, 'You suck!'

"Being a parent is *not* about being an advocate. It's about cheering my child on so he can do it himself. Cheerleaders are about rallying energy around the situation. They are responsible for maintaining a belief and a hope that, no matter what the circumstances, the possibility for a win is still there. Even if we lose this game, there is another one!"

Heather believes that children are responsible for themselves. She doesn't do things *for* her children. She makes sure that they are doing it all by themselves. Whether it's doing homework, figuring things out among friends, playing sports, or choosing clothes and getting dressed, she simply says, "I believe in you!"

I've noticed that the busier we get in our lives, the less patient we are in holding space for our children to do things themselves. We are in a rush, so we think it's easier just to move through the activity at our adult pace rather than hold the space for the child to figure it out in their own time. Because we may be worried about their future, and feel that they need our help to be successful in the world, we make decisions for them.

What if we could let go and simply hold space for our child's greatness to unfold? What if we could simply remind our child of her greatness—even when it's hard?

Sing your child's song.

> "Being a parent is *not* about being an advocate. It's about cheering my child on so he can do it himself."

There is a beautiful tradition among the people of a small tribe in Africa. They intuitively know what Heather knows. This custom, excerpted below, is from Alan Cohen's book *Wisdom of the Heart*[3]:

> "When a woman in a certain African tribe knows she is pregnant, she goes out into the wilderness with a few friends and together they pray and meditate until they hear the song of the child. They recognize that every soul has its own vibration that expresses its unique flavor and purpose. When the women attune to the song, they sing it out loud. Then they return to the tribe and teach it to everyone else.
>
> "When the child is born, the community gathers and sings the child's song to him or her. Later, when the child enters education, the village gathers and chants the child's song. When the child passes

through the initiation to adulthood, the people again come together and sing. At the time of marriage, the person hears his or her song.

"Finally, when the soul is about to pass from this world, the family and friends gather at the person's bed, just as they did at their birth, and they sing the person to the next life.

"In the African tribe there is one other occasion upon which the villagers sing to the child. If at any time during his or her life, the person commits a crime or aberrant social act, the individual is called to the center of the village and the people in the community form a circle around them. Then they sing their song to them.

The tribe recognizes that the correction for antisocial behavior is not punishment; it is love and the remembrance of identity. When you recognize your own song, you have no desire or need to do anything that would hurt another."

Review of Chapter 9: Remind Your Child of Their Greatness ... Always

- Remember your child's greatness, especially in the moments where they aren't being great. They will live up to your expectation.

- Reframe challenging thoughts about your children to focus on their greatness.

- Speak in a way that you can be heard by first connecting energetically.

- Separate undesirable behavior from the child by saying, "This behavior isn't like you. What's going on?"

- Acknowledge your child's greatness every chance you get.

- Say, "I believe in you," every chance you get.

- Hold the space for your child to be the best version of themselves.

See this strategy in action!

Check out the video on
Remind Your Child of Their Greatness ... Always

V
I
D
E
O

V
I
D
E
O

or visit
www.raiseahappychild.com/greatness

"Our deepest fear is not that we are inadequate. Our deepest fear is that we are powerful beyond measure. It is our light, not our darkness that most frightens us. We ask ourselves, who am I to be brilliant, gorgeous, talented, fabulous? Actually, who are you not to be? You are a child of God. Your playing small does not serve the world. There is nothing enlightened about shrinking so that other people won't feel insecure around you. We are all meant to shine, as children do. We were born to make manifest the glory of God that is within us. It's not just in some of us; it's in everyone. And as we let our own light shine, we unconsciously give other people permission to do the same. As we are liberated from our own fear, our presence automatically liberates others."

—*Marianne Williamson, spiritual activist and best-selling author*

PART 3

Put Happiness into Action

> "Everyone who got to where they are
> had to begin where they were."
>
> —*Richard Paul Evans, The New York Times best-selling author*

Let's recap what we've learned.

In *Chapter 10: Put It All Together*, you will see how to put together everything you've learned and apply it to a desirable day. We'll also share some great go-to phrases and one-liners that Heather frequently uses.

Once you've seen how it all comes together, you'll be ready for the last section, which includes 22 scenarios that will make sense because you will have a deep foundation of understanding by the time you get to them.

In *Part 1: Decide Who You Are as a Parent*, we looked at how to define your role as a parent and explored the following questions:

Chapter 1: How Do You Define "Success" as a Parent?

- It's important to decouple our feelings of "parenting success" from how our child "turns out." We cannot control their choices in life.

- We each have the opportunity to create our own definition of "parenting success." Achieving our definition of success must be entirely within our control of choices and behaviors.

- *Choices* can be successes or failures, but *human beings* are so much more than these labels.

- It is not our child's job to make *us* happy but to make *themselves* happy; it is not our job to make our *child* happy but to make *ourselves* happy.

Chapter 2: What Are Your Goals for Yourself and Desires for Your Child?

- Our goals determine our behavior. We consciously and subconsciously behave in ways that support our goals. Clearly defining our parenting goals will automatically result in parenting behaviors that support our goals.

- We can only set goals for ourselves, and they must be achievable by our own actions.

- We cannot set goals for our children because we cannot control their behavior.

- Modeling (verbally and behaviorally) is the most innate form of learning. We are powerful models for our children and can positively influence their behavior by consciously modeling it verbally or behaviorally in ourselves.

- It is not reasonable to expect our children to be more than we are willing to be ourselves.

Chapter 3: As a Parent, What Are You Really Responsible For?

- We have an opportunity to define what we are and are not responsible for as parents.

- When we define our responsibilities based on a positive intention (and not on a desire for control of a specific outcome), we create a healthier and more relaxed environment for everyone.

- The Triangle of Disempowerment has the roles of Perpetrator, Victim, and Rescuer. When we play these roles, we are acting in a disempowered state.

- The Triangle of Empowerment has the roles of Challenger, Creator, and Coach. When we play these roles, we are acting in an empowered state.

Chapter 4: What Is Your Definition of Happiness?

- Happiness is a choice. It comes from within and not from external factors, such as money, houses, or jobs.

- To be happy, choose "feel good" over "feel bad."

- To be happy, do what you want, when you want, how you want.

- Children are already doing everything in their power to feel happy. Our job is to recognize it and not squelch it with our beliefs about life.

Now let's recap *Part 2: Discover the 5 Ingredients for Parenting Success*. In this section, we explored the following strategies that parents can bring to any parenting situation:

Chapter 5: Choose the Energy You Bring to Every Situation

- We are all part of systems. Feed the family system with the energy you want to experience.

- Never engage in a conversation or dialog when you or your children are angry or frustrated.

- Short-circuit undesirable calibrated loops and create new "feel good" loops.

- We hear body language and feelings more than words. Shift your energy so your voice tonality and body language are communicating what you *really* want to say.

- Take your power back and put yourself in control of how you react to behavior. Choose the energy you bring to every situation and create the experience you want.

- If you want your children to learn how to effectively handle their anger, choose wisely how you handle your anger.

Chapter 6: Honor Your Feelings First and Then Your Child's

- Operate from a powerful guiding question: "How can we both get what we want here?"

- Check in with yourself and honor your own feelings and desires first.

- Understand how your child is feeling. Be a detective, if necessary.

- Create an outcome where you and your child can get your needs met. If you need help with a solution, ask your child.

- Think before you decide to force your child to exhibit good manners. Instead, see with the eyes of the heart.

Chapter 7: Focus on What You Do Want

- Make it a goal to create harmony and agreement in your interactions.

- Energy flows where attention goes. Choose what you feed your energy.

- Shift your attention away from what "needs improvement" with your kids, spouse, and employees, and change it to "acknowledge your greatness in every single moment I can."

- Ignore as much undesirable behavior as possible and just focus on the deal breakers.

- Use the technique for getting the behavior you *do* want. Explain once, ask a question that gets *them* (and not you) to say "no," and redirect the behavior to where they *can* do it.

- Rather than issue a command, instead say, "I need you to ..."

- Shift your approach of punishment (and rewards) by focusing on the desired outcome, which is to help your child learn how to express himself appropriately in any situation.

Chapter 8: Honor Every Choice Your Child Makes

- Choice always exists, in every moment of every day.

- Give your child lots of opportunities to practice decision making.

- Present choices with which you are comfortable and always honor the choice.

- Present choices within an experience that is not up for choice, such as going to the store or going to bed.

- Honor your children's choice, always and the first time.

- Honor the choice implicit in their behavior by saying, "When you do X, that tells me Y. I hear you."

- Be aware of what our behavior is communicating to our children. When they see us do things, it communicates a lot to them.

- Experience is the only true teacher. Let your child experience the natural consequence of every choice, even if it's hard to watch.

Chapter 9: Remind Your Child of Their Greatness ... Always

- Remember your child's greatness, especially in the moments where they aren't being great. They will live up to your expectation.

- Reframe challenging thoughts about your children to focus on their greatness.

- Speak in a way that you can be heard by first connecting energetically.

- Separate undesirable behavior from the child by saying, "This behavior isn't like you. What's going on?"

- Acknowledge your child's greatness every chance you get.

- Say, "I believe in you," every chance you get.

- Hold the space for your child to be the best version of themselves.

Does it make a bit more sense when you see it all together like this? With this recap in mind, let's put it together and see how Heather moves through a desirable day in her life as an entrepreneur, a wife, and a mom.

CHAPTER 10

Put It All Together

"It's interesting to see when a kid walks into the room
... does your face light up? That's what they're looking
for ... when my children used to walk in the room
when they were little, I looked at them to see if they
had buckled their trousers or if their hair was combed
or their socks were up ... so you think your affection
and your deep love is on display cause you're caring for
them, it's not. When they see you they see the critical
face ... What's wrong now? ... Let your face speak
what's in your heart ... it is just as small as that."

—*Toni Morrison, Nobel Prize-winning novelist*

Morning

As soon as I open my eyes, my day begins. I take a few minutes to remind myself why I am here on this planet, what I want for the day, and how thankful I am for my husband and children. (In my real life, I have one son but, to add depth to this scenario, let's say that I have two girls.)

I take a moment to lie in bed, feel the love, and remember the special bedtime story I shared with my girls, which filled my heart the night before. I remember sharing my feelings of sadness with my husband at the end of last night, and feeling his love and support for all of the perceived mistakes I had made in my business that day. I pet my dog to gather a little more tangible love, which inspires me to get out of bed. I make breakfast and lunch for my husband, and greet my children and my husband with fresh eyes. I remember that I am here on purpose. I remember that I have meaning and value to share with the world.

- *Goal met:* I cooperate and work in harmony (no resistance) to manage life together. It starts before I get out of bed. I decide how I want my day to go.

Still in bed, my eight-year-old daughter Elle comes in to tell me what she wants in her lunch today. I already feel a hint of frustration. I am instantly challenged to hold her in a good space; thankfully, I recall a great memory before she came into my room.

I respond with, "Good morning, love! I am so glad you are up and ready to start your day. I am glad that I got to roll out of bed to your smile today!"

I am genuinely happy to see her in the morning, to know that I have another day with her on this planet, so it is easy to say my truth out loud.

- *Goal met:* I acknowledge Elle's greatness in every opportunity that presents itself. When she shows her weaknesses, I see them as an opportunity to practice my focus.

My nine-year-old daughter Cora is busy getting herself ready for school. I make an effort to go into her room and acknowledge her. I remind her how proud I am that she's getting herself ready, and let her know that she is an inspiration for me to get myself ready as well. I take a moment to look in the mirror and have a happy, proud moment for myself and as a model to my daughter. It is actually more effort to be kind and loving to myself than to direct it to her. I know that it is important and valuable to do it for my well-being just as much, if not more, than for her well-being.

- *Goal met:* I hold myself in high esteem. When I look in the mirror and feel bad about myself—or verbalize that I feel bad about myself—it is an attack on her self-worth and self-esteem because she is a part of me. I want to model self-worth and self-esteem, even when it's difficult.

I am in the mood for an easy breakfast; the day is already moving quickly and I want to make it easier on myself. It's cereal for all! I give two choices for everyone. Elle immediately disagrees. She wants—demands—waffles for breakfast. I let her know that I hear her *and* that today is a cereal day. I remind her that she has a choice, always.

"Elle, you can have Cheerios or the almond crunch cereal."

She immediately responds with, "I don't want cereal."

I simply say, "Okay, I hear you. I accept your choice. No cereal today."

Elle continues with her plea for waffles.

I respond with, "I honor your choice not to eat cereal."

Elle goes to school hungry. I have a moment where I feel like a terrible parent, sending my daughter to school without breakfast. I need my children to understand that I also have the right to say what works for me in any given situation. I need to show cooperation and stay true to my needs. I know that she will not suffer from missing one breakfast. I make peace with the idea that her experience of consistency and her ability to make her own decision far outweighs the guilt I feel in the moment.

> I need to show cooperation and stay true to my needs.

- *Goal met:* I decide what I want before I present anything to anybody—especially my children—and own it. I have the right to make a decision and honor my desires.

- *Goal met:* I make sure that my child's voice is heard and acknowledged. I don't always have to agree with her, but I've heard her. We are human and have the ability and right to disagree. From disagreement often comes great revelation and understanding.

We gather our things for school and pile into the car. Elle is still feeling a little discord from her choice to skip cereal this morning. We are only five minutes away from home and Elle picks a fight with Cora because Cora was "looking at her."

Cora responds, "I can look at you if I want to."

The war begins. I make a decision to stay out of it. I know that Elle is angry about her choice and wants to vent her frustration on her sister. I see this as an opportunity for Cora to stand up for herself and practice her communication skills in a safe space, with a safe person.

I focus my attention on the radio, turning it up just a little bit ... okay, *a lot*. I ignore the situation and, when they do their best to rope me into it, I respond simply.

> I ignore as much undesirable behavior as I possibly can, as long as I can stay in a good space.

"This has nothing to do with me. I know that you guys will work it out."

I trust that sometimes my best plan of action is no action. I am happy that they are learning to communication with and through each other. I just need to stand back and watch the show—or change the channel!

- *Goal met:* I ignore as much undesirable behavior as I possibly can, as long as I can stay in a good space.

When we arrive at their school, it's time to drop them off for the day. They are still irritated with each other, but there's definitely an improvement. I remind them how much I love them and to look for the good in the day!

- *Goal met:* I gently remind them, and myself, to look for the good and focus on it.

After leaving their school, I receive a phone call regarding my business. There are major issues that need to be addressed, and I immediately move into work mode. I do my best to work out all the problems throughout the day, but it proves to take a complete toll on my mind, body, and spirit.

It is now time to pick up the girls from school. I know that I need to muster up the energy once again to be in a better space than where I am currently residing. I roll down the windows, put on "old school" music, turn it up loud, and sing hard. I feel better! I remember how good I feel with my children (most of the time) and focus my energy in the direction of love and appreciation.

- *Goal met:* Even if I'm rushed, tired, or frustrated, I take a moment to realize that this is just a small speck of time in the great scheme of things. I only have a limited amount of time to be with my children and embrace the time I have with them. In the moments when I'm frustrated, I remember the great times I've had with them and that these feelings shall pass. I shift my focus and give my attention to the moments I want to create, now.

After school

I pick up the girls and they are in great spirits! They had amazing days and are feeling frisky. It is a slight challenge to keep up with their energy, but I am up for it. I join them in the "feel good" space. We laugh, joke, act silly, and sing songs the whole ride home. It's more fun to match their energy than to bring them down by telling them—actually *convincing* them—how hard and terrible this day has been for me.

- *Goal met:* I make the effort to be in a joyful space when I see them again. If I haven't seen them all day, I need to make a choice of what feels better: Stay in my frustration about work or join them in joy because we're together.
- *Goal met:* I match their energy when they are in a good space. When they are in a bad space, I focus on being the energy I want them to be.

We arrive home and I immediately feel the pressure to get dinner going, homework completed, laundry folded, and emails answered. I feel overwhelmed, underappreciated, and all alone in my quest to run this home. At the height of my frustration, my daughters ask to go to the park down the street.

I check in with my desires. I would actually love to go to the park but feel that it is impossible. I have too much to do. I decide to enlist my daughters to help.

"I would *love* to go to the park! I have to get dinner going, fold the laundry, and get my emails answered. What do you guys need to do?"

They quickly respond, "All we have to do is our homework. That's it."

"I am willing to go to the park if you guys are willing to help get these chores done."

They agree. I ask who wants to be in charge of the laundry and who wants to be in charge of dinner. They work it out between them and we all commit to doing our part to make the park outing happen.

There is a moment where I feel as if "I shouldn't have to ask for help," but I know that my children, spouse, friends, and employees are not in my head. I know that, if I want something, I need to ask for it. They can't read my mind. (Often, I can't even read my *own* mind!) I know that I need to decide what I want and ask for what I need.

- *Goal met:* I work together in cooperation, not compromise. I decide what I need to have first, and then ask them to participate or not. It is their choice.

We go to the park and I sit on the bench, taking a moment to breathe in the air and appreciate my life. I watch them laugh, run, and enjoy the moment. I watch them gather pine cones and look at the differences in each one. I marvel at their wonder of the world. I am constantly reminded to enjoy the world and the miracles of it. I smile and allow great feelings to wash over me and literally take away the worries of the world. Everything seems to move in slow motion. It feels so good. I feel alive. I feel happy.

- *Goal met:* I put myself in situations that help us all live a full life (e.g., instead of feeling frustrated over my day, we go to the park). I make a conscious decision in the moment: "What's going to feel better as a parent when I'm done?" I'm going to feel better as a parent by going to the park versus stressing over daily problems.

- *Goal met:* I see the world through my children's eyes because their eyes are clean and pure, and mine have been around for some years and have a haze over them. When I see the world through their eyes, it's all new again and all beautiful.

- *Goal met:* I am open to their exploration and experiences. It proves to be much more fun!

We are home and the girls are hesitant to get back in the routine. (I think they are feeding off of my energy.) I actually had a very good time in the park, taking time to enjoy life. It was kind of a bummer to have to come back to laundry, cooking, homework, and emails. I am highly aware and decide to shift my energy again.

"I had such a great time in the park, girls! Let's get this stuff done so we can do something fun after dinner."

By shifting my energy, the girls are compliant and finish quickly. I give Elle the opportunity to choose what we eat for dinner and gather all the necessary items to prepare it. We work together while Cora folds the laundry.

> It was important for me to be aware of my energy and make a decision to change it. When I changed it, the girls' energy naturally matched my own.

It was important for me to be aware of my energy and make a decision to change it. When I changed it, the girls' energy naturally matched my own. I want Elle to see how quickly life can change. I want her to have the experience of cooking dinner to show that she *does* have control over her food decisions; however, sometimes control looks different.

- *Goal met:* I see each experience and feeling as an opportunity for all of us to learn. I'm not teaching them; we're teaching each other.

- *Goal met:* I include my children in many conversations and activities— even as simple and mundane as laundry, dishes, baking cookies, or running errands. I want them to know that they are not an inconvenience and that we're doing this together the best we can.

Chores are now done. Dinner is cooking in the oven. Dad is on his way home. Homework begins. I do my best to stay out of the homework process as much as possible. I allow them to make mistakes and have wrong answers. I allow them to leave their homework incomplete. I allow them to experience the natural consequences of their actions regarding their education. I trust that it will be okay.

It is often challenging to do this, especially because I am "Nosey Rosie," but I know that it will not serve my children now or in the future to be a warden of their educational experience. I trust that this is the perfect time to foster intrinsic value and support their learning process.

- *Goal met:* I give them the opportunity to grow in their own time and space—free from what I believe is right for them in this moment. If I think they need to learn something right now and aren't ready to learn it, then I need to let it go.

Dad pulls into the driveway. I remember that I also need to "show up" for him. I cherish and appreciate our relationship and want it to continue to thrive and grow. I make the effort to greet him at the door, give him a kiss, and tell him how happy I am that he is home. The girls follow right behind me. I want him to know his value and worth in my life. I want him to feel the love I have for him in every possible moment so that, when we struggle with communication or decisions, it is easy to reflect and appreciate our shared love.

- *Goal met:* I model successful, loving, and honest relationships for my daughters, so they will look for the same in their own lives.

Evening

We sit down for dinner and enjoy the meal that Elle helped prepare. Everyone enjoys it except Cora. She thinks it tastes terrible and tells Elle that she is not a good cook. My husband and I look at each other and smile.

My wise husband simply says, "Elle, I really appreciate your efforts to cook dinner. I know that it was a big help to your mom and a great surprise for me. Thank you."

Cora says, "I think it sucks."

I reply with, "I'm sorry you feel that way. You are welcome to put your dish in the sink and leave the table if you are that unhappy. We are enjoying our dinner."

Cora leaves and goes to her room. I am not interested in changing Cora's behavior or words to make me, my husband, and especially Elle feel better. It is my responsibility to stay in a "feel good" space, even if Cora is not being her charming self.

> I want him to feel the love I have for him in every possible moment so that, when we struggle with communication or decisions, it is easy to reflect and appreciate our shared love.

It is my responsibility to share my appreciation and delight for the meal with Elle, regardless of Cora's input.

- *Goal met:* I help Cora feel safe in being herself. She may make a choice with which I don't agree or that I dislike, but I'm not disappointed in her. I give her enough body language, context clues, and words to show that I never think badly of her as a human being.

- *Goal met:* I focused on what I *do* want: a nice, enjoyable meal. I let Cora know what she can do if she isn't enjoying her meal: put her dish in the sink and leave.

- *Goal met:* I'm lighthearted. It's not all "drama for your mama." I have awareness that every situation is not going to dictate whether my child is a good or a bad kid, or that every drama is not going to dictate their success or failure in life.

We decide to hang out in the living room and plan Elle's birthday. We are talking about all the fun things that we want to do. Cora overhears the conversation and decides to come out and join us. She tells us what she wants to do for her big 10th birthday.

"I want to rent a limo, go to a hotel, have a slumber party with my friends, and then come home and have a big cake and lots of presents."

My husband and I are taken aback. Last year, we went out to sushi and had a cake. This year, we have upgraded to a limo and a hotel? My husband and I have completely different reactions. I think it is awesome that Cora has such a big dream for herself; he speaks to me in a low voice, under his breath.

"What are we going to do? If she wants this now, what happens next year? Is she just being a spoiled brat? Has she watched too much TV? What's going on?"

I smile and simply say to Cora, "Wow! I think that is a great idea! I love how you have big dreams for yourself. It makes me think of my own big dreams. I can make sure that you have an amazing cake and lots of presents at home. I will be in charge of that for you!"

> I want her to have bigger dreams than I can even imagine. I want all of her dreams to supersede mine and come true. That is my greatest desire for both my children.

Cora says, "That's good. What about the limo and the hotel?"

My response is simple: "I love that idea. If you really want the limo and hotel to happen, I know that you will make it happen. When you have wanted other things before, you have always come up with a great plan to make it work. If you want some ideas, I am always willing to brainstorm with you—you know how much I love to brainstorm!

"When I was an eighth grader, I wanted to rent a limo for my eighth grade dance. Your grandparents thought I was crazy. I decided to save all my money from babysitting and use it for the dance night.

"My dad was talking to his golfing friend, who happened to own a limo service—and the rest is history. I had a limo for five of my friends and myself. We had a great time. I know that, if you really want it, it will work out. I am going to make sure that you have an *awesome* cake and great presents!"

I know intuitively how important it is to believe and dream with Cora. I know that a request for a limo and a hotel is not an indication of a brat. I know my child very well. I know her beauty and grace and the love she shares with the world. I want her to have bigger dreams than I can even imagine. I want *all* of her dreams to supersede mine and come true. That is my greatest desire for both my children. I am learning how to do it every day by watching and growing with them.

- *Goal met:* I let Cora know that I support and love her dreams, regardless of anyone else's opinions or judgments. She believes and knows that anything is possible. She can count on me for support and participation. She knows that I will say what I can do and hold to the commitment. I share a story from my childhood to model a possible way for her to get what she wants.

Elle is now inspired to dream big for her birthday. We decide to look through the cake decorating books to pick out her birthday cake. Cora joins in and we have fun dreaming together. The time passes and I feel a shift in my energy. I know that I am done being a mom for the night. I am ready to have "me time" ... now.

I am ready to spend some time with my husband in adult conversation. I am ready to spend some time with myself in silent contemplation or on the Internet, catching up on Facebook. I haven't decided.

Bedtime

I love everything about bedtime! Nobody can talk me out of my love, excitement, or pure joy that comes with bedtime; consequently, rarely is bedtime ever an issue.

I am very excited to get my children to bed. First and foremost, it pertains to my happiness and well-being; then, I also want them to be happy. I am happy, regardless of their behavior or attitudes in the moment.

I look at the clock and say, "Wow! Look how fast time flies! What time is it?"

In shock and despair, the girls say, "Bedtime."

"Yep! It sure is!"

I love knowing that, in 15 short minutes, I am able to experience a meaningful connection with my children, feel good about the end of my day with my children, and have freedom to do the things that matter to me before I go to bed.

I consistently follow a predictable (and some may say strict) schedule. The schedule is not in place for my children; it is established for me. It works for me, makes me happy, and gets me excited to put my children to bed.

Both children chime in, "We don't *want* to go to bed. We aren't tired. We want to stay up with you and Daddy."

My response is purposely limited: "I know."

They think my response is the ticket to stay up.

I simply add, "Your father and I need time to share together, and I need time for myself. When I give to your father and myself, I am a better mom to you guys. I need you both in your room, lights off. You are welcome to read with your flashlight or stay awake in your bed. It's your choice."

It really doesn't matter if they are asleep. I just want them in their room, quiet, and out of my space. I need to recharge.

The years of "convincing" children that bedtime or naptime is in their best interest is over. I know that I can't—nor do I want—to set a "rules" poster above their bed, dictating exactly how they are required to sleep. When my children are tired, they will naturally close their eyes and go to sleep. I am only interested in creating a routine on which my children can depend. It is none of my business whether they close their eyes or leave them open when the lights go out.

- *Goal met:* I state what I need, why I need it, and their choices, which also work for me.

My husband and I take the girls into their room. We both have our own special routine with each girl. I remind them individually of their greatness.

I whisper in Cora's ear, "You are such a great dreamer! I love how you think up amazing adventures. I love how you take care of yourself and know that you are a gift to the world. I appreciate how much you love your sister, especially when it feels hard to love her. I am so lucky to be your mom. I love spending time with you. I will wait to see your smiling face when I wake up. Until then, know how loved you are, always."

> I am only interested in creating a routine on which my children can depend.

I whisper in Elle's ear, "I am so thankful for this day with you. I learned so much from you. I love how you make choices for yourself. I love how you are learning to communicate with your sister, especially when you are feeling frustrated. I appreciate your effort and help in cooking dinner. I can't .thank you enough for being my daughter. I love sharing this life with you. I am so proud of you and can't wait to see what tomorrow holds. You are so loved and appreciated!"

- *Goal met:* I feel good about myself as a mom. They feel good that they are our daughters. I am proud of myself.

- *Goal met:* I remind my children, every chance I get, that they are great, amazing human beings. I focus on what I love and appreciate about them.

The girls are in bed. Cora is reading by flashlight and Elle is staring at the ceiling.

I offer a final reminder to Elle: "I know that you know your body best. I know that you will do what you need to do to feel good. I trust your decisions. You are a great decision maker!"

They whisper occasionally. I let the whispers happen. I put on my earphones and listen to some wonderful music to distract me. Eventually, quiet comes from their room.

My intention is to get my needs met. I need my children to stay in their room quietly. I need to have time for myself. I need to be free from interruptions and questions for the remainder of the evening. I know that my children will get adequate sleep, especially without rules, guidelines, and enforcements dictated by me. I accept their choice to stay awake or go to sleep. I know that the natural consequences they experience will influence their future decisions.

If, by chance, my child decides to stay up for the majority of the night and has a difficult time getting out of bed, I simply say, "Wow! I know that, when I stay up too late for my body, it is hard for me to get up. When that happens, I remember how I feel in the morning and decide to close my eyes earlier. Do what works best for you. I know that you will figure it out!"

I take some time to catch up with my husband. He decides to watch an episode of *Do It Yourself* TV, and I decided to catch up on my emails. We go to bed, ready to start the next day.

I had challenges throughout the day, but I know in my heart that I did the best I could. I know that tomorrow will offer even more challenges, but I also know that I will make it through and be better for it all.

> I know that I can show up with my children in anger and frustration or show up with support and love. Both take energy. I can spend my energy one way or the other. *It's my choice.*

I know that I can show up with my children in anger and frustration or show up with support and love. Both take energy. I can spend my energy one way or the other. *It's my choice.*

I need to remember to sprinkle in fun throughout the day; it's what makes this life worth the energy and the effort. I take the time to put myself to sleep, remembering all the great moments of the day. When my daughters wake me up at the crack of dawn, I will recall those moments and start the day with inspiration, enthusiasm, and a smile.

Use these great go-to phrases and one-liners.

After 25 years, I have mastered a few great phrases and one-liners that I use frequently with children. Remembering that communication is only 7% words, the energy, voice tone, and body language all need to come together to really get the desired result.

Take some time to burn these phrases into your memory. They definitely work better than "Because I said so!" or "Don't do that!" Watch the video (referenced at the end of this section) and see exactly how I use body language and voice tonality to convey the words. In the video, notice how I always get down to eye level and establish a connection with the child before I say a word.

Here are some phrases you can use to acknowledge your child's greatness:

- "I knew you could do it!"

- "I believe in you!"
- "I am so proud of you!"
- "Good choice!"
- "You are a great decision maker."
- "You're so loving."
- "You are always so kind and thoughtful. You always think of other people."
- "That's just like you! I knew you were amazing like that."
- "That just reminds me how special you are."
- "You are always surprising me. You're so smart. Just when I think you don't know, you know!"
- "You're amazing."

Here are some phrases you can use to stay in your power in challenging situations:

- "I am not comfortable with that."
- "That doesn't work for me."
- "I don't deserve this."
- "I don't appreciate that."
- "I'm not feeling good about this."
- "I'm sorry you feel that way."
- "Excuse me?" (Use all the internal energy you can muster, which really says, "Try that approach again in a different way.")
- "I can't hear you right now. Come back and talk to me when you can speak in a way that I can hear you."
- "I am not in a happy space right now. I need to take some time for myself to get back into a good space so I can be with you. I am going to go in my room to get there and I need my space. My door is going to be shut. I will come out when I am ready. Do you understand?"

Here are some phrases you can use to offer choices, model behavior, and guide behavior:

- "You have a choice. I need you to make a decision."

- "It's your choice."

- "If it were me, I would do something different right now [fill in the blank with whatever you would do], but that's just me."

- "When you do X, it tells me Y. If you didn't mean to tell me that, you'll know next time."

- "One time, when I was in a similar situation, I handled it like this [model a possible solution for your child]."

- "Where *can* you [describe an activity, such as yell, hit, scream, fight, bite, pinch, spit, jump, climb, or play with that thing]?"

Use these responses in everyday situations.

Here is a table with common phrases that parents say and examples of how I would say the same thing differently. As you read through them, practice saying the responses out loud and notice how you can:

- Present and honor choices in every experience.

- Clearly state what you need by saying, "I need ..."

- Confirm that you are being heard by asking, "Do you understand?" (Use this when what you need isn't up for negotiation.)

- Disengage from emotionally charged situations by saying, "When you are ready ..."

- Let the child know what their behavior is communicating by saying, "When you do X, it tells me Y."

- Hold the child in their greatness by saying, "This isn't like you."

Notice how it feels to be in your power without using threats, punishments, rewards, or bribery. You may find it helpful to read through this set of examples a few times to practice.

Common Parenting Response	Heather's Response
"Please sit down. We're going to eat now."	"We are eating dinner. If you would like to eat with us, I need you to choose a seat. It's your choice."
"I'm not giving you any more money."	"I know you will find a way to get the money you need. I can help you think of some ideas if you need my help."
"You can't go play until you have finished your homework."	"I need you to finish your homework. Do you understand?"
"Clean your room so we can go shopping."	"I need to leave the house soon. Will 15 minutes be enough time to clean your room, or do you need 20?"
"Don't touch that vase!"	"That's my vase. You can play with your toys."
"Don't hit your sister!"	"If you want to hit something, you can hit the pillow."
"Keep your room neat."	"I need to have your room neat. Do you understand? I can offer helpful tips if you need them. Just let me know."
"Get this room cleaned up right now, and I mean it!"	"I need to have your room clean. Do you understand?"
"Stop arguing with me!"	"I need to talk to you in a calm space. When you are ready, let me know."
"Don't shout at me!"	"I can't understand you when you yell at me. I am more than willing to talk to you with a lower voice. Let me know when you are ready."
"Please be quiet. I can't listen to your brother when you are both talking at the same time."	"I am talking to your brother right now. I need to finish my conversation with him, and then I can speak to you. Do you understand?"
"Don't talk while I'm reading to you."	"Do you want me to read or would you rather talk? It's your choice."
"Pay attention!"	"Let me know when you are ready to pay attention. Until then, I will wait."

Common Parenting Response	Heather's Response
"Stop bothering your sister!"	"Your sister needs her space. What can you do to help?"
"Keep your hands to yourself!"	"I need you to keep your hands off my body. I need my space. Do you understand?"
"Do your chores on time or you'll be grounded."	"I need your chores completed before anything else happens. Do you understand?"
"Don't talk to me in that tone of voice!"	"This isn't like you. When you are more like yourself, let me know and I will be happy to talk to you."
"You show some respect!"	"I appreciate and respect you. When you are willing to join me in that space, I will be happy to talk to you."
"Don't you come back to this room until you can show some respect!"	"I will only speak to you with respect. I am going to my room. When you would like to have a respectful conversation, I am willing to participate."
"Don't be late coming home from school."	"I need to leave home on time if you want to go to practice. It's your choice."
"I'm not picking up your dirty clothes!"	"I need all the clothes that need to be washed to go in the laundry room. Do you understand?"
"If you can't remember your lunchbox, you're just going to have to do without."	"What happens if you choose to leave your lunchbox at home?"
"You're not going out without your coat."	"I need you to wear your coat when we go outside. Do you understand?"
"You're not going to stay in this group and act like that."	"If you would like to continue hitting, you are welcome to leave the group and go hit the punching bag. It's your choice."
"Quit breaking the rules of the game."	"I need to play this game by the rules. If you are not interested in playing by the rules, I understand. You can leave the game."

Common Parenting Response	Heather's Response
"If you can't treat my paintbrushes right, you'll just have to sit out this project."	"I need you to take care of my paintbrushes. If you choose to hurt my brushes, it tells me that you don't want to do the project."
"If you forget your permission slip, you're going to miss the field trip."	"I need you to remember your permission slip for your field trip. What are the consequences if you choose to forget your permission slip?"

See these phrases in action!

Check out the video on
Great Go-To Phrases and One-Liners

V I D E O

V I D E O

or visit
www.raiseahappychild.com/phrases

PART 4

Feel Like a Parenting Pro with These Proven Scripts

"Child of mine, I will never do for you that which I know you can do for yourself. I will never rob you of an opportunity to show yourself your ability and talent. I will see you at all times as the capable, effective, powerful creator that you've come forth to be. And I will stand back as your most avid cheerleading section. But I will not do for you that which you have intended to do for yourself. Anything you need from me, ask. I'm always here to compliment or assist. I am here to encourage your growth, not to justify my experience through you."

— *Esther Hicks, inspirational speaker and best-selling author*

Great communication is possible when we are in rapport with our children.

In this book:

- We have become clear about our roles as parents.

- We have explored the five ingredients to bring to any parenting situation.

- We have discussed how to bring this all together in a typical day.

This section brings the five ingredients together in the most common parenting situations. Heather has honed these scripts and words over years of practice.

The children mentioned in the scripts are presented as an example and a model—a way to hear real conversations between Heather and the children, condensed into one scenario. Heather presents each scenario as the parent to model and offer the opportunity to see, feel, and experience the exchange. These scenarios offer a glimpse through Heather's eyes and in her heart.

As you read through these scenarios, you will notice how Heather does two very important things:

1. Builds rapport with the child and validates their wants, needs, and feelings by saying. "I have felt that way before. One time, something similar happened to me ..."

2. Models a possible answer for the child by sharing a story from her past on how she handled a similar situation by saying, "If it were me, I would ..."

By building rapport with her child, Heather creates an energetic space where both people can be heard. For example, when you call a friend and want to complain about a situation and just be heard, it feels good when your friend empathizes with you, lets you know that they really hear you, and says, "I know. That sounds really tough. I have felt like that before." A few small words create a large amount of rapport. True communication can only happen when we are in rapport with one another.

When Heather says, "I have felt that way before. One time, something similar happened to me ...," she is positioning herself verbally to be on the *same side* as the child. She instinctively knows that communication is far more effective when we are on the same side with someone, looking at a situation in front of us. It's natural for us to do this with our friends; however, for some reason, we don't often think to talk this way with our kids.

Heather always models possible answers for children to try on for themselves. She never tells them directly what to do. By telling someone what to do, it naturally creates resistance, and Heather is always working to foster harmony and agreement. Heather is intuitively in touch with human behavior. None of us wants to be told what to do. We all want to feel free to choose our next course of action.

When I hang out at the park with my niece and nephews, I notice how parents often miss the element of rapport when talking with their children. They talk *at* their child instead of talking *with* their child.

For example, the parents may:

- *Ignore what their child is saying:* "No! I don't want to hear it right now. Go away and play."
- *Deny how their child is feeling:* "You shouldn't be crying over that little scratch!"
- *Demand that their child feel a different way:* "You had better be nice and share the swings!"
- *Tell them what to do or bark a command:* "Don't climb up the slide like that!"

All of these approaches put parents and their children out of rapport, so it's no wonder that communication feels hard at times. Notice how Heather puts herself in a position to be heard in all of her scenarios, using simple phrases like "I know" or "I have been there before."

It's also important to notice a few things that Heather *never* does. As you read these scripts, you'll notice that Heather:

- *Never* says the word "no" to a child
- *Never* loses her cool or talks to a child from a charged emotional state
- *Never* takes a position of greater authority over the child

I invite you to read through all of these scripts, even if the situation doesn't apply to your or your life right in this moment. The scripts are filled with great teachings and great wisdom. In every one, you'll see Heather's consistency when communicating with children. You'll see how her behavior is always in support of her goals.

These scripts are, in my opinion, pure genius in action.

"Mom, he won't ..."

FIGHTS BETWEEN SIBLINGS OR FRIENDS

The situation

Four-year-old Chase and seven-year-old John are arguing in the living room, escalating to a battle cry from Chase while I am busy making dinner. I have had a long day at work. Chase runs into the kitchen, crying and giving me the gory details of the episode. John follows within seconds and begins to scream "his side" of the story.

What energy am I bringing to this situation?

I am exhausted and feel overwhelmed with the stress of getting dinner on the table and dealing with fighting kids. Based on my quick assessment, I know that I need to take a deep breath and change my attitude ... quickly!

Reframe: I know that my children can work this out. I know that this is a perfect opportunity for them to practice communication in a safe space.

What do I want?

For me: I want to finish making dinner for our family and do it free from drama or fights.

For my children: I want them to be able to work this out between them without killing each other—physically or emotionally.

The script

Chase: Mommm! John won't let me have a turn on the Wii. He just hit me and took it away.

Mom: Did John hit me?

Chase: No.

Mom: Then who do you need to talk to?

Chase: John.

Mom: Am I John?

Chase: No.

Mom: I know that you can handle this. I know that you can use your words to get this settled. I'm here if you need me.

Chase: Jasonnnnn, give me a turn!

Jason: NO!

Chase: Mom, he won't give me a turn!

Mom: I have faith in you guys. Remember, you both have a choice. You can settle this together and continue to play the game, or continue to fight and turn the game off. The choice is yours. I know that you both will make a great decision!

How does it end?

- They know that I will follow through with the choices I have offered. They decide to work it out and continue to play; *or*

- They continue to fight, giving me the opportunity to follow through (actually build trust in me) with the choices I have given. I turn the Wii off and proceed to offer another choice: "The fighting is not working for me. You can go in your rooms or outside. It's your choice."

Who's in control?

Mom: I am in control of exactly what I want. I have outlined acceptable choices and, regardless of their action, will follow through. I feel good.

Children: By giving them a choice, even though I set up the choice base, they feel power over their lives. They feel empowered and safe to make a decision and know either way that I am not going to judge them.

The gift

- My children gave me the chance to trust them, and to believe that they are capable of expressing their desires and getting what each one needs from the situation without me fixing it.

- They gave me the opportunity to build trust and boundaries with them in a neutral space, free from anger and frustration.

- They taught me to stand up for what I believe in and trust that this will all work out.

This is a popular scenario.

Check out the video on
Fights between Siblings or Friends

V
I
D
E
O

V
I
D
E
O

or visit
www.raiseahappychild.com/fights

"You're not the boss of me!"

BOSSINESS AND DISRESPECT

The situation

One Saturday morning, my 10-year-old daughter Melissa was very frustrated. She knew that she was responsible for cleaning her room before she went out to play with her friends. Her equally frustrated friends were outside and eventually decided to go to the park without her. This sent Melissa over the edge. I walked by her room and asked her how it was going ... *big mistake*. She lashed out at me, ending with, "You're not the boss of me!"

What energy am I bringing to this situation?

I am frustrated. All I did was ask a question, which prompted a terrible response. I feel bad that she missed the chance to play with her friends; at the same time, I feel fine because she understood and agreed to the commitment the night before.

Reframe: I know that my daughter is respectful and caring. I know that she is frustrated with herself and her response has nothing to do with me. I need to stay in a calm, respectful, loving energy. I repeat in my head, "This is not about me."

What do I want?

For me: I want to communicate with my child in a loving and respectful manner. I want to remain "disconnected" from the emotional frustration in this moment.

For my child: I want my child to know that she is in control of her life. She always has a choice. I want her to be aware of her emotions and help her recall dialogue to use when she is frustrated.

The script

Melissa: You're not the boss of me!

Mom: You are absolutely correct.

Melissa: I'm the boss of me.

Mom: You are, and I am the boss of me.

Melissa: Yeah, so?

Mom: As the boss of myself, I know that I will feel better leaving this conversation. When you are ready to talk with the respect that I deserve, you are welcome to come to my room.

Mom walks away; Melissa comes to Mom's room 20 minutes later.

Mom: Hi there!

Melissa: I'm done cleaning my room.

Mom: Good for you!

Melissa: Sorry that I was mean to you.

Mom: Yeah, I was surprised that you were so upset with me. You usually don't speak to me that way.

Melissa: I was just mad because I had to clean my room.

Mom: Who were you angry at?

Melissa: Myself.

Mom: I get angry at myself—well, *a lot*—and sometimes I say things to others that I don't mean or wish that I would not have said.

Melissa: I just get so mad!

Mom: Sometimes when I am angry, I say, "I just need some space."

Melissa: Maybe that would work for me.

Mom: Next time you are angry, you can practice.

Melissa: Thanks, Mom!

Mom: I am so proud of you for owning your responsibility in this situation. I love you and know that you will be able to handle this when it happens again. I love you!

How does it end?

- Melissa is able to catch up with her friends at the park and play for an hour before lunch; *or*
- Melissa misses her chance to play with her friends because she took too long and naturally realizes the consequences of her actions.

Who's in control?

Mom: I am proud of myself for staying calm when my daughter was struggling with conversation and actions. I took control of the only person I could—myself—by removing myself from the hostile environment.

Child: By giving her space, Melissa was able to gain control of herself on her own. She was allowed time to gather her thoughts and experience the consequences of her choices with her friends and family.

The gift

- This experience gave us both the opportunity to practice control of ourselves.
- It gave me the chance to voice my needs and desires in a calm, assertive way.
- Melissa was allowed to move through the frustration, even in a perceived disrespectful moment, on her own. When I removed myself from the equation, the only person she could blame, or get upset with,

was herself. When she made peace with her choice, she then made peace with me.

- We are clear of our value and know that, when we say or do things that seem disrespectful, it is not our intention.

- We understand that, when we speak from anger, frustration, or fear, it will not be heard.

- We expressed our love and sincere apologies.

"If I do ..., then I get ..."

REWARDS

The situation

My five-year-old son John came to the dinner table, ready to eat. He ate the majority of his food and left a big pile of green beans on his plate. He looked at me and then informed me how it works: "Grandma says if I eat all of my veggies, then I get to have dessert!" I am appalled. This is not how the dining experience works in our home. Eating vegetables has nothing to do with getting desert.

What energy am I bringing to this situation?

I am angry with my mother. I can't believe that she has been bribing my son to eat. I already have so many issues that I bring to the table with food; I don't want to add any more to the mix!

Reframe: I know that my past is not my son's future. I know that I can calmly explain my thoughts to my son without disrespecting or undermining my mother. I know that her intention was to have my son eat healthy foods.

What do I want?

For me: I want to have a healthy, casual relationship with food. I want to remember that the food we put in our mouth as well as the thoughts we put in our head are important.

For my child: I want my child to have a positive experience with food, free from negotiation. I want him to honor food and know that it is here to nourish our bodies. I want him to understand the value in all foods—from veggies to dessert.

The script

John: Grandma says if I eat all of my veggies, then I get to have dessert!

Mom: Really?

John: Yep!

Mom: How do you feel about that?

John: Well, some veggies I like, and some I don't.

Mom: Me too! What are your favorites?

John: I like corn, salad, carrots, broccoli, and green beans with those nuts you put on them.

Mom: Oh, you mean the almonds?

John: Yea.

Mom: Well, Grandma says to eat all your veggies because she wants you to be strong and healthy. When Grandma was growing up, her mom would tell her that she had to eat all her veggies to get dessert. So that's why she says it to you.

John: But you say I don't have to eat something if I don't want to.

Mom: There are plenty of foods that I don't like and so many foods that I absolutely love. I taste them a couple of times to make sure how I feel about them. Sometimes I like cauliflower; sometimes I don't. I have to taste them to see. You are a great taster! I trust that you know your body better than I do. If you are full or don't like the way something tastes, that's your decision. You make great decisions when you eat. I couldn't be more proud!

How does it end?

- John asks for almonds to add to his green beans and eats the entire pile on his plate and gets dessert; *or*

- John decides that he doesn't want the green beans and leaves them on his plate and gets dessert.

Who's in control?

Mom: I am happy that I was able to stay calm and objective in the conversation. I am proud of myself for staying neutral to a situation that has a lot of history for me. I am in control of the food choices that I give my son as the purchaser, preparer, and presenter. I can present choices with which I am comfortable and allow John to make his own decisions based on the options I provide.

Child: John knows that he is in control of his body and food consumption. He knows that I trust him and believes that he has the power to make his own decisions about something that is personal. He knows that eating food is not conditional.

The gift

- This experience gave me the gift of letting go of my "conditions" regarding food consumption.
- It allowed us to express our dislikes and likes, and be completely at peace with our decisions.
- It gave me the opportunity to remind John, in a subtle way, how I taste food a couple of times before I make a decision about whether I like it.
- It gave me an awareness of John's likes, so I can prepare his favorites once in a while.
- He knew that I trusted his judgment and decisions, which translated way beyond food choices.

"I'm not tired."

BEDTIME

The situation

My five-year-old daughter Ashley is playing with her dolls. It is 7:30 p.m. and time for bed. I ask Ashley to check the time and she reports back that it's time for bed. She informs me that she is not tired and doesn't need to go to bed, *especially* because she is not tired.

What energy am I bringing to this situation?

It has been a long day. I am exhausted and frustrated, and I want her to go to bed so I can have some peace and quiet. I know that I am not in the greatest space to address this situation.

Reframe: Ashley is genuinely not as tired as I am. I can honor her for how she feels and know that she is not being defiant. She is just having a very good time with her dolls. She also likes to spend time with us in the evening because we are away at work all day.

What do I want?

For me: I want to have an easy transition from being "on duty" with my child to having some "me" time.

For my child: I want my child to be self-sufficient and responsible for her well-being, especially when it comes to sleep, which is something we all need in order to survive.

The script

Mom: Hey, Ashley. What time is it?

Ashley: 7:30. Time for bed.

Mom: Good job reading the clock and knowing your schedule!

Ashley: I don't want to go to bed. I'm not tired.

Mom: I understand. Sometimes, when I have to go to bed, I'm not tired either. Sometimes my mind is racing, thinking of all the things I have to do at work or even at home.

Ashley: But I'm not tired.

Mom: The great thing is that you don't have to go to sleep to go to bed.

Ashley: What?

Mom: You are more than welcome to lie in your bed and read with your flashlight, or listen to your ocean wave music. So, if you are not tired, which one sounds better to you? The book and flashlight or your ocean wave music?

Ashley: I want my book and flashlight.

Mom: Great! Jump into bed and I will bring it right over to you.

Ashley: Thanks, Mommy!

Mom: Thanks for making a great choice!

How does it end?

- Ashley stays up for another hour. She is quiet and continues to read her book, occasionally making hand puppets on the wall; *or*

- Ashley really is tired and falls asleep within minutes—flashlight on, book open across her chest.

Who's in control?

Mom: I decided that I wanted an easy transition to bed and offered choices to Ashley that were acceptable to me. I now have time for myself and feel proud for handling the situation calmly in spite of my exhaustion.

Child: Ashley has a sense of control of her life. She expressed her feelings, felt heard, and even got a simple story from her mom to know that she is not alone in her feelings. She was given a choice and allowed to decide her own destiny, even if it was only a book.

The gift

- We were challenged to express our desires and get our needs met with each other.
- We both got what we wanted.
- We were able to work together to make it happen, free from a meltdown on both sides.
- We knew and felt that we have value to each other and to ourselves.
- Although for different reasons, we both felt good about going to bed.

"I don't want to do it!"

HOMEWORK

The situation

My eight-year-old son Tom has been struggling with his homework. He comes home and wants to play instead of doing it. He has a snack and the complaints come pouring out of his mouth. He is tired, bored, and mad at his teacher. He can't do his homework and doesn't want to do it.

What energy am I bringing to this situation?

I agree with him. I am angry that the kids have two to three hours of homework after eight to 10 hours at school. I don't even work that much! I am tired, and the last thing I want to do is be the police for my child and his homework.

Reframe: I need to focus and be clear on what I want from this situation. I need to approach the subject with an open mind and heart. I take a minute to focus on my heart, feel what is important to me, and know that I am coming from a loving space.

What do I want?

For me: I want to have time with my child, free from homework responsibilities. I want to offer my support and love to encourage his growth.

For my child: I want my child to feel good about the learning process. I want him to know that he has a choice regarding this situation and that I support his decision.

The script

Tom: Mom, the teacher gave us too much homework.

Mom: Really?

Tom: Yeah. It's too much and I don't want to do it.

Mom: I get it. Well, you know that you have a choice.

Tom: No, I don't!

Mom: When I am at work, sometimes my boss tells me that I have to finish a report before I go home. Do you think I have a choice?

Tom: No, because if you don't finish the report, you will get fired.

Mom: You are so smart! That is actually one of the choices. Can you think of the other choice?

Tom: You could do the report before you go home.

Mom: Exactly! What do your choices look like when you think of homework?

Tom: I can do my homework and get a good grade, or I can skip my homework and get a bad grade.

Mom: Close your eyes and think about it. Which one feels better to you?

Tom: Do my homework and get a good grade.

Mom: Do you need me to support you in any way?

Tom: No, I can do it by myself.

Mom: I know you can. You are a great decision maker. I can't wait for you to finish your homework so we can work on that model plane together. I hope you finish fast. You are my bright boy!

How does it end?

- Tom relies on himself to get his homework completed, and starts quickly so he has more time to play in the evening; *or*

- Tom decides to skip his homework and realizes the consequences from his decision. He decides quickly that he would rather complete his homework than feel the effects of his decision from school and home.

Who's in control?

Mom: I feel good about supporting Tom in his decision. I am excited to have extra time in the evening to enjoy each other rather than being the law enforcer.

Child: Tom appreciates the ability to make his own decision based on the options he defined. He knows what he wants—good grades—and has defined what he needs to do to get what he wants.

The gift

- This experience gave me the opportunity to let go of my "perceived" control, and trust that my son will make a decision from which he will learn, regardless of what he actually decides.
- I reminded myself that this was great practice for Tom to understand and feel the effects from the decisions we made. I was glad that he was learning it with homework instead of later with a job.
- Tom made a decision that he can live with and is more likely to follow through with because *he* made it.
- He understood that I am not responsible for his homework.
- He felt the love and support, and moved quickly through his homework, so we could spend extra special time together.

SCENARIO 6

"But *you* didn't say please."

MANNERS

The situation

We decided to go to our favorite restaurant for dinner together as a family. We have three children: three-year-old Allie, the middle child Andy, and our oldest Emily. As we wait patiently for the waitress, we all decide what we want to order. The waitress arrives at our table, begins to take our orders, and ends with Allie. Allie clearly states what she wants and "forgets" to say "thank you" to the waitress.

What energy am I bringing to this situation?

I am embarrassed because my child appears to have no manners. I am feeling self-conscious and wish that she had said "thank you."

Reframe: I know that Allie is a polite child, and it is not my job to prove this to this waitress. I recall many events in the past where Allie used her manners, and I am confident that I can have a calm conversation about this situation, even in public.

What do I want?

For me: I want to enjoy my meal with my family. I want to be a positive example of kindness and appreciation.

For my children: I want my children to feel safe to be themselves in any environment. I want them to be able to express the gratitude they have in their hearts.

The script

Allie: I will have the cheese pizza.

Waitress: Great. Thanks, sweetie!

The waitress walks away.

Andy: You didn't say "thank you"!

Allie: You can't tell me what to say!

Andy: Mom, Allie didn't say "thank you."

Mom: Andy, who do you need to take care of?

Andy: Myself.

Mom: Allie, I have a question for you.

Allie: What, Mommy?

Mom: Are you glad that the waitress came to our table and asked us what we wanted for dinner?

Allie: Yes.

Mom: How do we let others know that we are thankful for their help or service?

Allie: We say "thank you," but *you* didn't say "thank you" either.

Mom: Wow! You are absolutely correct.

Allie: Did you forget like I did?

Mom: I did! What do you think we can do to feel better about this?

Allie: We can say "thank you" when she comes back.

Mom: That's a great idea. I am so proud you!

How does it end?

● The waitress comes back and we both let her know that we are thankful for her service by saying "thank you"; *or*

- Allie is determined to say "thank you" for everything for the rest of the night.

Who's in control?

Mom: I feel good "owning" my actions with my child. When I was presented with the truth of my actions, I took responsibility and turned it into an opportunity to be a positive example for my family.

Children: Andy is aware of his responsibility and owns it. Allie was given permission to "forget," allowing her to figure out a way to remedy the situation. She is proud of her idea and feels good about herself and her family.

The gift

- Allie and I were reminded to share the gratitude we have in our hearts with others.
- This experience gave us permission to "forget" politeness, an opportunity to remember, and the courage to speak our gratitude, even if it is late.
- It gave me time to reflect on my unrealistic expectations for my children—expectations that I often don't live up to myself.
- I recalled all the ways that Allie is polite and knew in my heart that she is an amazing little girl.
- I was proud of Andy for acknowledging and accepting responsibility for himself.
- I was proud that my family had the courage to speak their truth and express the gratitude in our hearts.
- We all had a great dinner, full of "thank yous."

SCENARIO 7

"Why do I have to ...?"

SHARING

The situation

My eight-year-old son Eric is playing at his friend Mark's house, who is the same age. Mark's mom Amy and I have been friends for many years. Amy has always insisted that Mark share his toys with everyone, all the time. I have given Eric the chance to decide when and where he would like to share his toys. Sometimes it turns out great; other times he has regretted his decisions. Eric is playing with his monster truck, which he brought over to Mark's house. Mark decides that he wants to play with the truck and a war breaks out. Mark wants the truck and insists that Eric must share. Eric refuses.

What energy am I bringing to this situation?

I am embarrassed that Eric won't share, but I actually agree with him in this situation.

Reframe: Eric is a kind and loving boy. He often shares his toys and even his dessert. His behavior in this moment is not a reflection of his true self.

What do I want?

For me: I want to support my child and give him the tools to work this out amicably. I want to feel good about the situation with my friend Amy.

For my child: I want him to feel free, safe, and supported to state his desires.

The script

Mark: I want to play with the big monster truck and Eric won't share it!

Eric: I was playing with it first and I wasn't done yet, plus it's my truck. I can play with it if I want.

Mom: Eric, let Mark know how you feel.

Eric: Mark, I am not done with it, plus I don't have to share with you.

Mark: You *have* to share. It's the rule!

Mom: Actually, Mark, it is Eric's toy and he has the right to say whether or not he wants to share it with you. You have the same rights. You also have the right to share your toys or not. Sometimes I share and sometimes I don't. It's your decision. Now that you both have the information you need to make your decisions, we trust that you will work this out.

How does it end?

- Mark decides to share his toys, even when Eric won't share the monster truck. Eric eventually sees how good it feels to work together and appreciates Mark's generosity; *or*

- Both boys decide not to share with each other. Eric plays with his monster truck for the remainder of the visit and Mark plays with his toys.

Who's in control?

Mom: I feel good about the information that I shared with the boys and the opportunity for them to make their own decision. I am in control of my friendship. We agreed that the boys could handle this with a little input of information.

Children: The boys are in control of their friendship and the effects of decisions they make in that friendship. The boys feel heard and empowered to decide for themselves what works, separate from each other. Each may disagree or dislike the other's decision, but they know that they only have power over their decisions, not others.

The gift

- The boys gave the adults the opportunity to stay out of it.
- We allowed them to make a choice, even when we were uncomfortable with the way it would "look" to others.
- I was proud of my son for standing up for what he believed in, especially when others disagreed.
- I was happy that he felt safe enough to express himself in the moment, detouring feelings of bitterness or resentment.
- I was proud that Mark decided to go with what felt good for him.
- The boys reminded me that I have a choice in every situation. We all win!

SCENARIO 8

"I don't want the veggies!"

MEALTIME

The situation

We go out for a "nice" dinner as a family. My husband, my three-year-old daughter Sara, and my nine-year-old son Hunter are gathered around the big, round table. Sara begins to say what she wants (and what she doesn't want). The waitress delivers our food and there is broccoli on Sara's plate. Sara despises all vegetables. She refuses to eat and, in fact, gets so mad that she throws her plate on the ground.

What energy am I bringing to this situation?

I am furious. I am embarrassed and overwhelmed. I feel a lack of appreciation.

Reframe: I need to take a breath and remember that my happiness is not dependent on my children or their experiences. I have a choice with how I approach this situation.

What do I want?

For me: I want to enjoy a nice dinner out with my family. I want to actually taste my food instead of inhaling it. I want to enjoy my family.

For my children: I want my children to have the experience of dining out as a family.

The script

Sara: I didn't want broccoli on my plate!

Mom: You are welcome to take it off and put it on this plate.

Sara: I just don't want it!

Mom: You have a choice. You can leave it on your plate or put it on this plate.

Sara: I don't want it!

Sara throws her plate on the floor.

Mom: Wow! You added your own choice. I didn't think of that one. Well, I guess you are done.

Sara: I'M NOT DONE!

Mom: When I am not done with my food, I leave it on the table.

Sara: I want my plate!

Mom: I hear you. I understand.

How does it end?

- Sara has done this before and knew that I was going to ignore her behavior and continue with my meal. She realized one more time (hopefully the last time) that when she threw her food on the floor, it told me that she was done. She understood that she made a choice not to eat her dinner, and that she would not get anything else for the rest of the evening; *or*

- Sara had a complete meltdown and we needed to walk out of the restaurant to gain composure. After Sara screamed for 10 minutes— and I patiently waited, kept quiet, and took deep breaths—she calmed herself enough to have a conversation. We went back in and she waited for us to finish our food.

Who's in control?

Mom: I am in control of my emotions, especially when the overwhelming feeling of embarrassment arises. I calmly address the situation and know in my heart that whatever she "throws" my way, I will be able to handle it.

Children: Sara is in control of her life. She understands that she has a choice in every circumstance. She begins to realize the natural consequences for the choices she makes and processes the information deeply.

The gift

- This experience gave me the opportunity to practice responding calmly to an embarrassing situation.

- It reminded me that I too have a choice: I can get mad and ruin my meal, or I can handle the situation with a calm energy and finish my meal in peace.

- I understood that the food meltdown was not about broccoli, and look forward to the opportunity to tuck Sara into bed and have a "wise moment" with her, giving her the chance to express her feelings in a neutral, safe, comfortable setting.

- Sara knew that she was heard and valued.

- I know that Sara is an amazing little girl; she just had a moment, like I often do.

- I know that I am an amazing mom. I was given a challenge and I did it!

"I never get to play."

TEAM SPORTS

The situation

My 14-year-old son Chris comes home from soccer practice and is furious. His complaints begin: The coach is unfair, the players are mean, and he never gets to play in important games. He says that he only gets to play when they are winning by so many points that they can't possibly lose, or they are losing so badly that they couldn't possibly win.

What energy am I bringing to this situation?

I am angry. I was never really good at sports, so I totally understand what he is going through. I am upset that "certain" kids get to play and my son is continually benched.

Reframe: This is really none of my business. I need to stay as neutral as possible and be a sounding board and options communicator to my son. I can do this. This is not about me.

What do I want?

For me: I want to give my support and be a calm voice of reason and understanding for my son. I want to be understanding, kind, and compassionate yet disconnected from the outcome.

For my child: I want my child to be aware of his choices and have the courage to make the decisions he wants to make. I want him to know that we support his decisions, even if I would have chosen differently.

The script

Chris: This team sucks. I never get to play!

Mom: Really?

Chris: The coach is so unfair. He only puts in the best on the team to play and the rest of us sit on the bench. It's not cool!

Mom: What are your options?

Chris: I have no options.

Mom: Is that true?

Chris: I could quit.

Mom: That is an option.

Chris: Why should I quit? I really like soccer. I am just not as good as the other kids.

Mom: It's up to you. I am just here to listen and support you. When I was on the softball team—I guess I was about 12 or 13—I was confronted with a similar situation. I had to think about my choices and make a decision that made me feel good.

Chris: Grandma Mary didn't tell you what to do?

Mom: Nope, she wasn't into sports, so she really didn't have an opinion. She may have kept it to herself. She let me decide. She was a great teacher to me, so I am going to do the same for you.

Chris: Well, I don't know what to do.

Mom: How about listing a couple of options? I will write them down, and then you can see them on paper. They won't be floating around in your head, and then you can look at them and see what feels best.

Chris: Okay. I will get some paper.

Mom: Ready. What is the first option?

Chris: Quit the team.

Mom: Okay. Next?

Chris: I could talk to the coach and ask him to let me play more.

Mom: Great. Next?

Chris: I could practice more and get better at my skills.

Mom: Great thinking. Anything else?

Chris: I could sit on the bench for the rest of the season.

Mom: That is an option. Anything else?

Chris: I think that is it.

Mom: Okay. Now, look at your list and see what feels the best.

Chris: Well, it doesn't feel good to quit. I really like soccer. It doesn't feel good to sit on the bench. I already do that and it makes me mad.

Mom: So that leaves "talk to the coach" or "practice more."

Chris: Maybe I can go to the coach and ask him what I need to do to be able to play more.

Mom: You actually did a combo of these two. Awesome thinking!

Chris: Yeah, that's what I will do. Thanks, Mom!

Mom: I knew you had the answer in you. I am so proud of the choices you make and who you are as a person.

How does it end?

- Chris talks to his coach, focuses on his coach's suggestions for improvement, and plays longer and in more games; *or*

- Chris talks to his coach, follows his suggestions, and still doesn't get time in the game. Chris decides that he enjoys playing soccer with the neighborhood kids instead of in a team.

Who's in control?

Mom: It feels good to support my son and stay out of the drama of the situation. I am in control of my emotions by leaving the decision up to my son.

Child: My son feels empowered and supported to make a decision in his own best interest. He is able to define his options, with a little guidance, and be inspired to make a choice that feels good to him.

The gift

- This experience gave us both the opportunity to learn about choice.
- I realized that I had a choice: I could get angry, go to the coach and complain, fight for my son's rights, or give my son the chance to work this out on his own, support his decision, and be at peace with the result.
- My son was given the gift of choice and the power to make a very important decision in his life without my direct input.
- He was given the chance to practice speaking his truth to authority in a safe situation that was not life altering.
- He took responsibility for himself and was extremely successful.

SCENARIO 10

"I'm scared of the monsters."

BEDTIME FEARS

The situation

My four-year-old daughter Patty is going to bed. She tells me about a book they read at school that had really scary monsters in it. She let me know that the monsters lived in the closets of little kids' rooms and came out at night to scare them. We read our normal stories, I tuck her in, and she continues her "monster talk."

What energy am I bringing to this situation?

I am exhausted. I just want her to go to sleep so I can go to bed. I am aggravated with the school for reading a monster book that scared Patty so badly.

Reframe: I know that I can gather the energy to address this fear in a calm, positive manner. I know that it was not the intention of her teacher to scare Patty and have her take the story to heart. I know that I can help Patty move in a peaceful place before she goes to sleep.

What do I want?

For me: I want to have an easy transition from activity to sleep. I want to go to bed at a reasonable time and have my bed to myself in the middle of the night. I want to be an example of strength and courage.

For my child: I want my child to feel safe in her home, especially in her room. I want my child to know that she is always protected in many ways.

The script

Patty: I don't want you to leave me and have the monsters get me!

Mom: Have you ever had problems with monsters in your room before tonight?

Patty: No, but now I know about them.

Mom: I understand how you could feel scared. Sometimes, when I watch a movie that scares me, I also get nervous when I go to bed.

Patty: What do you do?

Mom: Well, I take a deep breath and think of all the people I love, deep in my heart, and know how protected I am at all times. I know I am always taken care of in some ways that I can see and some ways that I can't.

Patty: Will you protect me?

Mom: I will always be there with love for you. I am not the only one who looks out for you. You are so amazing that, even if you had monsters in your closet, you would show them so much love that they would be your best friend by the time morning came, just like in the movie *Monsters, Inc.*

Patty: What if they come out to scare me?

Mom: When I am scared, I just say out loud, "This is my room and you are not welcome here, so leave now!" and I feel better.

Patty: So I can tell them to leave?

Mom: Yep. It's your room. You sure can!

Patty: Thanks, Mama. I love you.

Mom: Remember your amazing dreams so we can talk about them in the morning! I love you, Patty-cakes.

How does it end?

- Patty falls asleep in the next 10 minutes and sleeps through the night; *or*

- Patty calls me back to her room within 10 minutes. I ask her to recall our conversation and remind her that she is safe and sound. I hear her yell, "*Get out!*" She goes to sleep 20 minutes later.

Who's in control?

Mom: I am in control by taking the time to share and remind Patty of all the ways she is loved and protected. I am clear in my mind and heart that I want her to stay in her room, saving my sleep for the night.

Child: Patty feels in control of her room. She knows that we are here to support and love her, and that she has the tools and awareness to take care of herself when she is in an uncomfortable situation. She is aware of all the ways that she is supported and protected. She understands that she has the power to handle this situation and that we are here to support her should she need backup.

The gift

- This experience gave us the opportunity to have a moment to share our fears and work through them together.
- It gave me the chance to share my spiritual beliefs and remind Patty how loved and protected she is at all times.
- By sharing my experiences with her, it empowered her to be aware of her wants and needs, and express them through her voice.
- Patty felt a sense of empowerment and control, knowing that I was there to support her, but she was not dependent on me to protect her.
- Since I would not always be there to protect her, I wanted her to know that she can protect herself and have a voice to get help, if she needed it.

"I hate you!"

BACK TALKING

The situation

My 15-year-old daughter Alexis came home with an invitation to the "biggest" party of the year. It is on the same weekend that we have already scheduled to go out of town for our big family trip to Yosemite National Park. It is a family reunion and we have been planning this event for over two years, uniting more than 20 families. I remind Alexis of the prearranged event. She is completely enraged and begins a rant, ending with "I hate you!"

What energy am I bringing to this situation?

I am angry. I don't deserve to have my daughter speak to me in such an ugly and nasty way. I feel bad because I understand how important these parties are to teenagers; at the same time, we have been working on this reunion for years, and it is not fair to our family members not to participate.

Reframe: I know that my daughter is a very respectful communicator. I know that she is disappointed beyond words. I know that she loves me, and "hate" is never in her vocabulary. I need to stay in an empathetic space to help her define and decide on the available options.

What do I want?

For me: I want to have my desires heard and understood. I want to have a conversation coming from a space of love and clarity. I want to keep our commitments with honor.

For my child: I want my daughter to learn the tools to communicate with clarity instead of anger. I want my daughter to feel that she has a choice. I want my daughter to understand and honor the commitments we have made to our family.

The script

Mom: I hear how upset you are about this situation. I need some space from this anger right now. I will be in my room when you want to talk.

Alexis: I hate you!

Mom: I'm sorry you feel that way.

Alexis storms off to her room and Mom goes to her room. Alexis takes one hour to calm down and then comes to Mom's room.

Alexis: Mom, can we talk?

Mom: I am here for you.

Alexis: I am not happy. I just want to go to the party this weekend.

Mom: I can understand that.

Alexis: I thought I could stay home and spend the night with Amanda. Her mom said I could.

Mom: That's an idea.

Alexis: Then can I stay at home?

Mom: May I ask you a question?

Alexis: Yes.

Mom: Did you tell your cousins that you were looking forward to seeing them this weekend?

Alexis: Yes, but they would understand. This is a big party!

Mom: I didn't ask if they would understand. I asked if you made a commitment to see them this weekend.

Alexis: I did.

Mom: I know you very well. I know that when you say you are going to do something, you do it.

Alexis: I know. This sucks!

Mom: When I was around your age, I had a similar experience. I made a choice to lie to my good friend and go to my other friend's party. I'm sure you can figure out what happened.

Alexis: Your friend found out and was mad at you?

Mom: Not only was she mad, but she ended our friendship. That taught me a lot about commitments. I missed having her as a friend and regretted my choice.

Alexis: I wish we were going another weekend.

Mom: I wish we were too, knowing what I know now.

Alexis: So, my choices are that I can go camping and be happy or I can go camping and be miserable.

Mom: I know what I would pick. It's your choice.

Alexis: Mom, I don't hate you.

Mom: Sometimes we say things that we don't mean, and I appreciate you telling me. I love you and always remember the love you give me and so many others.

How does it end?

- Alexis goes camping and decides to have a great time with her cousins and family; *or*
- Alexis is grumpy at the beginning of the car ride. She gets in a good space when she gets around her cousins.

Who's in control?

Mom: I am proud of myself for staying in a calm space and holding my daughter in her greatness. I was able to disengage from an angry conversation and stay patient with my daughter's timing. I let my daughter come to her own conclusions without my direct input. I held what I wanted in my mind and heart.

Child: Alexis is clear on her options and works through them by voicing them to me. She is aware of her disrespect and acknowledges her mistake. She takes responsibility for her words and behavior.

The gift

- This experience gave me the opportunity to allow Alexis to go through her feelings and come out on the other side.

- It gave me the chance to practice my reactions to situations that immediately made me feel angry.

- My daughter was aware of the choices she had and figured it out with little guidance and limited input.

- I was able to share a story that may have helped her understand my previous choices and the consequences which which I had to live.

- We were able to have a conversation that was clear and motivated by love.

"I got a D on my report card."

GRADES

The situation

My 15-year-old son John came home from school with his report card. He handed it over and had a look of disappointment in his eyes.

What energy am I bringing to this situation?

I feel worried and anxious. I am worried that he is having a difficult time, which could affect his college applications and so much more.

Reframe: I can consciously change my worried feelings to hope and be with my son in a space of understanding. I take a deep breath and connect in a space of love.

What do I want?

For me: I want to be clear, present, and honest in my communication. I want to understand my son and support him as best as I can.

For my child: I want my child to know and feel that his worth is not determined by a grade in school. I want him to remember that he is an amazing, bright, intelligent child on Earth for a reason.

The script

John: I got a D in chemistry and a C in math.

Mom: Really?

John: Yeah. I'm just no good in those classes.

Mom: In what classes *do* you feel good?

John: Well, I really like English and theater.

Mom: Great! Did you give your best "you" in chemistry and math?

John: I did the best I could in chemistry, but I know that I could do better in math. I just need to ask my teacher for some time after class to ask a couple of questions.

Mom: Well, it sounds like you know what you need to do.

John: You're not mad?

Mom: Nope. This is your life. I know that you will do great. You already have and you are only 15! I didn't get As in every class. Some courses didn't fill me up and some did. That's what school is about: the opportunity to test what you like and what you don't. When I do my best, that's all I can do.

John: Thanks, Mom!

Mom: You are so welcome. By the way, I got a D in chemistry and your grandpa said the same thing to me. Look how great I turned out! I love you.

How does it end?

- John has a D on his permanent record, talks to his math teacher, brings up his grade to a B, and still gets into the college of his choice; *or*

- John looks at school through a new set of eyes. He realizes and embraces his real passion—writing screenplays—and goes to college with his passion ignited.

Who's in control?

Mom: I am clear with my expectations that John does his best. I feel good. I was honest and clear with our talk and feel connected to myself and to my son.

Child: John is in control of his life. He understands his choices and takes responsibility for himself. He knows what he needs to do to feel better and do his best.

The gift

- This experience gave us the opportunity to be okay with ourselves.
- It gave me the chance to forgive myself as a teenager. (It's no coincidence that we both got a D in chemistry!)
- John knew that I love and support him in everything he does.
- He tapped into his wisdom to remedy the part of the situation that he wanted to change.
- I was reminded of what a great role model my father was.
- I smiled, knowing that, over 20 years later, the D did not affect my success in any way.
- John was relieved that I was not expecting him to be great at every subject, and knew in his heart that I just wanted him to share *his* greatness with the world.

SCENARIO 13

"Whatever!"

POUTING

The situation

My eight-year-old daughter Lisa is angry with our choice to go to a special dinner without her. She loves to go to "fancy" dinners with my husband and me. We decided to have a date night, which did not include Lisa.

What energy am I bringing to this situation?

I am feeling guilty. I know how much Lisa loves going to dinner with us. I feel bad that I have been working all week and that she feels left out and sad.

Reframe: I spend a lot of time with my daughter. We often bring her to our fancy restaurants so she can have a great dining experience. It is important to take care of my relationship and myself by having a night "off." I know that, if I let go of the guilt, she will naturally adjust to the situation.

What do I want?

For me: I want to enjoy a nice dinner with my husband, having an adult, kid-free conversation. I want to nurture my relationship with my husband. I want to be an example of someone who is taking care of her needs.

For my child: I want my daughter to understand how important it is to take care of yourself and your relationship with your partner. I want my daughter to know how much we value her and appreciate her wanting to spend time with us.

The script

Lisa: It's not fair! I want to go eat with you and Daddy!

Mom: I understand. You do get to pick dinner for yourself tonight. You can have pizza or mac-n-cheese.

Lisa: Whatever.

Mom: I deserve to have a respectful conversation. When you are ready, I am here.

Lisa: Whatever!

Lisa runs to her room, slams the door, and starts crying. We are ready to leave, and Lisa is still in her room. I go to Lisa's room and knock on the door.

Mom: May I come in?

Lisa: Yes.

Mom: I just wanted to let you know that we are leaving. I love you and I am so sad for our conversation earlier. I know that you are always so respectful, and usually pick better words to communicate your feelings. I want you to know that we love you and we will be home later. Miss Allison is downstairs and ready to fix you dinner when you are ready.

Lisa (crying): I just want to go with you!

Mom: I know. Sometimes my mom and dad would go to dinner without me. I felt left out and not important—except your grandparents would go to yucky dinner places, so I didn't want to go for the food. I just wanted to be with my parents.

Lisa: What did you do?

Mom: Well, my mom and dad were going whether I liked it or not, so I decided to have the best time I could with my babysitter ... and I did. She would play all the games my parents didn't want to play. We would make special art projects, and sometimes even make brownies!

Lisa: She was a good babysitter?

Mom: Yep ... like Miss Allison. Hey, I bet we have some brownie mix in the cabinet. Maybe you could surprise me!

Lisa: Okay. I love you.

Mom: I love you, baby! We will be home late, but I will come in and give you a kiss when we get home.

How does it end?

- Lisa has a great time with Miss Allison and makes amazing brownies to surprise us when we get home; *or*
- Lisa has a rough night missing us, but feels better when we get home and give her a kiss.

Who's in control?

Mom: I am proud of myself for staying calm and not letting Lisa's behavior affect my mood or decision to go out with my husband. I let her know that I deserve a respectful conversation and modeled a respectful conversation, even in conflict. I am able to leave in peace and enjoy an amazing dinner with my husband.

Child: Lisa has control of her happiness. She knows that, if she makes a choice to speak disrespectfully, our conversation will end and then resume when we can have respectful communication. She knows that we are going out to dinner without her. She has a choice: to enjoy her time with the babysitter or not.

The gift

- This experience gave me the opportunity to declare what I need and follow through with the action.
- It made me aware of my hidden feelings of guilt, the ability to work through the feelings, and follow through with my desires in peace and happiness.
- My daughter was given the chance to express her desires and work her way through her emotions to come to a place of peace with the situation.

- She was aware of and acknowledged the importance of nurturing self and our relationships.
- She knew that attending dinner didn't determine our love and respect for her.

SCENARIO 14

"Is Santa real?"

LYING

The situation

My six-year-old daughter Jade comes home from school right before winter break. She is noticeably bothered, and I'm not sure why. She immediately goes to her room and says that she needs space. I give her time and remind her that I will be in the kitchen if she needs me. She eventually comes out to talk to me, and tells me that the kids at school are making fun of her because she believes that Santa Claus is real. She looks at me and asks one question: "Is Santa real?"

What energy am I bringing to this situation?

I feel horrible and heartbroken. I preached over and over to my children how important it is to tell the truth, and here I am about to tell my child that I have lied to her about something that means so much to her.

Reframe: My intention is to give my daughter a loving experience of magic and joy. I know that I can tell the truth and recover from this situation.

What do I want?

For me: I want to celebrate the "magic" of Christmas with my daughter. I want to be truthful and honest about Santa Claus. I want to communicate from a loving place, absent of guilt.

For my child: I want my child to understand my intention for lying. I want her to have an appreciation and love for Christmas, even if Santa is not real.

The script

Jade: Is Santa real?

Mom: When you ask that, what do you mean?

Jade: Does the Santa at the mall come down our chimney, eat our cookies, and leave me presents?

Mom: No, that Santa doesn't do that.

Jade: Then why did I go and sit on his lap and ask him for presents?

Mom: Well, honestly, it's a tradition that many families do over the years.

Jade: But it's a lie.

Mom: Technically, you are right.

Jade: Why did you lie to me?

Mom: Well, I didn't think of it as a lie. I thought of it as magical or pretend.

Jade: But you said he ate our cookies.

Mom: You are right.

Jade: You always tell me to speak my truth. You didn't do that. You lied!

Mom: You are right.

Jade: Why did you lie?

Mom: Well, it has been a tradition for years to pretend that there is a Santa Claus. The man we now know as Santa Claus is based on a man who lived many centuries ago. He was a saint—Saint Nicholas—and he gave many presents to those in need, and helped many children and families throughout his life. We have kept the tradition to remind all of us about the hope, wonder, and miracles that happen in the world. That was our intention for continuing the tradition with you.

Jade: Well, why didn't you just say that from the beginning?

Mom: You're right. I wish that I would have done it differently. I am learning how to do things in life, just like you. Sometimes I wish that I had done things differently, but I can't change them now. All I can do is learn and grow from it.

Jade: So now we will not have Santa anymore?

Mom: Well, maybe not the way we have had Santa in the past. I think this is a chance for us to see and experience Santa in a different way.

Jade: Like how?

Mom: Well, the intention of St. Nick was to provide a little hope and wonder for those who didn't have much to hope for. What if we looked at Christmas as a time to honor what St. Nick was doing for others? What if we were "Santa" to others and to each other? What if we made Christmas a special time for *us* to be Santa?

Jade: Does that mean that I won't get presents anymore?

Mom: Absolutely not! You don't get presents because of Santa, or if you are good or bad. You get presents because you dream of things that you want in your life, and your family and friends do everything in their power to honor and support your dreams. That is why you get presents.

Jade: Oh, I get it! So I can also help other people's dreams come true by being Santa.

Mom: Exactly.

Jade: That sounds like fun!

Mom: It sounds like a *lot* of fun!

How does it end?

- Jade is super excited with all of the possibilities that lay ahead. She has come up with many ways to be "Santa" to our friends, family, and even the homeless man on the street corner; *or*

- Jade returns to school and says that *she* is Santa, confusing all her friends!

Who's in control?

Mom: I am proud of myself for owning my mistake about lying, and allowing my child to experience me as a human, still learning and growing. I also honored her truth in the experience. I took the opportunity to create a new tradition—one that feels better to me—and included my child in it. I experienced the magic and miracles of Christmas in a new way.

Child: Jade knows the value of the truth, and understands and appreciates the meaning of Christmas even more now. She knows that she still has the power to manifest her dreams and desires *and* can help others by inspiring and uplifting them when she is "Santa."

The gift

- We learned a very valuable lesson in truth.
- We were able to see Christmas and Santa in a new way that was true, felt good, and inspired others on their journey in this life.
- We were given the opportunity to learn and grow together.
- We honored each other's feelings.
- We were reminded of the true meaning of Christmas and were able to create the experience that we both desire.

SCENARIO 15

"You're an asshole."

SWEARING

The situation

My 10-year-old son Alex is walking in the grocery store with me, and he spots his friend Max on the next aisle. They exchange some words. I'm not paying too much attention until I hear my son scream across the store, "You're an asshole!" He is laughing and smiling; I am not.

What energy am I bringing to this situation?

I am embarrassed and humiliated. It's a small town and word always gets around. I am angry that this is how my son chooses to communicate in a public place. I am angry with myself because I swear at times and know that I have added to this situation. I know that now is not the time or place to talk about this. I am too angry and need to get out of this store!

Reframe: I know that my son's intention is not to be disrespectful or embarrass me in the store.

What do I want?

For me: I want to release my guilt for the years of swearing I have done in front of my child. I want to be aware of my communication and how it affects others.

For my child: I want my child to be able to communicate his feelings and thoughts clearly in any situation, and understand the language that is acceptable in each environment.

The script

We are home now. I have had time to cool down and regroup my thoughts.

Mom: So, Alex, can we have a moment?

Alex: What kind of moment?

Mom: A moment to share some thoughts together.

Alex: Umm, okay.

Mom: I was kind of shocked to hear your conversation with Max in the grocery store.

Alex: What part?

Mom: The part where you called him an asshole.

Alex: Oh, Mom. I didn't mean it. I was just messing with him. We say that to each other all the time!

Mom: I get it. I know that I swear at times.

Alex: At times?

Mom: Okay. I know that, when I get angry, I can sound like a sailor or a pirate!

Alex: That's true.

Mom: Well, you helped me see how inappropriate it is to swear like that in a place where other people are minding their own business.

Alex: So are you saying that I am not allowed to swear?

Mom: I am saying that you have a choice in every situation, as I do. I am going to make an effort to pay attention to the words I choose in public places. I know that I would feel terrible if a little boy or girl heard those words and repeated them to their parents.

Alex: I would also feel bad.

Mom: I know you would. I can't stop you from swearing. I am not interested in stopping you. I am letting you know what works for me. I appreciate when you communicate with me and around me, free from swear words. Does that make sense?

Alex: Okay, Mom. I get it.

Mom: Thanks. I knew you would!

How does it end?

- Alex is mindful of our conversation and decides to save his "sailor" talk for his friends in private; *or*

- Alex slips up and swears in front of me again. I simply remind him that we had a conversation and he agreed to it. He gets it.

Who's in control?

Mom: I have accepted responsibility for my swearing and made a commitment to myself to be more aware. I no longer feel guilty for the "pirate" mouth I often have. I controlled my anger by waiting to discuss the situation when we got home. I am proud that I offered my child a choice.

Child: My child has been given permission to be in charge of his own voice. He understands how his actions can affect others in a negative way and knows that he has the tools to make a conscious decision.

The gift

- This experience gave us the opportunity to share with each other in a safe, understanding environment.

- We understood our participation and have committed to being more aware of ourselves.

- My child knew that I was not there to tell him what to do.

- He knew that I trusted him to make a wise decision, and he respected me to acknowledge and appreciate my needs in the situation.

"Meltdown on Aisle 7."

PUBLIC TEMPER TANTRUMS

The situation

My four-year-old son Devin and I are shopping. On the way home, we stop at Target to pick up a few items. Devin is clearly done with the shopping experience. I decide to hurry through the store so we can leave quickly and get home. I make the mistake of going by the DVD aisle, which Devin notices immediately. He lets me know that he wants to get the Scooby-Doo DVD ... *now*. I tell him that we are in a hurry and don't have time to look today. He has a complete meltdown. The entire store is now aware of Devin's desire for Scooby-Doo.

What energy am I bringing to this situation?

I am embarrassed and not sure how to handle this situation in public. I am frustrated and tired from the day. I just want to go home.

Reframe: I know that I can handle this. I really don't care what the people in Target think of my child or me. I need to get a clear game plan in my head and stay as calm as possible.

What do I want?

For me: I want to get the rest of the items that I need from Target, check out, and go home. I want to be able to clearly communicate my desires and work to acknowledge and consider my son's desires as well.

For my child: I want my child to feel heard and acknowledged. I want him to be aware of his choices. I want to support his decision.

The script

Devin: I want Scooby-Doo.

Mom: I understand.

Devin: Mommmmmmeeeee! *I want Scooby-Doo!*

Mom: I hear you. Can you hear me?

Devin: Nooo!

Mom: I'll wait.

Devin: I just want the movie.

Mom: You have a choice. We can talk about this in the store or out of the store.

Devin: I just want Scooby-Doo.

Mom: If you continue screaming, you are making a choice to go out of the store to talk. Do you understand?

Devin: Yes, but I WANT SCOOBY-DOO.

Mom: I accept your choice. We will go outside the store to talk about this.

Devin: NOOOOO! I just want the movie ... that's all!

Mom: You made your choice and I am standing by it.

Mom takes Devin to the car to talk once he gathers himself.

Mom: When you are able to talk, I am listening.

After five minutes of crying, Devin calms down.

Devin: I am ready to talk.

Mom: What would you like to say?

Devin: I want Scooby-Doo.

Mom: Trust me. There is nothing I want you to have more than the Scooby-Doo DVD right now. Did you see the list in my hand?

Devin: Yes.

Mom: Was a Scooby-Doo DVD on my list?

Devin: I don't think so.

Mom: That's right. I didn't plan to get Scooby-Doo today. Do you have a way to get your Scooby-Doo DVD?

Devin: I don't have any money.

Mom: Can you think of any other ways to get your DVD?

Devin: I don't know.

Mom: What if we went through the rest of the store, gathered all the items we need, and think of different ways that you could get that DVD?

Devin: But I want it today!

Mom: Well, we still have eight hours left in today. That's plenty of time.

Devin: But I want it *right now*!

Mom: I hear you. I'm ready to go in the store and think up some ideas.

Devin: Okay.

How does it end?

- Devin comes up with an idea to call his grandma and ask her for the DVD. Grandma tells us to pick it up and she will pay for it later; *or*

- Devin gets tired of thinking up ideas, becomes distracted, and completely forgets about Scooby-Doo; *or*

- Devin never forgets about Scooby-Doo and talks about it until he goes to bed.

Who's in control?

Mom: I am proud of myself for staying in a calm space, even when I felt completely out of control. I stayed true to myself by offering my child a choice, and then honoring his decision. I took the time, even though I was exhausted and frustrated, to go to the car and give him the time he needed to gather himself. I stayed true to my desires by going back into the store and gathering the rest of my items. I remained neutral to his desire for the DVD and allowed him the opportunity to figure it out for himself.

Child: Devin was given the choice to talk in or out of the store. When he decided to go outside, somewhat by default, he was given the space to allow his emotions to run and exit his body. He was reminded of his power to create his own destiny and was given the opportunity to work it out on his own. He was also made aware that things we want can come from various avenues. I am not his only way to receive the items he desires. He is challenged to think outside of the box if he really wants the DVD, or let it go if it's not that important to him. The choice is his.

The gift

- When I let go of the labels that I have been conditioned to put on my child (e.g., "He's just being a brat," "He is spoiled rotten," or "He just wants his way"), I can see the truth of the situation.

- He was tired. I was tired. We were both in an undesirable emotional state.

- I was given another opportunity to practice what I wanted in a desperate situation.

- The experience gave me the chance to disregard external judgment and focus on my needs in the moment.

- I am pleased that I gave my son the chance to express his frustration, in his own time. Even though, in the moment, it felt slightly inconvenient for me, it was much easier to go to the car versus staying in the store for the event.

- My son was reminded of his ability to choose at any given moment and his power to create his desires.

- I was able to get in and out of the store with the items I desired (with only a five-minute intermission in the car).

SCENARIO 17

"Uh oh ..."

POTTY TRAINING

The situation

My two-year-old daughter Amber has shown interest in going potty on the "big" toilet and seems ready to train. She has been doing well, but when she is playing with her friends, she has "uh oh" moments. Now she is covered in urine, making each Lego float. Oh, it's not just urine this time. She adds a bonus surprise ... a little poop!

What energy am I bringing to this situation?

I am annoyed, tired of cleaning urine off the floor, tired of cleaning toys soaked in urine, and want to give up.

Reframe: I know that Amber is ready for the potty. She has been doing great. I know that it takes time and patience to make it through this process. I know that she will get it soon. I need to focus on the great feeling of never buying diapers again!

What do I want?

For me: I want to do less laundry and clean the floors once a week instead of twice a day. I want to support and love my child through this experience.

For my child: I want my child to wear dry clothing while she is playing with her friends. I want her to be aware of her body, even when she is having fun with a friend.

The script

Amber: Uh oh, Mommy. I went pee pee in my panties.

Mom: Wow, that's surprising!

Amber: I went poop too!

Mom: Hmmm. What are you going to do?

Amber: You need to clean me.

Mom: I didn't poop and pee on you. You pooped and peed on you. When I have an accident, I have to clean myself.

Amber: But I don't want to clean myself!

Mom: It's your body and your mess. I will be here to help you, if you need it. I know you can do this!

Amber (sobbing): I don't like it. I don't like to clean my poop!

Mom: I don't like cleaning my poop either. When I am playing with my friends, I make sure that I go potty so I don't have an accident. Then I won't have to clean myself.

Amber reluctantly cleans herself.

Amber: I am done.

Mom: Where do your dirty clothes go?

Amber: In the laundry room.

Mom: You are so smart. I know that you will remember the potty next time!

How does it end?

- Amber puts her clothes in the laundry room, helps her mom clean the toys and floor she peed on, and makes an effort to go to the bathroom so she doesn't have to clean herself and her mess again; *or*

- Amber has another accident and she cleans herself each time, with Mom watching for moral support.

Who's in control?

Mom: I have control of my thoughts. I am able to keep my frustration under control. I allow Amber to take care of the situation without me attempting to control her.

Child: Amber is inspired, through action, to be aware of her body while she is busy playing. She is in control of her time and enjoyment. She understands that it is her responsibility to clean herself. She begins to understand the power of choice. She can take a few minutes to go potty or many minutes to clean herself.

The gift

- We were given an opportunity to grow from this experience.
- I was able to practice patience, even though I knew that it would have been much easier and faster for me to clean Amber than wait for her to do it herself.
- Amber was aware of the natural—not forced—consequences of soiling her clothes. She knew that she would have to clean herself and the mess she created.
- She understood that I was there to support her and believed that she could go potty and take care of herself.
- I felt good because I stayed out of it.
- We were both proud of ourselves.

"I'm *not* sorry!"

APOLOGIES

The situation

My 11-year-old daughter Maria is playing hide-and-go-seek on the playground with a little boy named Carter. Maria is running from Carter. He grabs her hoodie to catch her. It startles her and she pushes Carter down. Both are angry, crying, and blaming each other for their pain. They come running to the bench where I am sitting.

What energy am I bringing to this situation?

I am peaceful, sitting and minding my own business, and honestly can't be bothered by the drama.

Reframe: I am going to stay in this space of peace and calm, regardless of what is going on with the kids.

What do I want?

For me: I want to enjoy the sun on my skin, sinking into this bench with peace and quiet.

For my children: I want them to work this out with as little input from me as possible. I want them to know that I support them and that they can take care of this situation without me.

The script

Maria: Mom, Carter pulled my hoodie and choked me. He could have killed me!

Carter: She pushed me down. She *has* to say sorry!

Mom: Maria, why are you talking to me? This has nothing to do with me. Carter, nobody *has* to say anything.

Maria: Carter, you are not supposed to pull on my hoodie. That's not how you play.

Carter: That's how *I* play. You have to say sorry for pushing me.

Maria: But I'm not sorry!

Carter: Then I am not going to play with you.

Maria: Fine. I'm not going to play with you either.

Mom: Great! You both have decided not to play with each other. I think you both made a great decision. Go and have fun playing by yourselves. Bye!

How does it end?

- Maria and Carter venture off on the playground, going their separate ways and enjoying the rest of their time; *or*
- Maria and Carter have a private conversation, away from me, and resolve the issue. They resume playing together as if nothing happened.

Who's in control?

Mom: I am proud of myself for staying calm and at peace. I am in control of my reaction to the situation and, the more I stay out of it, the more at peace I feel.

Children: Both children feel a sense of empowerment by expressing their feelings and being allowed the "space" to work it out for themselves.

The gift

- This experience gave me the opportunity to practice staying out of drama that has nothing to do with me.

- It reminded me that sometimes I am also not sorry in a situation in which I often feel "forced" to apologize.

- It reminded me that saying sorry when I'm not just makes me more mad, bitter, and resentful.

- The children taught me that sometimes it's better to go our separate ways, regroup our thoughts, and come together when we are in a better space.

- The children felt good about handling it on their own (with a little guidance) and can reflect on this time when they are in a situation in which I am not able to help them.

- They were empowered ... and I was at peace!

"I am *not* …!"

LABELS

The situation

My seven-year-old son Brad is sent home with a "red" card from school. He gives me the card and proceeds to tell me about his "red" day. He is upset and frustrated because the kids at recess said that he is mean and they are not going to play with him. The teacher interjected and added, "Brad, if you were nice to your friends instead of being mean, they would like you and play with you." Brad is very angry.

What energy am I bringing to this situation?

I am defensive. I am wondering what happened at recess for the kids to call him mean. I am sad that my child is angry, upset, and longing to belong with his friends.

Reframe: I know that my child is kind and loving. I know that the most important thing for me to do is stay clearheaded and keep my thoughts moving towards love and support for my child.

What do I want?

For me: I want to be there emotionally for my child and leave my own "recess memories" out of the conversation.

For my child: I want Brad to remember that he doesn't have to "be" a certain way for people to like him. I want him to feel his value and worth on this planet.

The script

Brad: I got a "red" card and it's stupid! The kids were calling me mean. I am not mean. I just wanted to do something else.

Mom: I get that.

Brad: Then, my teacher said that I was mean and the kids won't play with me unless I am nice.

Mom: Do you think that is true?

Brad: No. There are lots of kids who are mean, and people play with them all the time.

Mom: I know that when I am mean to a friend, we take some time away from each other. We talk and work it out, and then we are friends again.

Brad: Does your friend give you a "red" card for being mean?

Mom: No. We don't get cards to make us feel even worse about it. We just work it out.

Brad: But does she call *you* mean?

Mom: Sometimes, but I know that's not who I am. I know that we are just upset and frustrated. I know it's not true.

Brad: How do I play with the kids so they don't think that I am mean?

Mom: I only play with friends who I enjoy playing with. If people say that I am something I am not, I don't play with them. You have to decide if you enjoy spending time with those friends.

Brad: I don't really like playing with them, but I don't want to be alone.

Mom: Sometimes when I let one friend go, I am alone for a little bit, and then a new friend shows up!

Brad: I hope a new one comes. I'm not going to play with them for a little while and see.

Mom: What I know for sure is that you are an amazing boy, a good friend, and a good decision maker. I know that this will work out for you. I am here for you always.

Brad: Thanks, Mom!

How does it end?

- Brad takes a break from the "cool kids" and is able to find a new friendship that better matches his wants and needs; *or*
- Brad takes a break from the "cool kids" and realizes that he really does like playing with them and he just had a bad day.

Who's in control?

Mom: I am proud of myself for staying out of the drama of the situation. I gave Brad clear examples of how I choose to handle these situations and allowed him to make is own decision. I stayed in a clearly defined space of "knowing" that my child is not mean and may have mean moments, but inherently he is loving and kind.

Child: Brad feels in control of his choices and safe in his decisions. He sees the truth for himself and maps out a plan on his own.

The gift

- Brad gave me the gift of wisdom regarding "labels" that I put on others or myself.
- He reminded me that labels are not "who" we are; they are just a way we define the actions that are taking place.
- He let me know that the "red" card did not help him feel better about the situation.
- This experience gave us the opportunity to be reminded that our actions do not define us as human beings.
- I was inspired by the courage Brad showed to be open to letting go of a friendship that was not working, and then being open to a new friendship.

"Can I have a sticker for …?"

REWARD/CHORE CHARTS

The situation

My six-year-old son Jack comes home from school with a sticker chart that his teacher made, highlighting all of Jack's chores and responsibilities in our home. Jack informs me that we are supposed to put a sticker in each column when he does that task. He lets me know that, when he has filled up the column, I need to give him a surprise.

What energy am I bringing to this situation?

I am very angry. Jack is a member of this house and he already knows that we all have our "chores" to do—some more than others. Now he expects me to buy stickers, keep track of his every move, hold him accountable, and reward him for participating in our family? *Ridiculous!*

Reframe: I can feel this anger in my belly. I know that I need to take at least 10 minutes to calm down. I am going to the bathroom, splash some cool water on my face, and come into a better space where I am cool, calm, and collected.

What do I want?

For me: I want to share my opinions with my child in a calm space, free from blame and judgment.

For my child: I want my child to know that his contributions to this family are valued and appreciated, always. I want him to be inspired and intrinsically motivated to participate in family chores and responsibilities.

The script

Jack: Mom, Ms. Sterling gave us these charts to bring home today.

Mom: How exciting!

Jack: Yeah. When I make my bed or get dressed or brush my teeth, I get a sticker. Then, at the end of the week, you give me a prize.

Mom: That's interesting. I have a question for you.

Jack: What?

Mom: You do all these things so great already, and you know how proud I am of you. Right?

Jack: Yep!

Mom: Remind me why I need to give you a sticker for all the great things you do already?

Jack: So I can get a prize at the end of the week.

Mom: What kind of prize are you thinking about?

Jack: Maybe go to the store and get a toy, go to the beach and play, or go play at the park.

Mom: We already do all those things—just because you are you, and not because of the chores you do. Remind me why we need a chart.

Jack: Because it's fun!

Mom: I'm glad that you think it will be fun. Go ahead and do that. You could use your stickers and find treasures to give yourself from your room or even outside.

Jack: No, *you* are supposed to give me the stickers and the prize.

Mom: I love you and I am so proud of how you take care of yourself. I really appreciate all the help you give to keep our house healthy and happy. I don't need a chart to tell me how great you are. I already know!

How does it end?

- Jack decides to do the chart himself and realizes that it's too much work to keep up with it; *or*
- Jack realizes that his mom is not going to participate in this activity and decides to forget about the chart.

Who's in control?

Mom: I am proud that I kept my communication in a positive space, leaving judgment regarding the situation out of the conversation. I stated my opinion in a loving way, complimenting my son at the same time. I was clear that I would not participate in this project and felt good about it.

Child: Jack has the power to make his own decision. He feels good about having the option to do the chart. He feels creative and empowered.

The gift

- This experience showed me that, when I let go of my "agenda" blame and judgment, I can approach a situation from a win-win perspective.
- It reminded me to take a few minutes to "get my head on" before I talk to my child about a subject that obviously pushes a hot button for me.
- This was an opportunity to share how thankful I am for all the help he provides in our family and how much I really love and adore him!

"She said that I'm not her friend!"

FRIENDSHIP

The situation

My nine-year-old daughter Susie decides that she is going to have a slumber party for her birthday. We work on the invitation list, gather all of the necessary party supplies, and make a cake. The big night comes and our house is full of sleeping bags, makeup, candy ... and 10 little girls! They are all having a great time, and then it happens (there is always one in the group): Julie shouts out to the entire party, "I'm not your friend, Susie!" The party immediately divides and war is declared.

What energy am I bringing to this situation?

I am instantly transported back 30 years to my first slumber party. I am sad for my daughter. I want this to be a great experience for her. I am angry at Julie for hurting my daughter on her special day.

Reframe: I know that this is not about Julie or her actions. This is a chance for my daughter to practice what she is going to do in these types of situations in the safety of her home. I am here to support her and allow her to walk through this fire alone (well, with a little guidance).

What do I want?

For me: I want to stay as neutral as possible and allow my daughter to spread her wings. I want to cheer her on from the sidelines.

For my child: I want my daughter to have the support she needs from me. I want her to embrace her courage and inner wisdom to stay true to herself and her desires.

The script

Julie: I'm not your friend, Susie!

The room divides and it's "us" against "them."

Susie: I don't care!

Julie: We are going to go play in the other room, away from you guys.

Susie to Julie: So?

Susie to Mom (in private): She said that I am not her friend. She is ruining my party!

Mom: Hmmm. That's too bad. What are you going to do now?

Susie: I don't know what to do.

Mom: What are your options?

Susie: Well, I can talk to her in private and make up, or I can tell her to go home.

Mom: Sounds like a big decision.

Susie: It is! What should I do?

Mom: Which one feels better to you?

Susie: Well, I don't want to tell her to go home because that would be mean and the other girls might get mad at me.

Mom: How does it feel when you think of her staying at the party?

Susie: It doesn't feel good. She always tries to pick fights with us. I knew I shouldn't have invited her. I just didn't want to be mean.

Mom: Sometimes I make decisions that I know are not good for me just so I don't look mean. What I know for sure is that I have better experiences when I listen to my heart and go with what feels good to me—not with how I look.

Susie: Okay. Thanks, Mom. I am going to go talk to Julie.

How does it end?

- Susie talks to Julie in private. Julie decides to change her attitude and presence in the party. She stays and they have a great time; *or*
- Susie talks to Julie and they decide that Julie needs to go home. Julie calls her mom and leaves the party.

Who's in control?

Mom: I am proud of myself for staying out of it and still being a strong support for my daughter. I kept my feelings out of the situation.

Child: Susie was challenged to stay true to her heart's desires. She created options and decided how she was going to handle the situation. She initially hesitated to speak her truth, and then opted to walk through the fire. She was proud of herself for having the courage to stand up for what she wanted, even if she was standing alone.

The gift

- This experience gave us very unique gifts.
- Susie reminded me to stay true to my heart and my desires, even when it looks mean.
- As Susie picked her options, I was instantly reminded that we all have a choice.
- I was proud to see Susie initiate communication without my direction.
- Susie was given the opportunity to practice staying true to herself and her heart.
- She has added to her confidence and is proud of herself.

"He said that I'm fat and ugly!"

HURT FEELINGS

The situation

My eight-year-old daughter Maddy comes home from school and is not her normal, cheerful self. I wonder what happened. Does she need to talk? A big tear streams down her face. She says one sentence: "Adam, in my class, was singing 'Maddy, Maddy, she's a fatty. Oh, and she's ugly too!'"

What energy am I bringing to this situation?

I take a moment to check in with myself. I too was overweight as a child and was absolutely terrorized every day at school. I am sad, angry, and disgusted all at once. I know that I need to get myself in a more neutral emotional state before I speak. It may require biting my tongue for a whole minute.

Reframe: I need to remind myself that this is Maddy's experience, not mine. I know that this is an opportunity for Maddy to be reminded of her greatness and a chance for Maddy to embrace her greatness, especially when the world has a different opinion.

What do I want?

For me: I want to be there for my child emotionally and take this opportunity to heal from my experience.

For my child: I want my daughter to have the tools to feel empowered and safe in her body, and be reminded of her worth.

The script

Mom: I noticed a big tear coming down your cheek. Can I help?

Maddy: Adam, in my class, was singing "Maddy, Maddy, she's a fatty. Oh, and she's ugly too!"

Mom: What do you need from me? A talk? A hug? Do you need me to just be quiet with you?

Maddy: I need to talk.

Mom: I'm listening.

Maddy: Why does Adam have to be so mean?

There is a long pause.

Mom: Do you want me to answer that or do you still want me to listen?

Maddy: Can you answer it?

Mom: I can't tell you what Adam is thinking or feeling because I am not Adam. What I can say is that often, when others don't feel good about themselves, they make fun of or hurt others with the hopes that it will make them feel better. Can I tell you a special story about me?

Maddy: Yes.

Mom: I was made fun of *a lot* in school for being fat. There was a little boy, who I went to school with for six years. He would say, "Heather, Heather, not light as a feather!" I would come home and cry to my mom—Grandma Mary— almost every day ... well, not really, but it felt that way. I would tell her that the kids would call me all sorts of names and say that I shouldn't have been born because I was so ugly and fat.

Maddy: What did Grandma Mary say?

Mom: Grandma Mary was a beautiful, wise woman—just like you will be. She said something very important. Something I never forgot.

Maddy: What did she say?

Mom: She said that they were wrong. She said that I was a miracle baby, born on purpose, and that I was here to do great things.

Maddy: That would make me feel better!

Mom: It sure did. Even though he kept teasing me over the years, I knew a secret.

Maddy: What was the secret?

Mom: That he was wrong.

Maddy: How can I get Adam to stop?

Mom: I couldn't make this boy stop. I even beat him up one day because I was so mad, but it just made it worse. I decided to believe my mom instead of the little boy. Every time he said something mean to me, I decided to tell myself that I was a miracle and I mattered. I trusted my mom more than him.

Maddy: But it's hard and embarrassing!

Mom: I hear you. Know that I am here for you and I believe in you. Know that you will make it through this. If you ever feel that you need help, I am here. I know it will work out for you. It did for me!

How does it end?

- Maddy goes back to school and the teasing subsides, at least enough for her to deal with. She occasionally talks to me about it, and then I remind her of her unique value on this planet; *or*

- Maddy continues to be teased and is given the opportunity to feel her feelings, talk about them, and move through them, gaining courage and strength with my support.

Who's in control?

Mom: I am in control of my feelings. I give examples in a story to inspire courage, understanding, and triumph. I give Maddy the truth of my experience, allowing me to heal as well. I feel good.

Child: Maddy feels aware of and in control of her feelings. She knows and agrees that Adam is wrong. She knows that she is valued and supported. She knows that she has a choice: She can choose to believe him or not. She feels empowered and loved.

The gift

- This experience has given us the opportunity to feel our feelings, to be sad, and to know that there is always a choice to change our minds.

- We have been given the gift of connection by sharing difficult experiences and loving each other through it.

- My daughter knew that her feelings were safe with me and, at the same time, I knew that she could handle this situation.

- I trusted her and believed in her, and she believed in me.

- We both felt great!

Check out our website (www.raiseahappychild.com) and blog for more scenarios. We are adding new ones all the time!

Email us at hello@raiseahappychild.com if you have a scenario with your child and would like some help.

PART 5

Closing Thoughts

There is so much we can't know.

The vast majority of people in the field of psychology believe that our behavior is formed by our past. Conventional thinking states that our past experiences, external influences, environment, and even our parents' DNA determine why we do what we do in the world.

However, have you ever considered that behavior can be formed retroactively by the future? How about the idea that behavior can be formed by the intuition of where our calling will take us and what we are destined to become?

In *The New York Times* best-selling book, *The Soul's Code: In Search of Character and Calling*,[1] psychologist James Hillman offers a view of child psychology based on the idea of the personal daimon. The "daimon" is an old word with many meanings in many circles:

- To Christians, it is the "guardian angel."

- To Greeks, it is the "genius."

- To shamans, it is the "attendant spirit" or the "soul."

- To others, it is simply "our calling."[2]

Hillman calls it the "Acorn Theory," which holds that "each person bears a uniqueness that asks to be lived and that is already present before it can be lived. ... [E]very single person is born with a defining image... The entire image of a destiny is packed into a tiny acorn, the seed of a huge oak on small shoulders."[3]

Put another way, we have come to this planet with a specific purpose, and we will stubbornly create our life—and the experiences in our life—to fulfill our soul's calling. We are each an acorn that already contains a specific blueprint for a magnificent, unique oak tree. The soul knows who it is from the beginning.

Hillman shares examples of several famous people where it seems as if they, as young children, knew what they might become. For example, Yehudi Menuhin, one of the greatest violinists of the 20th century, insisted as a tiny child on having a violin, yet he smashed the toy violin he was given. His "soul" (daimon) was already grown up, and it disdained to play a child's toy! It seems that he wanted—demanded—his young fingers to practice on the real instrument in his future.

Maybe the child knows what he must become and fears it. For example, Manolete, the bravest and best Spanish bullfighter, was a terrified child, who clung to his mother's apron strings as if he already knew the dangers he would have to encounter as an adult.

Winston Churchill was a poor scholar. He was consigned to what we would now call a "remedial reading class," as if putting off the moment when he would have to labor for his Nobel Prize for Literature. He also stuttered. As Hillman points out, Churchill had to save the Western world through his speech. Of course he had a speech defect and couldn't speak easily when he was 11 or 14! The calling was too much for a small-sized schoolboy to carry.[4]

Many in the field of psychology would say that Manolete became a bullfighter because he wanted to prove to himself and to the world that he was not a scared, weak little boy, but what if Manolete knew—in some part of his soul—that one day he would be facing thousand-pound bulls and, as a little boy, was terrified at that thought? Was he perhaps practicing with his mother's apron for the cape he would one day hold?

Here are some things that we don't know:

- We don't know why we get our parents,.
- We don't know why our children get us.
- We don't know that flunking a high school math class and then having to attend more of a "safety school" is worse than going to Harvard.
- We don't know that an obsession with comic books at a young age is a "waste of time."
- We don't know that attention deficit disorder (ADD) behavior is really a problem. What if children with ADD behavior are just bored with a

class situation and textbook learning that they know they will not need in their later life?

We don't know how the acorn will grow or what shape the tree will take. From our vantage point of linear time and traditional psychology, we make judgments, but we really don't know.

As parents, we must live with the unknowable. We must trust that each soul will achieve its destiny with a stubborn force of will. Our job is to have faith and then cheerlead our children along the way. Our job is to trust that they, as little acorns, already know how to become magnificent, unique trees.

Steve Jobs gave a famous commencement address to the 2005 Stanford graduating class. He talked about his life and the things he did along the way. He talked about his time at Reed College and the calligraphy class he took, which later fueled his passion for great fonts and became one of the hallmarks of Apple's famous user interface design.

As Steve Jobs so wisely told these students, "You can't connect the dots looking forward; you can only connect them looking backwards."[5] Steve Jobs knew what James Hillman knew: Our future often influences our current behavior. Parents think they know more than their kids. They think they have more wisdom and can guide their children based on their experiences with the world. However, can anyone ever *really* know what experiences our soul needs for its growth into that tree?

Can we only connect the dots of our life by looking backwards?

"The geniuses on our planet are young, free from the details of the future, live from one fun moment to the next, and are always moving towards happiness. Our children are paving the way. I plan on joining them in every moment I can with a smile on my face and love in my heart."

—*Heather Criswell*

**Download the poster for free at
www.raiseahappychild.com/poster**

List of Videos

Video / Chapter	URL Link	QR Code
Introduction	www.raiseahappychild.com/intro-video	
Chapter 5: Choose the Energy You Bring to Every Situation	www.raiseahappychild.com/energy	

Video / Chapter	URL Link	QR Code
Chapter 6: Honor Your Feelings First and Then Your Child's	www.raiseahappychild.com/feelings	
Chapter 7: Focus on What You *Do* Want	www.raiseahappychild.com/focus	
Chapter 8: Honor Every Choice Your Child Makes	www.raiseahappychild.com/choice	
Chapter 9: Remind Your Child of Their Greatness ... Always	www.raiseahappychild.com/greatness	

Video / Chapter	URL Link	QR Code
Chapter 10: Put It All Together	www.raiseahappychild.com/phrases	
Scenario 1: "Mom, he won't ..."— *Fights between Siblings or Friends*	www.raiseahappychild.com/fights	

Endnotes

Chapter 1: How Do You Define Your Success as a Parent?

1. Robert Collier, *The Secret of the Ages* (New York: Robert Collier Publications, Inc., First Printing, 1926).

Chapter 3: As a Parent, What Are You Really Responsible For?

1. Doc Lew Childre, Howard Martin, and Donna Beech, *The HeartMath Solution: The Institute of HeartMath's Revolutionary Program for Engaging the Power of the Heart's Intelligence* (New York: HarperCollins Publishers, 1999).

2. Lynne Namka, Ed.D, "The Drama Triangle: The Three Roles of Victimhood" (2004) (www.angriesout.com/grown20.htm).

3. David Emerald, *The Power of TED* (*The Empowerment Dynamic)* (Bainbridge Island, WA: Polaris Publishing, 2009).

Chapter 4: What Is Your Definition of Happiness?

1. Allen Klein, "Laughter and Humor: Myths and Realities," study by cardiologists at the University of Maryland (www.allenklein.com/articles/laughterhumormyth. htm; www.hunterhome.net/triviamar06.html). Emphasis in original.

2. *Time* magazine cover, "The Science of Happiness" (Jan. 17, 2005).

Chapter 5: Choose the Energy You Bring to Every Situation

1. A. Mehrabian and M. Wiener, "Decoding of inconsistent communications," *Journal of Personality and Social Psychology* 6 (1967): 109–114; A. Mehrabian and S. R. Ferris, "Inference of Attitudes from Nonverbal Communication in Two Channels," *Journal of Consulting Psychology* 31: 3 (1967): 48–258.

Chapter 6: Honor Your Feelings First and Then Your Child's

1. *Webster's New World Dictionary, Fourth Edition* (Cleveland: Wiley Publishing, 2002), p. 300.
2. *Ibid.,* p. 320.

Chapter 7: Focus on What You *Do* Want

1. Alfie Kohn, *Punished by Rewards: The Trouble with Gold Stars, Incentive Plans, A's, Praise, and Other Bribes* (New York: Houghton Mifflin Company, 1993).
2. Alfie Kohn, "Why Incentive Plans Cannot Work," *Harvard Business Review* (September-October 1993). Copyright © 1993 by the Harvard Business School Publishing Corporation. All rights reserved. Reprinted by permission of *Harvard Business Review.*

Chapter 8: Honor Every Choice Your Child Makes

1. *Webster's New World Dictionary, Fourth Edition* (Cleveland: Wiley Publishing, 2002), p. 317.
2. *Ibid.,* p. 258.
3. Foster Cline and Jim Fay, *Parenting with Love and Logic* (Colorado Springs: NavPress, 2006), p. 84.
4. Amy McCready, *Positive Parenting Solutions* blog (www.positiveparentingsolutions.com/parenting/how-can-i-get-my-kids-to-clean-their-rooms).
5. *Ibid.*

6. http://abcnews.go.com/blogs/headlines/2012/09/mom-angry-that-male-vice-principal-spanked-her-daughter.

7. *Ibid.*

8. *Ibid.*

9. *Ibid.*

Chapter 9: Remind Your Child of Their Greatness ... Always

1. *Webster's New World Dictionary, Fourth Edition* (Cleveland: Wiley Publishing, 2002), p. 822.

2. Robert Rosenthal and Lenore Jacobson, *Pygmalion in the Classroom: Teacher Expectation and Pupils' Intellectual Development* (Norwalk, CT: Crown House Publishing, 2003).

3. Alan Cohen, *Wisdom of the Heart* (Carlsbad, CA: Hay House, 2002), p. 4. Quote used with permission from the author.

Part 5: Closing Thoughts

1. James Hillman, *The Soul's Code: In Search of Character and Calling* (New York: Warner Books, 1997).

2. *Ibid.*, p. 9.

3. *Ibid.*, pp. 6-13.

4. *Ibid.*, p. 107.

5. http://news.stanford.edu/news/2005/june15/jobs-061505.html.

Meet the Authors

Heather Criswell

've spent my entire life working with and loving children. After 25 years of working with over 30,000 kids, I have developed a unique approach to parenting.

When I was 21 years old, my father believed in my dream to open a different kind of preschool where children were empowered, celebrated for their unique gifts, and unconditionally loved. My family contributed time, energy, and money to make this dream a reality ... and See World Learning Center was born in Las Vegas, Nevada.

For nearly a decade, I raised a generation of children, who believed that they were a gift to the world, and taught them how to share those gifts with others. My husband and I fostered many children over the years. All of these amazing children had so much to teach me about how to communicate with them.

Years later, my passion spread to impacting the lives of entire families. I established the Touch of Life Wellness Center, also in Las Vegas, which was a place where people could come for healing and personal transformation. After that, I launched WiseInside, a company that creates products for kids and adults to connect and feel good. I am also a public speaker and coach parents and teachers.

This book project and the accompanying website (www.raiseahappychild.com) are my latest creations. They bring together all of my experience and wisdom. My goal is to bring the world the most effective and loving parenting tools, techniques, and approaches so they can raise happy children (and be happy too).

Taryn Voget

I am the chief executive officer and cofounder of the Everyday Genius Institute, based in San Francisco, California. My company deconstructs how the world's best do what they do, and shares their strategies in our educational book and video series (see the back of the book for this information). We also help individuals discover and expand their unique genius.

I have had the true honor and privilege of working with Heather Criswell. She has let me crawl inside her mind to understand exactly how she gets such amazing results with children. Our work has been full of joy and light and laughter and learning. It is my great pleasure to be a part of bringing this extraordinary thinking to you.

Before designing my dream job of rubbing elbows with geniuses, I studied at Georgetown University and Oxford University, and spent 13 years as a strategy and operations consultant for the top companies in the world. Out of sheer necessity while consulting with the Fortune 100, I developed an uncanny knack for analyzing and streamlining complex processes. Through my years of working with dozens of businesses and thousands of people, I have developed the unwavering belief that genius is always in simplicity.

My desire to reveal strategies of genius and make them accessible to everyone ignited my inspiration for the Everyday Genius Institute. I research, write, speak, teach, consult, and coach around the world on the subject of genius and human potential.

Create Heartfelt Connections in Minutes with WiseTalk for Families®

WiseTalk for Families is a communication "tool" for parents and "game" for children that provides a simple way for families to share more quality time & have heartfelt conversations in just a few minutes a day.

- Share quality time with your child
- Discover what your child is really thinking and feeling
- Create heartfelt conversations
- Open the door for difficult topics
- Let your child know that she is loved

www.wiseinside.com

WiseInside
wisdom shared from the inside out

More titles from the Everyday Genius Institute

Study Smarter, Not Harder
Think like a Genius Straight A+ Student

Write Words That Sell
Think like a Genius Marketing Copywriter

Taste Wine Like a Pro
Think like a Genius Wine Master

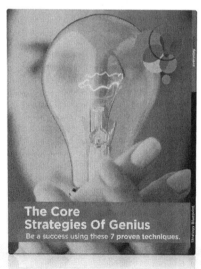

The Core Strategies Of Genius
Be a success using these 7 proven techniques.

available at

Thank you!